WHAT PEOPLE ARE

THICKER THAN BLOOD?

What a huge amount of work went into this book! It obviously involved massive research, and I am sure it will be invaluable for either people who want to adopt a child, or for a child who has been adopted and needs more understanding of why their particular adoptive parents came to adopt them. The author shows great insight into how circumstances are often related to past lives and can come up for healing in this present life.
Reverend Leonora van Gils, Inter-Faith Minister & Spiritual Counsellor, Allergy Specialist

Thanks to Ann, a book that was long missing is finally a reality. She has, not only through her personal experience but also through her professional therapeutic experience, provided us with insights on a subject that has indeed up till now been neglected in the literature of the regression therapy field. If life is a school of the soul and the purpose of the soul is to collect experiences and act out the Life Plan, then one hard but useful way to do this is to live through the feeling of rejection by the biological parents and hopefully be compensated by the subsequent compassionate warmth of adoption and fostering. When I encounter such cases in my own practice I show the pattern that Ann is suggesting in her book: that soul bonds may very likely be thicker than blood and stronger than nurture.
Athanasios Komianos, President of the Earth Association for Regression Therapy (EARTh)

It is to be expected that adoption and fostering would normally give rise to fairly difficult dynamic situations in which the baby/child might, say, consequently harbour a strong unconscious feeling of abandonment. This can often also wreak havoc

in their later relationships. The psychology is in itself complicated enough, but here Ann Merivale investigates and catalogues an aspect that usually goes totally unrecognised by materialistic social services, as well as by most of those people who are seeking a child. Her thought-provoking thesis, as a regression therapist and believer in reincarnation, is that the set-up may be an arranged karmic re-assembly of relationships among persons who were previously connected and have in their current life-plan agreed to be together again – perhaps to resolve issues that are still outstanding or to build up a greater love over lifetimes. Many readers will be stirred by this exciting and insightful spiritual account of numerous real, and very varied, case histories.
Keith M. Hearne, BSc, MSc, PhD. Psychologist

Thicker Than Blood?

A Fresh Look at Adoption, Fostering and Step Families

Thicker Than Blood?

A Fresh Look at Adoption, Fostering and Step Families

Ann Merivale

6th BOOKS

Winchester, UK
Washington, USA

First published by Sixth Books, 2015
Sixth Books is an imprint of John Hunt Publishing Ltd., Laurel House, Station Approach, Alresford, Hants, SO24 9JH, UK
office1@jhpbooks.net
www.johnhuntpublishing.com
www.6th-books.com

For distributor details and how to order please visit the 'Ordering' section on our website.

ISBN: 978 1 78279 836 1
Library of Congress Control Number: 2014946461

A CIP catalogue record for this book is available from the British Library.

Design: Stuart Davies

Printed and bound by CPI Group (UK) Ltd, Croydon, CR0 4YY, UK

CONTENTS

For DELILAH

Acknowledgements

First of all, I should like to express my gratitude to all those whose stories are to be found herein, with a 'special mention' for those who wrote them for me themselves. I am sure that they will be valued by readers who are able to relate to them personally.

Secondly, I am grateful as always to my supportive family and to Lawrence for constantly egging me on and on occasion giving constructive criticism and suggestions.

I also owe a lot to the 'great writers' on the subject, especially Nancy Newton Verrier and the deceased Betty Jean Lifton.

The spiritual teachers from whom I have learnt so much over the years are too many to name, but my gratitude for this education is unbounded.

Finally, I am again grateful to all the efficient staff of 6th Books, John Hunt Publishing, without whom this book would have remained permanently stuck inside my computer!

Introduction

After she had prayed, the goddess Ninsun,
the wise, the all-knowing, came down from the roof
and summoned Enkidu. "Dear child," she said,
"you were not born from my womb, but now
I adopt you as my son." She hung a jewelled
Amulet around Enkidu's neck.
from Gilgamesh[1]

I was the eldest of six children and learnt to cook at my mother's knee. As a consequence, sixty plus years on, I am still reluctant to use recipes when I cook, finding it too much trouble and/or time consuming to do so. Recently I got an urge to try making a Bakewell tart. I knew an important ingredient of the filling to be ground almonds, and assumed that it would also contain butter, sugar, egg and possibly a little bit of flour. So I made a pastry case in my usual way, spread jam over the bottom and then hastily threw ingredients for the filling into my food processor and put the final article into the oven. The result was eatable, but it bore little resemblance to the delicacy that I remembered having once purchased in Bakewell. When I mentioned this to my daughter on her next visit, she commented, "Why didn't you Google for a recipe?" I replied that I had simply not thought of that, but that it would be a good idea another time. When "another time" came round, I found that I did not need to go up to my computer because my husband's battered old Marguerite Patten that was standing right there in the kitchen contained a recipe for Bakewell tart. Had I thought to look there in the first place, I would have seen that one of its most important ingredients was cake crumbs. This was in fact the *only* ingredient I had omitted when I tried to use my head rather than a cookery book. So now I can make Bakewell tarts that don't disgrace their namesake!

Of course missing ingredients affect more than just cookery. At a critical time during the upbringing of our third child, whom we had adopted at two weeks when our two natural children were three years old and almost five, and wondering where I was going wrong, my sister who had herself adopted two children gave me Nancy Newton Verrier's book *The Primal Wound*[2]. This was tremendously helpful and consoling because I found that it described absolutely all the problems that we were having with our younger son. However, in common with any subsequent book that I have read on adoption, I find it to be lacking one vital ingredient, it does not explain the intense love that I felt for our baby Christopher from the moment I first set eyes on him in the foster home, nor the fierceness of the bond between us even through our 'darkest hours', nor his older brother's reluctance to start school two months later because he could not bear to be separated from his baby brother, nor his brother's extraordinary tolerance of his bad behavior, nor his sister's frequent resentment of his presence in our family, nor my husband's reluctance to send him away to boarding school even when my own 'survival' seemed to be at stake. Yet it was to be a few more years until I came to identify this vital missing ingredient as KARMA, i.e. the previous relationships that all four of us have had with Christopher and the consequent Plan that we made to be together as a family this time round.

There is nothing new about adoption. In fact the above quotation is taken from the oldest book in the world! The first surviving version of the epic *Gilgamesh*, written on cuneiform baked clay tablets, which were discovered in 1853 among the ruins of Nineveh (now Mosul), dates from around the eighteenth century BC and thus precedes the Iliad by a thousand years. What *has* changed over the centuries – and indeed even in my own lifetime – are attitudes towards the question, as well as the many ways in which adoption has been handled.

"There *is* no right way to do adoption," commented my friend Athene when I had voiced to her my question as to whether we had done the right thing by not adopting a younger sibling for our son Christopher. Athene (whose story is recounted in Chapter Eighteen) is a strong character who has worked through the problems that being adopted gave her, but anyone who is still wrestling with the complicated issues surrounding adoption, fostering or stepfamilies should rest assured that they are far from being alone in having so far failed to pin them down.

My own interest in this subject dates from my late teens or early twenties, when an unknown Australian cousin suddenly entered our lives. Her rather sad story shows the extent to which attitudes can change so radically in a single lifetime. My maternal grandparents had emigrated from London to Sydney for my grandfather's work and, when they returned to England upon his retirement from conducting the Theatre Orchestra there, my mother came back with them, but her younger brother did not. He in due course married and had a son, of whom my family saw quite a lot during periods when he was living with his father, who returned to England following his divorce. It later transpired that my uncle's wife had got pregnant when they were engaged and that, not having the courage to tell their Catholic parents about it, they had had the child adopted, and the cousin whom we did know had always been taken to be an only child. The adoptive parents never told the poor girl (whose name, coincidentally, is Ann!) that she was adopted, but she nevertheless instinctively knew from her earliest childhood that this was so and resolved as soon as she was old enough to find her birth parents. By the time that she had made her way over to England to meet her father, she had been diagnosed as severely schizophrenic. Although I myself cannot have met this other Ann more than a couple of times, my mother kept in touch with her for a while after she had returned to Australia. She has never met her younger brother, but I have good reason to believe that she is now being well cared for in a home.

Later, but while still in my twenties, I worked for a short period as a care worker in a school for deeply disturbed children. This experience gave me the desire, should I ever marry, to give a home to a 'problem toddler'. But once I had married, given birth twice, and found out how tricky and demanding bringing up 'normal' children was, I changed my desire to adopting a baby, laboring under the naïve assumption that it would not be very different from having a child naturally. Since the philosophy of the school in which I had worked was based on the findings of the English pediatrician and psychoanalyst Donald Winnicott (1896–1971), I should perhaps have been more aware of the implications of adoption at any age. But I can now see that my desire stemmed from the Plan that I had made before birth to come together again with all the members of my present family. Why Christopher and I should have agreed that he would join us via a biological mother other than myself is not a hundred percent clear, but life experience has taught me that there must have been very good reasons for it.

Konrad Lorenz (1903–89) was an Austrian zoologist, ornithologist and ethologist, who (despite his Nazi sympathies!) is well known for his studies of goslings and 'imprinting' (forming a primary attachment). Ethology is the study of animals in their natural environment, and Lorenz found the crucial time for imprinting to be, in the case of goslings, between twelve and seventeen hours after birth. An English contemporary of Lorenz's, the psychologist John Bowlby (1907–90), developed the attachment theory with regard to human babies to their mothers, and Winnicott believed that, in order for integration of the personality to be achieved, it was essential for the child's primary attachment to be uniquely to the mother or mother substitute throughout the first year of life. Although I knew all this – and had seen with my own eyes the devastating effects of early maternal deprivation – I did not reckon with the full implications of separation from the birth mother. No doubt I was imagining myself as an adequate 'mother substitute' rather than thinking about imprinting during a baby's first few hours of life!

Anyway my ambition to adopt was achieved in 1979, when David and I were given by Barnardo's the immense privilege of being able to receive into our family the two-week-old, half Sierra-Leonean baby Thomas. (We added the names Christopher and Kandeh, and nowadays his friends call him Chris or C.P., though we his family still prefer not to abbreviate his name.)

I greatly enjoyed seeing an award-winning (2008) French film/movie, which is the début of the novelist Philippe Claudel. Entitled *Il ya longtemps que je t'aime* (translated as *I've Loved You So Long*), it is superbly acted, extraordinarily moving, and I would strongly recommend it to anyone who fancies being totally absorbed for almost two hours. However, despite Claudel's wonderfully sensitive and realistic handling of the issue of imprisonment and its aftermath, I could not help being struck by the *unrealistic* picture that he gave of an adoptive family. This is not intended as negative criticism, for a single delicate subject is quite enough for a single film to deal with, but one aim of this book of mine is to dispel any idealistic notions that anyone might have on the question of adoption. Would it were true that a couple who were either unable or unwilling to produce children of their own could simply go over to Vietnam, return with two adorable, bright, little girls, and meld them instantly into a perfect, happy family, but alas real life is not like that!

Very many people have, like me, been greatly helped by the work of Nancy Newton Verrier, an adoptive mother who has devoted herself to writing about and speaking on the subject of adoption. Her understanding of the difficulties is profound, and I know that I am not alone in having, after first reading *The Primal Wound*[2], exclaimed to myself, "So it's not just that I'm a bad mother!" She has also written a second useful book[3] that is addressed more to adoptees themselves.

Verrier's thesis briefly is that all adopted children, whatever the circumstances that caused their birth mothers to give them up, suffer from a *subconscious* feeling of having been rejected, and that this can lead to behavioral problems such as lying and stealing or 'attachment disorder'. I underline the word 'subconscious' because it is precisely this that makes for the child's difficulties. If they had a conscious understanding of exactly what it was they were battling with, they might have less need to either 'act out' or 'suppress' (which in Verrier's experience is even worse) their problems. And she argues in consequence that children are always better off staying with their birth mothers, however ill-equipped they are to bring them up.

Another author for whom I have a very strong admiration is Betty Jean Lifton, an adoptee who had already established herself as a successful writer before becoming a psychotherapist and running an adoption counselling practice in Cambridge, Massachusetts. Until her death in 2010, she was also a leading advocate for adoption reform. I regret having only discovered her two books[4] on the subject some time after Christopher had left home, but would now label them a 'must' for all those involved in the adoption process. My own desire to dig 'deeper still' stems from a further layer to my education, which I shall now explain.

Finding all the difficulties that our family were going through mentioned in *The Primal Wound* was, as I have said, extraordinarily helpful to me, and now, many years later, I feel a strong desire to help others in a similar way. Where, however, things are different for me nowadays is in the fact that my conversion to belief in reincarnation firstly gave me still more help in understanding my own life, and secondly led me to train with the renowned, now deceased, Jungian psychotherapist Dr. Roger Woolger, who developed his own unique form of Deep Memory Process (formerly known as integral regression) therapy. I had already started researching reincarnation and related spiritual topics, and writing books based on this research, even before training as a therapist, and all that I have learnt since I first read *The Primal Wound* causes me now to want to add to other writers' insights.

So my thesis – no doubt in contradiction to most or all other books on Adoption – is that everyone is in the family they are in for a good reason. That, whether or not they feel that theirs is the family that could have brought them the most happiness, they are in the right family for achieving a purpose that was planned before they were conceived. (The same applies equally of course to natural children who feel that they are in the 'wrong' family, but that issue was covered in one of my previous books. The aim of *DISCOVERING THE LIFE PLAN*[5] was to show that *every* life has a purpose that was planned broadly beforehand, and to demonstrate, by going through all the stages of life from pre-conception to post-death, how and/or when people tended to discover what was their Life Plan.) I firmly believe that Betty Jean Lifton is a clear case of someone who *chose* before coming in to her present life to have first-hand experience of being adopted because of the help that this would enable her to offer to others, and her own wonderful memoirs[6] are a very moving read. In fact I recently had a chat with her on one of my regular shamanic journeys[7], and she assured me that had she still been incarnate, she would have been happy to write an endorsement for this book!

It is in *no way* my intention to belittle the difficulties and the pain suffered by adopted people, the parents who have charge of them, or the parents who – for whatever reason – have felt obliged to give up a child for adoption. Far from it since, as both an adoptive mother and a therapist, I speak from personal experience. Nor am I aiming – if indeed it were possible, which I doubt – to prove my belief that people who have known each other before come together in families in order to work out issues that have their roots in the past, or to continue loving connections. I am simply recounting my own and others' experiences, in the hope that they will offer interest, explanation or consolation to those who are still in difficulty.

One of many questions that my husband and I were asked when our application to adopt a child was being considered was "How would you feel about welcoming into your family a child who was less intelligent than your other two?" We replied firstly that the idea did not bother us at all; and secondly that we would welcome the opportunity of testing the 'nature versus nurture' debate. In the event that opportunity was not given to us since Christopher's birth parents are both university graduates and he has an extremely high IQ, but my belief remains nevertheless the same – that genetics and upbringing are of equal importance. Whether anyone would ever find a way of proving a percentage such as fifty-fifty seems somewhat doubtful, but in any case I have myself in more recent years moved towards seeing the picture as one third genes, one third environment and another third what the child brings in with him or her from his or her previous incarnations. The exact proportions are immaterial – even if it were possible to calculate them – but what *does* matter to my mind is that the importance of all three factors should be appreciated and that each child should be given the best opportunity for realizing his or her potential in the most supportive and happiest possible environment. Fortunately we have moved on a lot since Polly was born before the beginning of the Second World War (see Chapter Three), but I fear that we still have quite a long way to go.

Although I have made no attempt to write a history of adoption[8], the scope of this book is broad, reflecting the fact that I see the whole issue of adoption as a broad one. Besides the three that I have just mentioned – children (who of course will hopefully become adults), adoptive parents and birth parents – I am touching on other types of relationship which I see as not totally dissimilar: foster parents, step parents (even grand step parents!), and I have in addition a chapter on pets. After all, many people do actually adopt their stepchildren and, even when there is no legal adoption, the issues around creating a new family are similar. As for pets, for some people these *are* their children, they are always (or anyway should be!) an important part of the family, and it is my belief that animals too come into our lives for a reason and because of previous connections.

All the stories I have recounted are true, though names, and sometimes precise circumstances and events, have often been changed for the sake of anonymity; and I am deeply indebted to the clients, friends and acquaintances who have generously permitted me to include their experiences. Very special thanks go to those who have chosen to recount their stories in their own words.

My own specialty as a therapist is, as I have already made clear, Deep Memory Process (DMP). This means that, as a general rule, the clients who come to see me believe in reincarnation and, often having failed to find a resolution to their problems through other therapies, hope to find an explanation for them in their distant (or occasionally less distant) past. Working through 'outdated' issues and then releasing them can be extraordinarily effective, but this book is confined neither to people who have come to me for therapy, nor to people who believe in reincarnation. In these chapters you will find the stories of some (for instance Jan in Chapter Fifteen, and in fact my own children) who do not share my beliefs in any way, so I am aiming to speak to a wider audience than I did in most of my previous books.

This wider audience may benefit from a little explanation of terms, which people with my beliefs nowadays tend to take for granted, so I should now like to ask the rest of you please to be patient for a tiny moment. First of all, you will find the word 'karma', plus its adjective 'karmic' and its adverb 'karmicly', used fairly liberally. 'Karma', which is the Sanskrit word for 'action', is a term used generally to denote 'cause and effect'. "What goes around comes around," as the saying goes: When you throw a stone into a pool, there will inevitably be ripples, even though on occasion the ripples will not reach you until several centuries later, in a subsequent life. So 'karmic links' exist between people who have known each other before and who come together again for a reason, whether it be for one of them to pay an outstanding debt to the other, because of some problem that they need to work through together, or simply because of long standing love and affection.

People who practice regression therapy do not do so in order to satisfy curiosity as to who someone might have been in a previous life. Nor are we interested in 'proving' reincarnation. The purpose is purely to help people to improve their lives *at the present moment*, and part of this process often involves finding out about past trauma in order to let go of it, and discovering the lessons that one still needs to learn. In a therapy session much of all this is revealed and dealt with in the 'inter-life' state – i.e. after the client has gone through a death in a previous life – and to this we give the Tibetan name of 'Bardo' (which literally means 'between islands'). (Dr. Roger Woolger also used the term 'mini Bardo' when he was helping a client to re-program a certain trauma, but there is no need to go into that here since it is not my present intention to write a textbook for DMP.)

After conceiving the idea for this book, people with varying problems, but a similar theme, kept landing in my lap. I do not believe this to have been coincidence, but rather that our meeting was organized by spirit beings 'on the other side'. Then, when I mentioned the idea to my client Loraine (see Chapter Nineteen), she replied encouragingly, "That's a book that needs to be written!" So here now is my humble offering, and if any readers find themselves able to identify with any of the stories and find them helpful, that will bring me great joy.

Notes

1. Taken from a new English version of *Gilgamesh,* Stephen Mitchell, Free Press, Simon and Schuster, US, 2004 and Profile Books, London, 2004.
2. *The Primal Wound – Understanding the Adopted Child,* Nancy Newton Verrier, Gateway Books, USA, 2009.
3. *Coming Home to Self – The Adopted Child Grows Up,* Nancy Newton Verrier, Gateway Books, USA, 1993.
4. *Lost And Found – The Adoption Experience,* The University of Michigan Press, USA, Third edition 2009, and *Journey of the Adopted Self – A Quest for Wholeness,* Basic Books (Perseus Books), USA, 1994, Betty Jean Lifton, Ph.D.
5. See my third book, *Discovering the Life Plan – Eleven Steps to Your Destiny,* Ann Merivale, 6th Books, John Hunt Publishing, 2012.
6. *Twice Born – Memoirs of an Adopted Daughter,* Betty Jean Lifton, McGraw Hill, New York, 1975.
7. For an explanation of this, and of reasons for practicing it, see my book *Delayed Departure – A Beginner's Guide to Soul Rescue,* 6th Books, 2013.
8. For that I strongly recommend *Love Child,* Sue Elliot, Random House, 2011. In her book this author skillfully weaves her own fascinating story around a wealth of well researched and interesting historical information.

PART ONE – FOSTERING

Anger is the second universal emotion. It is also the most difficult emotion to deal with, especially in its extreme form, rage. It is difficult to deal with because we either repress it or we explode. We seldom know the cause of our rage, but often act upon it anyway. It is the source of much unhappiness and violence; yet it is also the initiator of change both personal and societal.
Nancy Newton Verrier[1]

Many people foster professionally – some long term, others short term. (Our own adopted son spent the first ten days after leaving the maternity hospital in a foster home, in order to give his birth mother a little more opportunity to change her mind about surrendering him.) Obviously, whatever the circumstances, the most important thing is to ensure that every child is given love and security, and the latter will be particularly difficult for a child who is moved repeatedly. A quick check on the Amazon website immediately brought up numerous books on fostering, and it is not the main focus of this book of mine. There are, however, two points that I do want to bring in to this book. Firstly – as my first four stories demonstrate – that fostering can be a substitute for adoption when the foster parents or parent would have preferred to adopt had it been possible, and secondly that many of the same issues surround both fostering and adoption.

My personal experience of fostering is very limited indeed. When our own adopted son was about seven or eight we were asked by a Namibian mature student of our acquaintance to give a home to his son of about the same age, whom he wanted to be educated in England. At the time we were very much involved with an anti-racist organization, which made us feel concerned that there were not enough black children in our area for Christopher to mix with, and so we agreed to give it a try mainly for that reason. I cannot, however, say that the placement was in any way successful. For one thing the poor child was very upset at being uprooted from his home country and his family, and for another – and as a natural consequence of that – his behavior both in our home and at Christopher's school was very disruptive. Also, as our older son Paul mentions in his piece in Part Four, our own children did not get on at all well with him and found his living with us very difficult to cope with. After a couple of school terms, while wishing that we could be of help, we felt obliged to tell the young boy's father that we could not continue with the arrangement. I consequently have an unbounded admiration for people who foster difficult children long term. We all have different vocations and that one is not mine!

Fortunately, however, there are people in the world who are very different from me. On March 28th, 2010, I heard the distinguished film star and writer Emma Thompson talking on the British radio program 'Desert Island Discs'. Even though her choice of music was very different from mine, I found everything she said extremely interesting. But I pricked up my ears particularly when she spoke of the Rwandan refugee whom she and her husband Greg Wise adopted informally at the age of sixteen and whose deportation they subsequently fought successfully. A great political activist, one of a number of organizations that Emma Thompson supports is the Refugee Council and, when she first became acquainted with the young lad, he bonded immediately with her whole family. This is of course to my mind a clear indication of strong karmic links between them all, but what Emma further said supports my view that everything that happens is part of a Plan and that there is good reason for it. She talked about having had a miscarriage as well as about the birth of her daughter Gaia, and she said that if she had not lost a child they would probably not have felt able to take on their "son." Since he is now studying for a Master's degree in Human Rights at the School of Oriental and African Studies in London, it is clear to me firstly that the fostering/adoption has been overwhelmingly successful and secondly that there was a reason for the young man being forced to leave Rwanda at an early age.

Even when the fostering is short term, I still believe that the child is always placed in a particular family for some karmic reason. Our experience with Naphtali, the child whom we fostered briefly, is not, however, something I have to date felt a need to explore. (He has not turned up in any of my regressions, but that need not mean that he does not have some past life link with me. Perhaps the lesson was simply that I was not cut out for fostering!).

I am starting off in India simply because it is there that I began writing up the stories. I hope you will find them as interesting as I do.

Note

1. *The Adopted Child Grows Up – Coming Home To Self,* Nancy Newton Verrier, Gateway Press, Baltimore, 2003.

CHAPTER ONE

RAJU'S STORY

Now it is not good for the Christian's health to try to hustle the Hindu brown.
For the Christian riles and the Hindu smiles and weareth the Christian down;
And the end of the fight is a tombstone.... with the epitaph drear
'A fool lies here who tried to hustle the east'.
Rudyard Kipling

One hot day in about 1968 – the exact date is neither known nor of great relevance to this tale – a little boy named Velmurugan ran away from home. He was probably about seven or eight, though his date of birth, again, will never be certain. His parents' marriage had never been good, and when his father took up with another woman his mother had no choice but to return to her parents' very small home in a different village. Velmurugan was the eldest of three children and, though he is sure that he and his younger brother were both left behind, he can no longer remember whether or not his sister went with his mother. Sometimes when we suffer a great deal of pain, we cope with it by cutting off from our feelings, and memories can then consequently get suppressed. What Velmurugan did remember all too clearly was the cruelty of his stepmother, which drove him to take such drastic action on that now distant day.

Though he was not yet old enough to be aware of its geographical location, home for this little boy was a village in Tamil Nadu, not far from the southernmost tip of the subcontinent of India. After fleeing a certain distance, he somehow managed to board a train, eventually ending up in Chennai (then Madras), some four hundred and fifty miles to the north. Then, not even knowing the name of his village and not having the slightest idea how to get home again, he simply joined the bands of homeless children who then, as now, thronged the streets of that enormous city.

For about two years Velmurugan wandered the streets of Chennai and, being brighter than the average child in the same predicament, he took several premature steps into adulthood. He earned a bit of money from washing cars, he always had a spare shirt and made use of a particular tap for washing the dirty one, and he secured for himself a permanent 'bed' in the form of a little platform at a bus stop. By day, when he was not washing cars, he roamed the city just like all the other homeless children, begging from passers-by.

The support network on the streets of Chennai was strong, and Velmurugan made some firm friends, one of whom worked in a restaurant and used to bring him leftover food each evening. His good friend Paul was not homeless, but nevertheless joined with him in the car cleaning, and his closest friend of all was called Raju. In fact the bond between Velmurugan and Raju was so strong that at one point they decided to get each other's names tattooed onto their arms.

In 1970, Judith and Klaus, a young Australian-German couple, were taken to Chennai for several months by Klaus's work in the field of law. They shared the desire nowadays widespread among Westerners to help the 'exploited' countries through development projects and social reform rather than by handing out little sums to individuals. However, when one day Velmurugan approached them for food, their kind hearts were touched. Rather than giving him a rupee or a banana, they took him to their home and gave him a meal. Seeing Raju inscribed on his arm, they assumed that this was his name, and he has consequently been known as Raju ever since.

Raju's appreciation of his new friends' hospitality was such that meals at their abode rapidly became a daily occurrence, and

Judith and Klaus also adopted the habit of giving him the bus fare 'home' to his bus stop each evening. One day Raju decided that he wanted to write his generous hosts a letter and so, being of course illiterate, he found someone to whom to dictate it, putting the address as "Bus stop"!

After a little while Judith and Klaus decided that they might as well let Raju sleep at their place rather than always giving him the fare back to the bus stop. When the time for their return to Germany was approaching, they found that they did not like the thought of saying goodbye to their protégé, but Indian law made adoption difficult, if not impossible. So, after a lawyer had been approached, legal guardianship was agreed upon. They had, by the way, at some point during the interim, taken Raju to see a doctor, who, when they asked him the child's age, had replied, "Something between six and ten"!

Though he came from one of India's lowliest castes, his prospective guardians were quick to recognize Raju's intelligence and potential. Judith, being of a wonderfully motherly disposition, would have been only too happy to take him home with them straight away, but Klaus wisely felt that it would be better for the child not to be removed from his own culture. So they decided to put him into a boarding school, choosing for the purpose one of the very best schools in Chennai. Judith says now that she wonders whether this was in fact the best decision – whether Raju might have been better off in a school frequented by children of less high castes – but personally I feel that the struggle that he had in that school, where many of the other children looked down upon him, must have strengthened his character and given him some preparation for his role in later life. In England or America it is not that difficult for a bright child to escape from a lowly background, but Indian society is structured very differently. If one's name does not give one's caste away – after all names can (as we have just seen!) always be changed – one's features will most certainly do so.

At boarding school Raju had to learn not only the three 'Rs', but also to be a child again. Each summer, when the school was closed, Judith and Klaus had him to stay in their home in Germany. Two miscarriages and five years later their three natural children started to make their appearance. Far from being jealous, Raju, who had begun calling Judith "Mummy" even in the very early days of their acquaintance (though Klaus, for some reason, always remained "Klaus), proudly helped to push the pram, his dark Dravidian skin forming a striking contrast to his little siblings' pale complexions.

Like all parents – and particularly all adoptive parents – this wonderful couple had their ups and downs with their Indian son. But, as will be seen throughout this book, 'downs' are often converted into 'ups', and one instance of this was when Judith and Klaus had to contend with the 'beggar mentality', which is such a strong feature of Raju's caste. As he was completing his education, this firmly ingrained pattern of thinking made Raju feel that his foster parents should continue supporting him for life – that he did not need to earn his own living. Judith and Klaus were consequently forced to point out kindly but firmly that, since they had spent so much money on his education, it was then up to him to make use of it and to stand on his own feet. Before long their three younger children would be preparing to obtain university degrees and enter good professions, and there was of course no reason why Raju should be treated any differently.

After finishing school, Raju read for a degree in Mathematics at the University of Chennai (still at that point Madras). Before he had completed his studies, he obtained a little bit of part time employment teaching some of the younger undergraduates. One of his pupils was a student of History named Sheela, whose strong point was not mathematics but whose course included a certain amount of study of that subject. They fell in love, but in India marriages are always arranged by the parents, so what chance had Raju, an 'orphan', of persuading Sheela's parents to let her marry him? Furthermore, her family's reaction, which was a perfectly normal one in their stratum of society, was that Raju's mother must have been a prostitute and would consequently be totally unacceptable as a mother-in-law for their daughter.

During the many years that had elapsed since Raju had first left the extreme south, the place of his birth had never faded completely from his memory and he regularly described it to his friends and teachers. Although he did not know its name, certain images of his village, such as its very large tree, were indelibly engraved upon his mind, and he knew that he would recognize it immediately were he ever to find it. Once, not long before making the acquaintance of Sheela, Raju had been very ill and, with "Mummy" (i.e. Judith) far away in Germany, he had felt an intense longing to see his first parents again and to be cared for by his birth mother. So Sheela's parents' reaction gave him a further impetus; he knew for certain that his birth mother was not a prostitute and resolved to prove this to Sheela's family.

When he had first arrived in Chennai, Raju did not even know whether he had travelled from the north, south or west of his vast country, but he remembered something about the climate of his original home and so his studies of Indian geography at school helped him to realize that he had most likely come from the south. Other than that he had no clues. Miraculously, however, one of the teachers he talked to turned out to be from the very same village! This teacher was of course able to tell him how to get there and, on completing the journey, Raju asked around for anyone who had lost a child. The village barber was soon able to put him in touch with his mother, and the emotions engendered by this reunion can be left to the reader's imagination. His birth mother told Raju that his father was dead, but he was in due course able to meet up also with his younger brother and sister, who had both married and gone to live in neighboring villages. Once Raju had produced a genuine family (a German-Australian couple, wonderful foster parents though they were, could not count as 'parents' in India!), Sheela's parents were eventually persuaded to give their assent to the match.

After completing his degree, Raju took Klaus and Judith's firm words to heart and started seriously to develop his remarkable talents and business acumen. (Judith recounts how, when in the early days of their acquaintance she had asked him whether he could add two and two, he had replied negatively, but that when she asked, "What are two rupees plus two rupees?" he replied, "Four rupees," without a moment's hesitation!) He worked very hard, mainly as a tour guide for the Indian Government, for which of course his fluent German and English proved very useful. He bought a house in Chennai, and Sheela and he had three children.

Raju worked and he saved, and he worked and he saved, until eventually his roots began to pull him once again southwards – southwards to near the meeting point of the Bay of Bengal, the Indian Ocean and the Arabian Sea, each of which wash up different colored sands onto the shore, and where people throng daily to watch both the sunrise and the sunset. To near the rock just off the coast, where the great sage Vivekananda meditated and found inspiration to embark upon his preaching mission. To a part of this amazing land where huge flocks of egrets grace the paddy fields, where beautiful butterflies abound and enormous monkeys chase each other from tree to tree. Where peacocks roam freely, green parrots flit happily about in the early morn, and the hue of the kingfishers completely dazzles the incredulous Western eye. Here in this 'Earthly Paradise', at the foothills of the Western Ghats and on the edge of one of India's great national parks, Raju not only, in true Indian tradition, built a house for his mother in her own village, but also, in 2003, bought a sizeable plot of land, just a stone's throw away from where he had been born.

His plan for this land was to build a resort hotel, designed in the style of traditional Indian architecture, and, in December 2006, the Indien Hermitage (German spelling since 'Indian' was already patented) was opened. Raju's ultimate aim was to be able to accommodate forty-four guests in spacious bungalows, but the first stage was six one- or two-bedroomed cottages, set in gardens that were already being made beautiful, with also a wonderful swimming pool – one of the largest in the whole state – together with a spacious, open, reception and dining area, and of course a kitchen. They also planned to have Ayurvedic massage and an Ayurvedic doctor 'on tap', and did in fact already arrange that for one group who visited almost as soon as the hotel had opened.

In early February 2007, my husband David and I were near the start of seven weeks of travelling around India. Being a bit green and not realizing the full implications of the height of the Indian tourist season, we got caught out in Pondicherry, where we had immense difficulty in securing a hotel. Following this experience we resolved from then on always to try harder to book ahead, and one day, when we were making use of some public internet facilities, the man seated at the next computer overheard me asking David to look up Kanniyakumari hotels in the guidebook. He told us that he was a travel agent and could book us into a very nice resort hotel near to Kanniyakumari, which was too new to be in the guide books. The price he quoted was rather more than our normal daily budget, but nevertheless still less than an average British youth hostel, and so, following some partly negative experiences with hotels in Pondicherry, we leapt at the chance and asked him to book us in there for three nights a couple of weeks later.

In the meantime we visited Tiruvannamalai, where we followed the custom of walking round Ramana Maharshi's famous Arunachala Hill at full moon, Chennai, Marmallapuram, Madurai and Rameswara, and we also succeeded in booking train tickets from Madurai to Nagercoil, the nearest town to the

Indien Hermitage. Anyone who has ever done any travelling at all in India will appreciate that this train journey was in itself a challenge. It began with an argument with a porter, who (typically!) wanted to charge us four times the going rate, and ended with total failure to locate a porter at all. In between we regarded descent from the train with our heavy cases, in the dark with no announcement or any way of reading the name of the station, as quite an achievement. What is more, our arrival was a couple of hours later than we had been hoping and, once a porter in the form of a taxi driver had finally been secured, he had never heard of the brand new hotel into which we were booked. Fortunately, however, he had a mobile phone and was apparently able to understand the directions that he was given.

In one of the Indian cities that we visited, we were at one point driven past a very small eating establishment that was labelled "DINNING HALL." When I saw this, it occurred to me that it was something of an appropriate epithet for the whole of India! In streets where dogs bark and traffic roars all night, and where there are always so many people that everyone thinks that they need to shout louder than anyone else in order to be heard, the non-stop din is indescribable. It was not until I had suddenly escaped from it that I realized the extent to which it had been getting me down. Remote by day, Raju's resort hotel seemed even more remote by night, and our joy when we were greeted firstly by the blissful silence and secondly by the sweet, smiling face of Ayappam (whom we later discovered to be the cook) knew no bounds. After making us a cup of tea, Ayappam escorted us to our comfortable cottage and we sank quickly into some much needed sleep.

This sleep was, however, for both of us rudely interrupted in the early morning by a rather severe dose of the inevitable 'Indian tummy' (which I can't call 'Delhi belly' since we had not at that point yet been to Delhi!). David's intermittent stomach pains and concomitant symptoms had started a couple of days before my more or less identical ones, which made it look unlikely to have been caused by something we had eaten, but on the day of the train journey to Nagercoil we had both believed ourselves to be well on the road to recovery. However, being used to India because of my seven previous visits to Sai Baba's ashram, I was not unduly surprised and – once my intestines had turned themselves completely inside out – I quickly resigned myself to the thought of twenty-four hours of nothing but bed and water. Unable to sleep until well after it had got dark again, I simply lay in bed all day reveling in the silence, and I rapidly decided to extend our stay in the Indien Hermitage by at least another couple of nights.

David, however, prior to sleeping almost solidly for twenty-four hours (as is his enviable wont when he is unwell!) decided to put in an appearance at breakfast. He was greeted warmly not by Ayappam or Raju, but by Judith, now in her sixties and in a wheelchair. Five years previously she had had a spinal operation which had gone sadly wrong, but her indomitable spirit had prevented her from either succumbing to bitterness or anger, or from allowing her inability to walk to curtail her and Klaus' zest for travel. She explained to David that the hotel belonged to her foster son, for whom she was standing in for a month, and David readily joined in Ayappam's fortieth birthday breakfast party, where he also met Sheela, who had left the children in the care of her sister and come down to help as well. Raju and Sheela were planning, as soon as they could afford it, to build a house on the premises for the whole family, but for the moment the hotel building had naturally depleted their financial resources and so, when the opportunity of leading a group of Germans on a month's tour of India had come up, Raju had seized it. Judith and Klaus had of course been eager to see their eldest son's latest venture and, after spending a month there together, Klaus had had to return to Germany whereas she had succeeded in taking off an additional month from her work in order to help Sheela run the hotel.

We were at that moment the hotel's only guests, and the next day, after an excellent night's sleep, I felt ready, if not to eat, at least to enjoy having the large swimming pool entirely to myself. We both still felt a need to be very cautious about food but, while watching Sheela and Judith share one of Ayappam's delicious meals, we enjoyed conversing about our experiences of India and about our respective families. Little by little Judith recounted to us her fascinating tale and, when evening came, we also made the acquaintance of Raju's birth mother. Since my Tamil is even more non-existent than her English, anything more than a very sweet smile and a "Good morning," (which she says both morning and evening!) was impossible, but Judith explained to us that, in true Indian tradition, during Raju's absence both he and his mother felt that Sheela should not be allowed to sleep alone. Raju's birth mother's village is, as I said, not very far away, and so she arrived at the hotel each evening, and each morning she returned by taxi to her herd of goats.

After some much needed rest, David and I both soon became fit enough to do the touristy things in the area, but our first port of call had to be the station in order to book a train for our next destination. Reluctant though we were to tear ourselves away from such an idyllic spot and Judith's excellent company, we had an appointment in Mysore and had also booked a flight from Bangalore to Pune. Mysore is a long way from Nagercoil, and Kozhikode seemed from the map to be a good halfway point. Sheela kindly volunteered to telephone Raju for advice on hotels there, and she discovered that he was going to be in Bangalore with his German group on the very same night as we were! He was keen to meet us, and so I told him the name of our hotel and urged him to come and join us for a meal there. In the end we stayed six nights at the Indien Hermitage before heading northwards again, and our visit to Mysore will come into the next chapter.

On arrival at the hotel in Bangalore, I was just completing the form at the hotel reception desk when Raju telephoned. He needed to be with his group for the evening meal, but said that he could come round for a coffee within half an hour. The meeting had unfortunately to be brief, but it was long enough for me to tell him about the book I was planning to write, gain permission to use his story, and ask him a few questions.

During the conversations that we had had over five days, we felt that people who had named two of their children after Mozart and Bach would have to become good friends of ours, and Judith and I also discovered a number of other things that we had in common. One of these was Catholicism, but, unlike myself who had some years previously become interested in regression therapy, Judith and Klaus have never had any reason to study the Gnostics or the great Christian clairvoyant Edgar Cayce, or to consider the fact that belief in reincarnation was widespread in the early Church until it was suppressed at the Council of Constantinople in AD 553. But they are very open-minded people and, like his Christian headmistress, they never attempted to foist their own religious beliefs onto Raju, who has always been left free to find his own way spiritually. Hinduism, with its concomitant belief in reincarnation and karma, pervades the air he breathes, and Sheela, too, comes from a Hindu family. When I asked him whether he believed that he had chosen Judith and Klaus because of having known them before, Raju replied very emphatically in the affirmative.

"When I was living on the streets," he said, "there was once an American woman who took me many times to eat in restaurants, but when she offered to take me back with her to America, I said, 'No thank you,' that I was happier where I was. On the other hand, when on one occasion Judith had to go to Sri Lanka, I cried bitter tears and begged her to take me with her. Obviously my bond with these two wonderful people was much, much stronger than the one with the American woman, and that can only have come from previous acquaintance." Though he has never had any means of proving it, Raju believes it to be very likely that Judith and Klaus have been his parents before, and he thinks that it is mainly for that reason that he feels more attachment to them than he does to his birth mother. The same is true for all his siblings. His three German siblings have always talked of him as their Indian brother, and he feels much closer to them than he does to his younger brother and sister in Tamil Nadu.

In talking with Raju, it became clear that he believes very firmly in destiny – that we make a plan for our lives – and that people come together for a reason. After all, we agreed, what were the chances of my 'happening' to sit next to that travel agent when I was on the internet in Pondicherry? And in such a vast country as India, when we were both travelling around all over the place, could our coinciding for just one night in Bangalore have been entirely due to chance? Personally I believe that it was not. I had had the idea for a book on adoption at the back of my mind for quite a long time, and I know that I have guides on the other side who help me with my writing. Why did I on this particular trip feel so very strongly drawn to Kanniyakumari, when there are so many places in northern India that are generally more popular with tourists? Why was I prepared to miss out even the Ganga (Varanasi, and Rishikesh, which friends had recommended so strongly) in favor of a part of the country whose climate my long-suffering husband found more difficult to cope with? Why, when we had done a bit of travelling in southern India three years previously – three years before the Indien Hermitage had opened – had I suggested Kerala rather than the southernmost tip? Was it because the time was not then ripe for us all to meet? Personally I firmly believe this to be the case, as does Raju.

Alas, as soon as Raju had finished his coffee, he had to return to the hotel where his German group were having dinner, but we parted 'friends for life', knowing for sure that we would one day meet again for longer in his welcoming hotel (where I am certain that we will never again be the only visitors, because once it has got into the guide books it should, I believe, become very popular).

Until we do meet again (and possibly for the rest of my life) questions will linger in my mind, but on the other hand I feel no urgency to get them answered. Anyone who has already read my third book will be aware of my belief in a Life Plan made before we come in to each of our incarnations – a belief which Raju shares. To me it is already clear that Raju needed to have parents like Judith and Klaus to help him to realize his potential, but what is less clear is his reason for choosing different parents initially. Obviously he had work to do in India rather than in Germany, but why the need for him to endure such a difficult childhood? For sure it must have strengthened his character, and is it not also a wonderful example for his country of what *can* be done – proof that caste boundaries *can* be broken? Probably, too, his birth mother needed to learn about loss; and also, if she had not suffered his loss for so many years, Raju would not now be in a position to help her in the way that he has been doing recently.

CHAPTER TWO

KATE AND NANDA'S STORY

The Indian way of life provides the vision of the natural, real way of life. We veil ourselves with unnatural masks. On the face of India are the tender expressions which carry the mark of the Creator's hand.

George Bernard Shaw

David and I had been intending to explore the backwaters of Kerala but, after having for such good reasons prolonged our stay near the southernmost tip of India, that had to be left for another occasion. We carried on to the state of Karnataka, where we had arranged to visit my English friend Kate, her Indian husband Anil, and the small home that they were running for children who are either orphans or whose families are unable to care for them. Since Kate and I had first met in a Sai Baba group[1], when she was in Europe seeking funding for their work, I knew that she would share my views on the fact that people come together again who have known each other in previous lives, and that they do so for good reasons. I was interested to know whether, among the many children that Kate had cared for over a number of years, there were some to whom she had felt closer than others, i.e. some with whom she believed her karmic links to be particularly strong.

Kate had when we first made friends told me how she had always longed for children of her own, and how she had had to come to terms with the disappointment of that dream not being fulfilled, and this, my first, visit to her Indian home gave us time for further conversation. She told me about a clairvoyant reading she had once had, in which she had been informed of a lifetime in which she had been cruel to children. This was hard to imagine, seeing her now as such a wonderful mother figure for the those in her care, but she herself appreciates that she is paying a debt from that previous lifetime, firstly by not being able to conceive successfully herself, and secondly by caring for children who are in such great need of a good home.

When I put my question to her, Kate told me about the child, now a married adult, whom she had tried to adopt when she had been working in an orphanage in Tamil Nadu, before she and Anil had married. Nanda was only about four or five when they first met, and his parents had brought him from Sri Lanka to the orphanage because they could not afford to keep him. The mutual attraction had been instantaneous and, although the attempts Kate made to adopt him legally were thwarted, she explained that he is still like a son to her and that they are in very regular communication despite the distance between the states in which they each live. After she had moved to Karnataka with Anil, and Nanda had left the orphanage, Kate supported him financially through further education, and she still gives him all the support she can in his work as an artist. Recently, when his birth mother got in touch with him about resuming contact, Nanda refused to meet her once he had realized that she was only hoping to get money from him. He clearly regards Kate as his 'real' mother and the bond between them remains as strong as ever despite their failure nowadays to meet very often.

Following my return from this trip to India something prompted me to do a regression on the question of my relationship with Kate. When I told her later about what it had revealed both about that *and* about her previous relationship with Nanda, she found it as interesting as I had!

My Regression

"Priya, Priya, come here! Your mother's got the meal ready, and anyway it's time for you to stop playing such boyish games. Tell your friends they should go home too. You're a young lady now.

We need to talk to you soon about something very important."

Bother! Why did father have to go and spoil things? I was having such fun showing Bandhu that I could climb that tree faster than he could. Of course Father, being so high up in the temple, disapproved of my playing with boys of a lower caste. In fact he really disapproved of my playing with boys at all. It was silly – and annoying – but I suppose the sun would soon be going down now anyway, and maybe I was getting a bit hungry.

The food was good, as always, but I was not in the least prepared for what came with it. "Your mother and I," said my father seriously, "think that it is time for you to prepare for marriage."

"Marriage!" I exclaimed in horror. "I'm much too young for that, and anyway who would want a young girl like me as a wife when I would much rather be playing with Bandhu and his friends than cooking or sweeping?"

"It's more than time that you grew out of those boyish games," replied my father. "And Bhardwajj and I think that Chetan would be a very suitable husband for you – especially since you share so much talent for music."

Bhardwajj was my father's closest colleague in the temple, and Chetan was about five years older than me. I loved him a lot and he taught me to play the sitar and encouraged my *bhajan* (devotional song) singing, but I didn't love him in the sort of way that I would want to love a husband. In any case I knew that Chetan was in love with Chaaya. I had seen them more than once sneaking off into the woods together; but I sensed that they would want to keep that a secret and nothing would make me be disloyal to Chetan. I did not know what to say, so I simply protested, "I'm sure Chetan wouldn't want such a marriage."

My father replied coolly, "It isn't up to him. You know perfectly well that it is the parents' duty to choose partners for their children. Bhardwajj and his wife discussed this matter with us some time ago and we just had to wait until you were both old enough to inform you of our decision."

I decided to plead tiredness and retired to bed to think about what to do. Had Chetan been informed of this, I wondered to myself, or would he be as shocked as I was? Well, I could find out the very next morning, when we were due to meet for my music lesson. In the meantime there was nothing to be done but sleep, though that clearly wasn't going to be easy when I had something so big to worry about. Ah well, I could pray to Krishna, I suppose. Chetan was such an ardent devotee of Krishna's, and He would surely be sympathetic about our dilemma.

Morning did eventually come, and it was just as I had feared: Chetan seemed if anything to be even more shocked than I was. "It's not that I'm not fond of you—" he stammered, but I interrupted.

"Don't worry about explaining. I've noticed you with Chaaya and I'm sure she really loves you. She's older than me anyway, and no doubt much more ready for marriage."

"Oh dear, so you've seen us sneaking off together? I thought we'd managed to keep it a secret. Have you told anyone?"

"Can't you trust me? I'd never do that!"

"Of course I trust you," said Chetan fondly. "And it's good to have a friend who understands. If only our fathers weren't so high up in the temple, it might not be such a problem for a Brahmin to marry someone of a lower caste, but as it is I don't see how my parents can ever be persuaded. I just don't know what to do. I don't think I could live without Chaaya, and we'd both really love to have children."

"Well, if your parents refuse to agree to the match, why don't you just run away together?"

"If only we could! Life doesn't seem so complicated when you're only fourteen, but by the time you're my age you have to think about earning a living. If I stay here in our village I'll always be sure of employment in the temple, but if I went elsewhere, what could I do to support us both, and where could we live?"

"No problem!" I replied. "You're such a gifted musician, and you can make wonderful instruments as well as playing them and teaching, so why don't you just concentrate on that and not worry about whether another temple would take you on? But in any case how can you be sure your father will say 'no' until you've asked him?"

"Well, I suppose there's no harm in telling him what you've just told me, and making it clear that neither of us wants this marriage."

In fact Chetan turned out to be quite right, alas. His parents were furious when he told them about his love for Chaaya. They came straight over to our house to tell my parents, and they were equally angry. My father accused me of encouraging Chetan's 'disgraceful' relationship and forbade me to see him or to go out and play with my friends. I was depressed, but determined nevertheless to help Chetan and Chaaya. So gradually I hatched a plan.

As well as being musical, Chetan had a great love of elephants. One of his duties was the charge of the temple elephant, his family owned two other elephants besides, and he had taught me to ride one just a couple of years previously – a thing which greatly suited my tomboyish nature. I chose a moment to slip out of the house when I knew that my father would be busy working with Bhardwajj and Chetan would be giving the temple elephant its last feed, taking with me some food from the large store at the back of our house. "Since your family have two elephants and several servants," I said to Chetan when I'd sneaked in, "why don't you and Chaaya elope with one of each? You would all three fit on the elephant's back, and you can take this food for the journey, which I know my mother won't miss as we have so much."

"What a girl you are!" laughed Chetan in reply. "Well, Dhiraj has always been good to me. Perhaps he'd be willing to show us the way to his village. He goes back there from time to time to visit his ageing parents, and I'm sure that they're good people. Do you think you could possibly go and ask Chaaya what she thinks of the idea while I talk to Dhiraj? If we do go, I think there's no time to waste. Could you ask her, if she's willing, to come and meet me here in about an hour's time? Tell her to bring a few clothes with her of course, but nothing else. I'll have to take my sitar and all the tools I use for making instruments."

How exciting! Even though I would still have to endure my father's wrath, I loved the thought of an adventure. I found Chaaya, who was fortunately alone outside her house, and needless to say she was more than willing. Then I sneaked back into the house before my parents realized that I had gone.

What a to-do the next morning! I feigned complete surprise of course, and succeeded in appearing to be very upset. So much so that my father repented slightly of his harsh treatment and promised to look for another music teacher for me. From the reports I got, it sounded as though Bhardwajj's family were even angrier about the loss of the elephant and the servant than they were about the elopement. I thought that my parents might now let me be a child again, at least for a while, and my mother did indeed agree to let me out of the house when I offered to go and search for clues as to where the guilty foursome might have headed for. "Just so long as you don't stray beyond the confines of the village…" But she didn't think to forbid me to go and look for Bandhu.

I didn't even confide to Bandhu my knowledge of what had happened. Rumors always spread so fast in this little world of ours, and I didn't want to be disloyal to Chetan and Chaaya. But then a whole month went by and I began really to miss Chetan and my music lessons very much. When we went to the temple for worship I couldn't put the same zest into my singing, and Father hadn't got round to looking for another teacher for me.

Then suddenly one day the missing servant returned with news. His master was doing fine, he said, having secured a post as a music teacher in the village where Dhiraj, the servant himself, came from, and as for the beautiful Miss Chaaya, she was much in demand for her skills in sewing and weaving. They had secured a modest home for themselves, and no one disapproved of their living together because they had not realized that they were not married. When my father heard this he became angrier than ever but, to my great surprise, he agreed to let me go and visit them in the company of the servant, whom Bhardwajj refused to take back into his employment because of his disloyalty. He said that I could go there for two days on condition that Dhiraj then brought me straight home again.

What a wonderful two days they were! It was so good to be away from home for the first time in my life, and better still to see my dear friends so happy together. Chetan was truly delighted to see me again too, and we spent some joyful hours making music, with Chetan also showing me the instruments that he was busy making. Since Chaaya was not a Brahmin, I had never really had the opportunity to get to know her before they left, but she greeted me most warmly and we began to form a strong bond. To my amazement, when I returned home again, my father agreed to allow me to continue to visit them once a month, but it gradually became apparent that his reason for permitting this was a hope that Chetan would change his mind and transfer his affections from Chaaya to me. A hope that was of course completely unfounded.

Two years went by, Chaaya gave birth to their first child, and Chetan was selling so many of his instruments that he was able to save enough money to buy the family a larger house. Then adventure came to me too! One day a handsome man turned up in our village and came to show my father and Bharwajj some instruments that he had made. They agreed to commission some, since they had been missing Chetan's talent and of course refused to buy any instruments from him. This man, whose name I later found out to be Ganesh, noticed me as he was leaving the temple and made eyes at me. At sixteen I was developing into an attractive girl and beginning to push my boyish ways aside, and when I felt his gaze, it sent a rush of blood to my head and my heart started to throb in a way that I had never before experienced. So I yearned to see him again, and sure enough he came back a few days later with the first commissioned instrument completed. I happened to be walking past the temple as he arrived, and this time he spoke to me somewhat flirtatiously. I explained who I was, and he commented on the beautiful color of my sari, and my eyes, which he said were like deep pools into which he would love to sink. When he expressed a wish to meet me again, I did not know what to say, fearing that it would only cause trouble if I suggested that he talk to my father. So I simply ran home rather fast, but that night I had great difficulty in sleeping!

I hardly like to recount the rest of the tale – so very painful is it for me – but when Ganesh finally disappeared for good a year or so later, and my father somehow found out about our relationship, it seemed like the end of the world for me. My parents were in total despair as to what to do, since losing my virginity had made me now 'unmarriageable', but then my good friend Chetan came to the rescue.

"You could come and live here," he said. "You would be good company for Chaaya and the child when I have to go off on my travels selling my instruments." They had sadly lost their first child, but little Kamlesh, whom I loved dearly, was already learning to walk and becoming quite a handful. I was delighted at the suggestion and didn't even tell my parents, but simply decided not to return home after my next visit. Before long I had become noted for my *bhajan* singing in the temple that Chetan's family attended, and the chief priest there offered me a small salary in return for performing various minor duties. What is more, I got given an important role on the joyous day when Chetan and Chaaya finally married!

I wondered at first how long it would be until my parents came looking for me, but in fact they never did. News of my new life reached them somehow or other, and they sent messages back which implied that they felt themselves to be well rid of me. I grieved much more for Ganesh than for them, but gradually Chaaya convinced me that he was not worth weeping over. More worthy of my tears were their subsequent three children who lived only briefly, but in due course Kamlesh acquired a sister who was strong and healthy, and we all felt happy and rewarded by such a lovely family. Chetan did so well with his work that in time he even saved enough to build me a little house adjoining theirs. This was an ideal arrangement, as it meant that I was close enough to be of real help to Chaaya when he was away, without having to be under their feet when the family wanted privacy.

* * *

Well, that regression was a surprise! But should it have been? Kate, who was Chetan in that Indian life, had clearly had very many previous lives in India, which she had now made her home, she had learnt to speak three Indian languages, and one of her present greatest joys in life was teaching the children in her care to sing *bhajans*. The fact that we had made friends very quickly suggested that we must have known each other well in at least one previous life. Since I have not yet met Nanda, I have no way of proving that he was previously Chaaya (and even if I did meet him, I would still be unable to prove it to anyone else!), but I somehow felt sure that he was. When I told Kate about what I had seen, it made a good deal of sense to her. She commented that it explained why Anil felt a bit jealous of Nanda, even though he had no obvious reason to be, since theirs had always been a mother/son type of relationship without any sexual element at all. It made her happy too, not having been able to achieve a successful pregnancy this time round, to think that the bond between her and her – for want of a better adjective – 'adopted' son was so strong.

As for me, it appears that I have a karmic debt to Kate from a lifetime in which she (then he) had cared for me better than had my parents. No doubt that is partly why I always feel such a strong desire to give what financial support I can for her work with the children!

Note

1. Sathya Sai Baba is an Indian *avatar* (divine incarnation). For more information about Him see my book *Souls United – The Power of Divine Connection*, Llewellyn, USA, 2009.

CHAPTER THREE

HOGARTH AND THE FOUNDLING HOSPITAL

> *...glass cabinets filled with buttons, acorns, hairclips...tiny, pathetic keepsakes mums left behind for their babies to remember them by. A pointless exercise, it turns out, because the first thing the orphanage did was to change the baby's name. With a different name their old history would end...*
> From 'Mister Pip' by Lloyd Jones

The renowned British artist William Hogarth was born in 1697 into a Britain which was not only the richest nation on Earth, but also comfortable in just about every way and proud of the great improvements it had made in society and in public affairs. Yet, as the art historian Malcolm Oxley[1] points out, the eighteenth-century British were very far from excelling in the Arts. It was Italians who were dominant in the theatre, the French in dance and as for British music, well, that was Handel (who, being born German, should really be called Haendel!). Hogarth through his life gradually drew around himself quite a large circle of eminent men, and all of them were of the opinion that there was something amiss here. He himself was actually trained as an engraver, never as a painter, and Oxley, who likes to draw analogies with football leagues, says that he would put Hogarth only in the Third Division for his painting. His reputation probably stems more from his innovative approach and the subjects he chose for his paintings rather than their quality.

Hogarth's own father was a Latin teacher, who sadly spent five years in a debtor's prison following the failure of his Latin-speaking coffee house. This must have affected the young William, who was always on the side of the disadvantaged and a great supporter of charitable institutions. He hated Papism for its lack of emphasis on the importance of good works. He was from its beginning a governor of the Foundling Hospital, which continues today as the children's charity Coram, and he donated paintings to it as a method of self-promotion, as well as persuading other English painters to do the same. The Foundling Hospital had become a fashionable place to visit, its Art Gallery became Britain's first public one, and Georg Frideric Handel conducted benefit concerts in the Hospital chapel. In fact, after the first performance of *The Messiah*, in Dublin, had been something of a flop, Handel organized its next performance there in 1750 and in all he conducted the work at the Foundling Hospital nine times before his death in 1759.

The Foundling Hospital was established by Royal Charter in 1739, after a long struggle by Captain Thomas Coram (1668–1751), a successful shipwright and sailor who had returned to England to retire after a life's work in the New World of America. Coram had been appalled by the discarded and dying children in the streets of London and spent seventeen years campaigning for the establishment of a Foundling Hospital. Supported by the burgeoning fashion for charity and benevolence in eighteenth-century London, King George II signed the Charter on 17 October 1739 incorporating the hospital for the "Maintenance and Education of Exposed and Deserted Young Children." The first meeting of the Foundling Hospital Governors was held in November 1739, and the first children were received into the Hospital's care in 1741. After having been ousted from the Board for criticizing some of the other governors, Coram continued to visit the Hospital and he acted as godfather to more than twenty foundlings. He died in 1751 and his wish to be buried beneath the altar of the Hospital Chapel was granted.

Upon entering the hospital children were baptized and given a new name. Up until the end of the eighteenth century, mothers also left a token which could be used to identify the child if the parent made a request to claim him or her at a later date. As the city of London grew, it was decided in 1926 to move the hospital out of London and a new building was erected in Berkhamsted in Hertfordshire. The old site was sold and the hospital demolished, apart from a few fragments and interiors that can be seen in the Foundling Museum today. This Museum is in Brunswick Square, London, and the Foundling tokens are displayed there. Many of them bring tears to the eyes. The Foundling Hospital continued to operate until 1954, and during its two hundred and fifty years of operation it cared for over 25,000 children. When new social attitudes and approaches to childcare made the institutional model outdated, the hospital's last remaining children were placed in foster homes, and nowadays Coram, which was previously named the Thomas Coram Foundation for Children, aims to develop and promote good practice in the care of vulnerable children, young people and their families. This provides a living link with Thomas Coram's pioneering work and the original mission of the Foundling Hospital.

Noble though Coram's ideas were, however, there are still people alive today whose memories of living in such institutions are far from happy. In fact in March 2014 Macmillan published a book entitled *The Last Foundling*; its author, who was born in 1939 to Jean Craig, was renamed Tom when poor Jean surrendered him reluctantly to the Foundling Hospital to avoid the scandal of being an unmarried mother. He was fostered initially by a loving family, but at the age of five was forcibly returned to the hospital's boarding school, where he suffered not only a total absence of love and affection, but also a great deal of cruelty. Fortunately the 1946 Curtis Report, which looked into the needs of children in care, resulted in big improvements being made, but these came much too late for many, and Tom, whose real name was Derek, was in any case never told anything at all about his background. Always convinced that his birth mother was still "out there somewhere," he eventually succeeded in tracing her, and – most unusually I am sure – Jean and her husband Duncan adopted him just before he was twenty-one and he has since borne their surname, Mackenzie. He came to realize, through three failed marriages, that he was always searching for a mother rather than a wife, but it seems he has been 'fourth time lucky' as it was his present wife who encouraged him to write the book.

I query his claim to be "the last foundling" and here is the story of another one, who was even less fortunate than Derek/Tom, but who has nevertheless succeeded in making a great deal of her life.

A Dancer's Story

Patrick and Marion were deeply in love, but the problem was that she was a working class Catholic and he a fairly upper class Protestant, and their families would not agree to their marrying. When Marion found that she was pregnant, the stress proved too great for Patrick and he abandoned her. Marion's father's reaction was to say to her, "Don't ever bring that bastard into this house!" It was the 1930s, and there were insufficient adoptive families in England for the number of babies needing homes, so initially Marion left her little Rachel in the hospital and sneaked out to see her occasionally. Then, when the baby was a few months old, Marion reluctantly took her to the Foundling Hospital. The first thing that they did was to change all the baby's clothes to brown institutional ones, and the second thing was to change her name from Rachel Evans to Gertrude Polson. Then she was placed in a rural foster home, where, like Derek, she remained for about five years.

These foster parents, Mr. and Mrs. Robinson, were both very loving people, and they took to the baby instantly and treated her as their own. Disliking the name Gertrude, they decided to call her Polly, and their natural son, Norman, who was a few years older, loved her very much as well. Alas, after a while Norman became seriously ill and the authorities decided that the Robinsons must surrender Polly in order to be better able to care for their own child. She was then sent to a new foster home in a fairly unsavory part of outer London, but during term time she boarded at the Foundling Hospital's school.

Polly was infinitely less happy with the Locke family in this second foster home – especially since she missed the countryside – but had nevertheless to endure living there on and off until she was eleven. Wartime rations were inadequate for both her appetite and her health, and air raids also did a lot to increase her unhappiness. Polly says that she was born believing in reincarnation, which made her sure that things would get better for her one day, but she was of course severely reprimanded whenever she dared to voice her ideas in the Christian institution in which she was being educated. Nor were any of her natural talents encouraged. She was gifted at art, writing and singing, but her greatest passion was dancing. However, when she voiced her desire to become a professional dancer, she was told in no uncertain terms that the only work opportunities that would ever be available to her would be as either a cleaner or, if she was very lucky indeed, a nanny.

When the Locke parents at the second home told her that they were going to apply to adopt her, she immediately ran away. She knew that their reason was not love but the fact that they found her useful as a baby sitter for their own two children, and she was still badly missing the Robinsons, her first foster family. Many years later she was told in a clairvoyant reading that Mr. and Mrs. Robinson had been her natural parents in a previous life in France, and that she had been happily married to their son Norman in another lifetime in Egypt. This made a great deal of sense to her, and she eventually succeeded in tracking them down just before Mrs. Robinson's death. It was a very happy reunion, even though Mr. Robinson told her that they had never really got over losing her. Norman had eventually pulled through his illness and, by the time they met again, was married with a family of his own, but they have kept in touch. This friendship has been a great consolation at difficult times during Polly's life.

After running away from the second foster home, Polly realized that she had nowhere to go, which of course reinforced the feelings that being a foundling had always given her. Only the joy of dancing enabled her to cut off from those feelings, and the opportunities for doing that at school were few and far between. The first night after leaving the Lockes she slept under a tree in a London park (fortunately it was summer!), but when she was found the next day she was forced, if only through hunger, to admit where she had come from. She did not, however, mention the foster home but only the school, and so it was there that the police took her. She was greeted not by a meal but by a beating, but one of the staff eventually took pity on her when she gave the reasons for her unhappiness. So she was found another foster home with a family named Davis, where she settled quickly and happily. It was not the Foundling school's policy to place children in the same homes every holiday, but after sampling various different homes, Polly kicked up such a fuss when they tried to send her to anywhere but the Davises that they relented. The Davises would in fact have liked to adopt her, but could not afford to do so.

Although they were not well off, the Davises had an appreciation of the Arts and always encouraged their own two children's musical abilities. Michael, the older one, was learning to play the violin and would often when he was practicing, find little tunes for Polly to dance to. Since the whole family recognized her talent, she was not afraid to confide to them her ambition, and it was entirely thanks to their encouragement that she determined to pursue it. When it was time for her to leave school, securing funding for anything such as a ballet school was out of the question, but once she was too old for the Davises to continue to be paid for her care, they were happy for her to go on living with them while she did odd jobs to pay for her keep. She was so determined and so economical that she managed to save a good part of her earnings to spend on occasional dancing lessons.

In due course Polly's dancing got noticed and she was occasionally offered stage performances. The director of one such performance, whose name was Don, fell in love with her and, when she left the Davises to get married, her foster sister was bridesmaid and her foster brother played his violin at the wedding. The marriage lasted for some years, but having two children made it impossible for her to pursue a full time dancing career. She made up for that afterwards, however, by training as a dance teacher, and even now that she is well into her seventies and enjoying grandmotherhood, she is still able to give classes in such things as circle dancing. She succeeded for many years in suppressing all the pain of her past, but that is something that can never be done forever. Suppressing so much suffering will either little by little cause an illness such as cancer, or else it will force itself to the surface and then explode. The latter is (fortunately!) what happened with Polly, who is a survivor, and who no doubt knew deep down how much she had come to give to the world. It was incredibly hard for Don as well as for her, because she had frequent flashbacks to her ill treatment of the past, about which he had been given no preparation.

Marion eventually married and had more children, but she naturally never got over having had to give her baby up and she did in due course find her despite her new married name. Should we be surprised that Polly did not immediately welcome her birth mother with open arms? Besides any subconscious feelings of rejection that she was probably holding, Polly was consciously very aware that all the suffering inflicted on her both in school and by having been moved throughout her tender years from pillar to post was caused by Marion's "dumping" her in an institution as a tiny baby. The idea of meeting her mother consequently aroused quite a lot of anger, but she agreed to it nevertheless, if only as a means of expressing her feelings. The relationship was initially quite fraught, but one good effect it had was to push Polly into therapy.

Although she had in childhood been forced to suppress her conviction about having lived before, it never really left her and so, after reading various books on reincarnation making friends with people who were steeped in alternative medicine, she decided to try some regression sessions. From these she discovered a male lifetime in which she had been married to Marion and had abandoned her. This of course helped her to appreciate the karma that existed between them and also, as they communicated more, she came to understand what her birth mother had been through and to have compassion for her. They made peace before Marion died, and Polly was able to help her mother recognize the reasons for what had been in their Life Plans. Polly also found out through regression about some of her previous links with the Davises. These included a troubadour lifetime in which they had all been good friends as wandering musicians!

Although the therapy was invaluable for Polly, and Don was very supportive, it put a great strain on the marriage, which in due course ended amicably. While he has remarried, she is content to remain single, finding life very full with numerous activities besides her family commitments and occasional dancing classes. She kept in touch with Mr. and Mrs. Davis until their deaths and still sees their children occasionally. Don's main interest is still in dance, but he has never come round to her spiritual beliefs, which makes her feel that a separation at some point would always have been on the cards. Her children too, while being in no way hostile, laugh at many of her ideas. They have, however, no objection to her talking with her grandchildren about spiritual matters, and she says that two of them are "remarkably psychic." This accords with the view (which I am indeed finding with my own grandchildren) that numerous highly evolved souls are at present incarnating into our needy world. So we have good reason to hope for huge improvements in child care as well as numerous other things!

CHAPTER FOUR

A FOSTER SISTER'S STORY

Native Americans understand intuitively that all children deserve a symbolically crafted life story that includes origins; that "if you don't know who you are, you don't know where anything else fits."… Jerome Bruner … recalled that his mother used to save some old dough to make bread: "It's called Mother's Dough. You need a bit of the past to make the present."

Betty Jean Lifton, *Journey of the Adopted Self – A Quest for Wholeness*

Annabel's parents (Harry and Judy) were Somerset farmers and Methodists, and through their church they were put in touch in the 1950s with an orphanage in Bristol that was seeking farm holidays for some of the boys in its care. The couple had sadly lost their own son at an early age and partly for this reason they were happy to offer a home to boys in need. Gradually the holidays developed into something more permanent, and by the time Harry and Judy's first daughter was born they regularly had anything up to eight or nine boys living with them at any one time, some for short periods, others for longer. They were nevertheless always categorized as short-term foster parents, and in those days foster care was much less professional than it is now. Harry and Judy were paid nothing by the orphanage that sent the boys, and often the children were taken away from them suddenly and for no apparent reason. It was a labor of love, but at least it gave them some help on the farm. As for the boys (Harry and Judy never took girls), working on the farm served both to keep them out of trouble and to give them a sense of purpose. Some of them in due course made careers as farm laborers, while others went into the forces, and one that Annabel remembers even became a doctor.

Annabel was born ten and a half years after her sister Mary, and there was never a time in her childhood when there were no boys living in the house. She has memories of many of them and has kept in touch with several, but just two stand out as being people with whom she knows she has strong past life connections. Her parents never forced their religion on to their daughters and Annabel never took to Methodism, but she always knew that her path was a spiritual one and that she had lived many times before. Her father (who she says is undoubtedly an old soul) always supported her in everything she did, and she never had any reservations about sharing with him whatever she was learning or doing. As she grew up she developed interests in such things as Tarot and clairvoyance, and nowadays she works as a healer, counsellor, hypnotherapist and past life regression therapist. In fact Harry was sufficiently interested to actually do some regressions with Annabel. In one session he saw himself as a farmer on the Nottinghamshire border and even gave its name. It was not a place that either of them had ever heard of, but Annabel then did some research and succeeded in tracing the farm he had named.

So the two foster brothers in our story are Pete and Arthur, and they could hardly provide a greater contrast to one another. They also give support to my thesis that, while both 'nature and nurture' (i.e. genes and environment) are important in character formation, what is innate – and developed from past-life experiences – is at least equally so. Pete, who is nine years older than Annabel, has been her 'big brother' all her life. Harriet, his birth mother, whom he traced after reaching adulthood, was a teacher and an alcoholic, and he was the result of a brief fling that she had with an African. (Pete has not succeeded in tracing his father and so does not know his nationality.) As soon as he was born, Harriet, who never told her family that she had had a child, placed him in the Bristol orphanage with a view to his being adopted, but that sadly never happened. Harry and Judy, however, grew so fond of Pete while they were fostering him that they asked to adopt him. This was refused on the grounds that there were no other black children in the neighborhood and, when Judy became pregnant with Annabel, Pete was taken away from them. They managed to get him back soon after the birth, but over the ensuing years he was frequently taken back to the orphanage. In the orphanage the boys always wrapped themselves up in the sheets like mummies for security, and presents that foster families had given to them were always taken off them. Pete did, however, somehow manage to keep the torch that Harry and Judy had given him.

Though Pete never bonded with Mary, her older sister, the repeated toing and froing between the orphanage and the farm did not prevent him from forming an extraordinarily strong bond with Annabel. (Mary resented his existence, regarding him as a supposed replacement for her deceased brother; she has consequently always been rude to him.) He has had a highly successful life, becoming, after going to university, first a social worker and then a psychotherapist, and he is now happily married with two sons. The orphanage was fortunately closed many years ago, but Pete was once asked to go and talk to a 'survivors' group'. That laid his ghost about the time he spent there, and nowadays he never likes to talk about it.

Arthur on the other hand was sixteen when he first came to the farm. He had always been troublesome, was violent and drinking too much, and, after having been excluded from school, he had spent a brief time in borstal. Annabel, who was eighteen months at the time and upset at her beloved Pete having just been sent back to the orphanage, was throwing a temper tantrum when Arthur first walked into their kitchen upon arrival. He went over to her, picked her up and, she says, "That was it! From then on I followed him everywhere. We were inseparable, and I sobbed my heart out for a week when he went into the Army."

But Arthur's story, alas, does not have a happy ending, despite what Annabel describes as his "gorgeous looks." His attachment to Annabel and her family has always been over-possessive. He is also racist and had never liked Pete when they were both in the orphanage. So he did not share Annabel's joy when Pete returned 'home' and is still always jealous of him. He did not even like it at all when his own younger brother and sister joined the family. (Although Harry and Judy normally only took boys, they naturally felt it important to make an exception when it was a case of keeping siblings together.) They were by now expert at dealing with 'social outcasts', and they managed to get Arthur off drink for a while, but it sadly did not last. Now sixty-five, he is seriously alcoholic and has never been persuaded to try to do anything about it.

Arthur did stay in the Army for ten years, but then he was thrown out because of his constant fighting and boozing. After that he went through a series of jobs and relationships, but has now been out of work for twenty-three years. He married three times and has three daughters (two by the second wife and a third by the third, who was a prostitute). His wives all left him because of his violence and alcoholism, but he has always blamed others for what happens to him and has made several suicide attempts. Unable to tolerate his behavior any more, Harry and Judy lost touch with him for over twenty years. Judy predicted that he would "die lonely," and Annabel now fears that she was right. The eldest of his daughters is now twenty-three and a drug addict and alcoholic, but the younger two have nevertheless done miraculously well for themselves. The second one, now twenty-one, is an office manager and married, but Arthur, who has absolutely no social graces anyway, refused to attend the wedding because he did not like the man she was marrying.

It upset Annabel when her parents lost touch with Arthur for so long because, for some strange reason, until very recently he always continued to cling to her. It is hardly surprising that someone who had been in care until the age of sixteen (even if the care were considerably better than that provided by the Bristol orphanage concerned) would have many problems, but Annabel is also of the opinion that such problems would almost certainly date from longer ago than their present life. Long after Annabel had grown up and established herself in her own home and profession, Arthur would repeatedly turn up on her doorstep and make a nuisance of himself. When drunk, which was frequently, he would be abusive, and he would also on occasion try to interfere with another relationship that she was in at the time. By the time we discussed her story for this chapter she had done a regression to find out about the karma between herself and Arthur. What she found was that – probably in about the early 1800s – they had made a pact always to care for one another. She feels that their previous relationships have not been sexual, but rather of a brother/sister nature, and that he is a much younger soul. She says that in the past he was less destructive than in his present lifetime and that, when a few years ago he asked to come and live with her, she made it a condition that he would stop drinking. He, however, broke his side of the bargain so that Annabel eventually felt that she had no choice other than to break the pact they had made and cut ties with him all together. At the time of writing they have had no contact for several months.

Annabel's links with Pete, however, tell a completely different story. Apart from a period when he was researching his birth family, he has always kept good contact with Anabel's family, and she still sees him regularly. As well as tracing his birth mother (whom he supported until her death from alcohol), Pete met his grandmother and, though she died soon afterwards, it was a happy meeting since he was the only grandson. He was a real support to his foster family through both Judy's and Harry's deaths (the former in 2005 and the latter in 2011). He found it difficult not to be angry with his birth mother, but Annabel says that he got through it well because of being well balanced and having done a lot of work on himself.

When we talked the first time, Annabel said that she would like to come back for a regression to look for her karmic link(s) with Pete, who she was already sure was a member of her soul group[1], and this proved very interesting. (It was also a new experience for me because normally in DMP one is seeking the cause of a particular problem and past life connections tend to come up, or not come up, purely incidentally. Thanks, however, to her extensive experience in the field, Annabel was a very easy subject and it was not, as it often is, difficult for her to obtain the information we wanted.)

In the first life that she got into, the two of them were brothers in thirteenth-century England, and Pete (then named John) was a couple of years or so older and protective of his brother, who clearly had learning difficulties. They were a family of nine children, and their mother had died giving birth to one of their sisters when the boy who is now Annabel (then apparently known as 'Squig'!) was about six. Squig had no emotional attachment to either of his parents and was not particularly upset when his grandmother told the boys, who were busy playing outside at the time, that the baby had "killed" their mother. The oldest sister was married and living in another village, and the family then moved there, sleeping outside while the father built a house for them.

John grew up to be a competent woodsman, making such things as hurdles, and he continued to look after Squig after marrying and having a family of his own. Squig, who worked with him, in due course acquired a girlfriend named Matilda, who worked as a washerwoman and was not very bright. By this time the father had died, and John built a round house for the two of them. John suggested that Squig and Matilda should marry, but they felt no inclination to do so. When Matilda had a baby girl, Squig's comment was that he would have preferred to have a pig!

Tragedy struck when the village was hit by plague. John died at only thirty-five, shortly after Matilda and the rest of the family had perished, but Squig managed to escape to the woods when the village was cleansed by being burnt to the ground. He survived alone by begging for a few months while wondering what to do, and eventually ended up in Salisbury hoping to find his oldest brother, Rodney, there. Rodney was a stonemason and so Squig thought that he might be in Salisbury helping with the building of the cathedral. (I have checked the history of Salisbury cathedral, and the foundations stones were indeed laid on 28 April 1220!) Sadly he never found his brother, but he secured a bit of building work himself, living from hand to mouth and staying wherever he could find shelter. By the age of about forty he was sick and ready to go. His death was speedy, but the body, which was not found for several days, was simply chucked onto a cart and then into a sort of sewage system.

The first person Squig met on the other side was Sam, who is one of Annabel's spirit guides now, and he told Squig that the purpose of that life had been to "understand about learning difficulties and emotional detachment." It was agreed that he had succeeded in this purpose, Annabel commenting that Squig had "learnt to get by with a bit of laughter and to cope alone." He then met up with John, gave him a good hug, and they agreed that "We made good brothers." I then asked them to go and find Squig's body, and together they gave it a decent burial before agreeing to choose a better life next time.

The "better life" that Annabel then went into was one in which the two of them had fallen in love and married despite her family's total disapproval of the match. In the first scene she found herself as a girl of about fifteen named Isabella. She was living in a big house, where she was supposed to be attending her older sister's engagement ball. Isabella loved horses and didn't like having to wear a long dress and have her hair done up elaborately. Her father came to get her, and her mother, who was something of an eccentric and made her laugh, bribed her to attend the ball by promising that she could ride her horse all day the next day.

About two years later she had run away to Yorkshire with the stable lad, whose name was Jed. There they made money from breeding winning horses at Doncaster, and they lived in their own house in York. They had two sons, but she was not very maternal, preferring to be outside working with the horses. They had a housekeeper, who disapproved of Isabella for "not behaving like a lady." Later they had a daughter, who was also something of a tomboy. As they got older the boys both helped with the work. At some point Isabella's sister came to York and she recognized her, but they didn't speak. It later became clear that Isabella had cut off from her family completely after her father had given Jed a beating because of being concerned about what his friends would think of her relationship with the stable boy.

Jed died first, from a heart attack, and Isabella missed him dreadfully before dying herself about six months later. The family remained close and the children and grandchildren came and went. She died alone in her seventies after falling off a horse and damaging her back and legs. In the Bardo she recognized her father as a man with whom she has had an on and off relationship in her current life as Annabel, and with whom she has now finally cut ties because of his continued failure to make a lasting commitment to her. She then tried in vain to make peace with him. Her guide Sam appeared again and she asked him where her mother was. His reply was that she was "off doing what she wants to do," and Annabel realized that it was the same mother as she had had in her present life and that their relationship had not really changed. She had again learnt her intended lesson well: "To hold out for what you really want, not being swayed by other people." Annabel could well relate to that in her present life, and the regression confirmed what she had always felt – that Pete (who isn't fond of horses now, though he does, like her, still love the countryside) "has always been there for me and is always a gentle protector."

Note

1. On this topic, I recommend the books of Dr. Michael Newton, published by Llewellyn Worldwide, USA.

PART TWO – ADOPTERS

> *There are two myths which therapists need to purge from their understanding of adoptive families. Both myths perpetuate the adoptee's sense of unreality. These are the* chosen *myth and the* grateful child *myth. Being told that he is chosen places a great burden on a child to be the perfect child of his parents. It also runs contrary to the feeling that he was* unchosen *by the birth mother.*
> Nancy Newton Verrier, *Coming Home to Self*

Adopters come in different guises, ranging from those who adopt because they are unable to have children of their own, to those who (like me and my husband) wanted to add to the family they already had, to those who make a deliberate choice to give a good home to a child or children with problems or difficulties of one sort or another. There will inevitably be profound differences between those who adopt through 'necessity' (for want of a better word) and those who adopt through choice, and I have often wondered how much difference the reason for adopting makes to a parent-child relationship. I once had a conversation with someone who had adopted her first child after trying for a baby for several years and had subsequently had another three children naturally. She was quite honest about her feelings: "When Robbie, my second one, was born," she said, "I couldn't help being even more thrilled than I had been when we first got Alex, because he was SO gorgeous! I just couldn't help loving my second baby even more." I don't know how typical such feelings are, but I do know that conception often comes more easily after a couple have adopted or have been accepted as adopters. For this woman, I think, getting pregnant after long having seen it as an "impossible dream" influenced her feelings towards the new baby, whereas my own case was completely different. I had no difficulty at all in getting pregnant, but, much though I wanted the children, I did not enjoy pregnancy, and so having someone else produce our third child for me seemed an immense privilege.

I once met a very unfortunate case of a woman who came to me all too briefly for therapy. Her problems were immense and, in the short time that I had in which to attempt to help her before she gave up the idea of continuing with therapy, it was glaringly apparent that the prime cause of her difficulties was a father who had never accepted her for herself and always made her feel inferior to the child that he would have engendered had he been able to.

Fortunately such a case is probably not suggestive of a majority attitude, but it still seems clear to me that the dynamics in a family such as my own will be very different from those where the parents were unable to produce blood children. People who were as naïve as I was in imagining that adopting a young baby would be similar to giving birth may have had the same sort of shock as I did. I know that many people have not been as fortunate as I was in finding that the joys far outweighed the difficulties. I even know of 'failed' adoptions, where a child was either given up on and then placed elsewhere (thus no doubt increasing his or her problems still further), or where he or she went 'completely to the bad'. I pray that nothing like that will happen to anyone reading this book who might be contemplating adoption. The stories that follow are very different from each other, but they all have more or less happy endings. May you future adopters prepare yourselves for possible pitfalls, and may you be as fortunate as, say, Sharon!

CHAPTER FIVE

ADOPTING FROM ANOTHER COUNTRY

Sharon and Blanca's Story

There is no action in the world which is devoid of consequence. This is the law of nature... One who is aware of this truth is unlikely to commit any wrong deeds because he knows that good deeds produce good results and bad deeds lead to bad consequences...
Sathya Sai Baba

The following year (2008) I was again in India, but, apart from a brief visit at the end to Kate and Anil's place, I was simply spending a month in Sai Baba's ashram rather than travelling around. When I am there, I sometimes eat in the North Indian canteen, which tends to be frequented more by Indians than by Westerners, and they normally converse only with each other. Occasionally, however, I have made a friend over a meal, and that year I found myself one evening, just two days before I was due to leave, sitting opposite a delightful woman whom I soon learnt to be American. We found plenty to talk about besides Sai Baba's miracles – her work, my work, books (she decided to go and buy my first one[1] from the Sai Towers shop the next day) – and, just as we were consuming our respective last mouthfuls, I asked, "Do you have any children?"

"One adopted daughter," Sharon replied, and so (needless to say!) I promptly invited her for a cup of tea in my room. Time was short, since the ashram gates close at nine o'clock and she was staying outside it in a hotel in the village, but she kindly agreed to come and tell me her story.

Sharon had no children by her first husband, and they eventually divorced amicably. She was successful in her academic career, which she found fulfilling, but when she was in her forties, she decided that her life would be even more rewarding if she adopted a child. Also, she had already by then come to believe in reincarnation, and she felt that taking on a child who needed a good home would bring her some good karma. Enquiries led her to Uruguay, where she learnt about a Church organization that helped problem families, and she was in the process of making arrangements to go there when she suddenly met Lester at a friend's house. We have all heard of 'love at first sight', and Sharon was so sure that Les was right for her that she promptly arranged to give a party at her own house and invited him to it.

He worked for the Red Cross, was also divorced, and their relationship lost no time in taking off. When Sharon told him of her intention to visit Uruguay for the purpose of adopting a child, Les was not deterred in the least, having himself many years previously come to the rescue of a friend of his who had got a married woman pregnant. He and his then wife already had a daughter and were happy at the thought of adopting a son, and by the time that Sharon met the son he was well into his twenties and interested in Hindu philosophy. (He even accompanied her on her second visit to India and Sai Baba's ashram.)

So all of a sudden Sharon, who had been single for a number of years, found herself with a ready-made family. She and Les married soon after her return from Uruguay, but he sadly died in the year 2000. Blanca, however, who was twenty-six when Sharon and I met, took to Les immediately and he proved to be an excellent father to her.

Blanca was three and half years old when Sharon made her first visit to Uruguay. The child came from a large family, of whom the mother was badly schizophrenic and the father, who was considerably older, had heart trouble. When the 'Consejo de Niños' (Council for Children), the above-mentioned Church organization, had visited the home a year or so previously, they had found Blanca's blouse covered in blood and her brother's foot swollen from a snake bite. They were both taken to the orphanage where all of Blanca's other siblings were being cared for – apart from one, who had been adopted locally. Her older sister Rosa remained in the orphanage until she got married, and Sharon and Blanca still communicate with her today.

It was a priest who made the choice of child for adoption, and Sharon was completely bowled over as soon as she set eyes on the little Blanca in the orphanage. She says that she looked like Shirley Temple and is still radiantly lovely. In fact – and this has been confirmed by the photograph that Sharon has sent me – the two of them look so alike that people have often assumed that Blanca was Sharon's natural daughter. Once settled in America, Blanca learnt English very fast. As soon as she had mastered the language sufficiently, she would regularly say things such as "Mama, I love you and I like you," and she has always expressed gratitude for her adoption and her education.

Blanca has always been very sensitive, with a strong sense of morality, and as a young child she would often cry when she felt that she had done something wrong. A real charmer, she has never been short of friends, and now she is living happily with a boyfriend. She did not do particularly well at school to start with, but used to charm the teachers into giving her Bs and Cs, and then, thanks to Les helping her with her homework, she made it to university, where she studied management and catering. There she found herself, started getting grade As and Bs, and now she runs her own restaurant. (Being a Virgo, she is of course very practical.)

When Blanca was seventeen, Sharon took her back to Uruguay to meet her family. Although she had no memory of her time in the orphanage, the nuns remembered her, as did all her family. She was welcomed with a banner and a huge gathering, and she met all of her eight siblings as well as her parents. Her father, who Sharon says looks like Blanca, is very sweet, but Blanca was a little scared of her mother, who is on medication for the schizophrenia and chain smokes.

Since Sharon had to leave the ashram before the gates closed and I was tied up until the time of my departure soon after that evening, there was no time for us to perform the regression that Sharon might have liked in order to look for her past-life link(s) with Blanca. I consequently did some dowsing, which I often find a useful means of obtaining information. It is, however, worth noting that the pendulum tends to be much less reliable when one is not indifferent to the answers it gives. Obviously the subconscious can influence it, but when one is completely impartial to the results, as I was in this case, it is pretty dependable.

The answers I got on that evening in Baba's ashram were that, though Sharon and Blanca had never been mother and daughter before, they had been acquainted in many previous lifetimes. In the lifetime that was the most significant for their present one Blanca had been Sharon's older sister and had cared for her a great deal, particularly after their mother had died. Sharon and I happened to bump into each other the next day, and there was just time for me to tell her about this. She replied, "That figures, because she often reprimands me!" She then recounted an occasion when the two of them had been together and had walked past a group of young black people. Because of the way in which they were behaving, Sharon had stared at them, whereupon Blanca had said to her firmly, "Mother, those are not the kind of people you stare at."

After returning from India to our respective countries, Sharon and I remained in touch by email. She told Blanca about our meeting, about my writing this book, and about the information that I obtained with my pendulum. Apparently Blanca (who said that she would be happy for me to use her real name) also feels that a previous life as Sharon's elder sister rings true for her.

Sharon is, like myself, an Aquarian and, since I also have a

Virgo daughter who sometimes reprimands me, I am now wondering whether Alice has in the past been *my* older sister!

Note

1. *Karmic Release – Journeying Back to the Self,* Ann Merivale, Sai Towers Publishing, 2006.

CHAPTER SIX

ERIC AND LOIS'S STORY

The greatest achievement was at first and for a time a dream. The oak sleeps in the acorn, the bird waits in the egg. And in the highest vision of a soul a waking angel stirs. Dreams are the seedlings of realities.
James Allen (from *As a Man Thinketh*)

During the twelve years in which Eric and Lois tried for a baby Lois had two miscarriages and, once Eric had passed forty, their concern that time was running out increased. The turning point came for them just after a particularly bad time when they had both been feeling extremely depressed. On Eric's forty-sixth birthday (May 17th, 1992), the weather for the time of year was exceptionally good and they decided to go for a long walk in a very beautiful place in mid-Wales, not far from where they live. Somehow this wonderful walk caused them to view the world from a different perspective, and it was shortly afterwards that the possibility came up of their adopting a baby from Peru.

Eric and Lois had initially made some contacts in Mexico but, before those had borne any fruit, someone they knew told them that Peru had a better legal system, and this person was even able to introduce them to a lawyer there. It is easy to imagine their excitement at the prospect of their long-held dream being fulfilled, but it was of course some time later that they learned that the day of their wonderful walk was also the day on which the baby who was to become Rachael had been born thousands of miles away in a poor suburb of Lima! Was this pure coincidence, or was the fact of their daughter's birth on that special day being communicated to their subconscious through the ether?

This couple are both professional artists; Eric taught for some years, but gave it up when they decided to have a go at running their own business. Nowadays Lois designs and makes beautiful handicrafts and cards, for which Eric makes frames and other things she needs, and he is also kept endlessly busy organizing their attendance at events where they are able to sell their wares. Although they have now been successful in this venture for well over twenty years, it is very hard work and never easy to make ends meet, and so the couple had to save hard for quite a while in order to fund their trip to Peru.

Neither Eric nor Lois is strictly religious, though he was made to go to Sunday school as a child and she was brought up Church of England and is still spiritually inclined even though she no longer goes to church. They are open-minded people, but before meeting me (in our local swimming pool!) had never given any real thought to the question of reincarnation or the idea of coming together again with people we have known before. They are, however, firm believers in 'destiny' and in things happening for good reasons, and they see as significant the facts that their daughter and Eric have the same birthday, that Eric was forty-six when she was adopted in 1992, that Eric was born in 1946 and that ninety-two is twice forty-six.

When they first went to Peru they had to change flights in Amsterdam, where they were held up by a technical problem. While waiting for the airline to sort things out, they picked up a newspaper that had an article in it about international adoptions in Peru being impossible due to allegations suggesting that legal procedures had been corrupted. This naturally made them hesitate about continuing with their journey, but Lois's strong sense of destiny won the day.

The lawyer's wife picked them up at Lima airport, and so it was she who had to break the news that the mother of the baby who was originally being considered had changed her mind about giving up her child. However, hours before their flight arrived in Lima another mother had approached the lawyer asking if he could arrange the adoption of her newly born daughter, Lourdes. So, just a few hours after arriving at the airport, Eric and Lois went to the lawyer's office in downtown Lima. The lawyer told them that Lourdes and her mother would be there in about thirty minutes and that they would have temporary custody of Lourdes throughout the adoption process. Lourdes and her mother duly arrived, and Lois and Eric promised the mother that they would take very good care of her daughter. The three of them then straight away signed legal papers for Eric and Lois's custody of the baby. So there they were with responsibility for a twenty-six day old child just hours after arriving in Lima!

The new family then checked into their hotel accommodation, where Lourdes was fed and bathed. Eric and Lois decided to keep the name Lourdes as their child's first name but, since they knew it would be difficult for English people, they added the name Rachael, and it is by this latter name that she is now normally known. Although the baby's mother did not delay in agreeing to the adoption, there were many other delays, and the six weeks for which they had planned and budgeted gradually dragged on into five months.

By the time that I first espied Rachael in the swimming pool she was already an attractive teenager and easily able to overtake me while I was swimming my habitual mile. Since darker skinned people are unfortunately few and far between in the area in which I live, I noticed her straight away and, since her parents were also in the pool, it was immediately apparent to me that she was adopted. Eric, who was then able to find time to go swimming more frequently than either his wife or daughter, is a very sociable person and, with my special interest in the question of adoption, it did not take too many weeks for us to get into conversation on the subject. Eric told me that they were planning to make a second visit to Peru mainly for Rachael's sake, and he was interested when I told him how we had made a family trip to Sierra Leone when our son had become old enough to remember it. I also talked to Eric about this book that I was writing and, since it is easier to talk at home than under the public shower, he kindly agreed to my suggestion of bringing Lois round some time for a coffee.

We all lead busy lives, and by the time the three of us had got round to agreeing on a mutually convenient date, their family holiday in Peru had already taken place. But we started our conversation by going back to the beginning, and Lois recounted how she remembered crying over the length of time that the bonding with Rachael had seemed to take, despite the fact that it had been "love at first sight" at least on her and Eric's part. What Lois found particularly hard was the fact that little Lourdes took so long to accept comfort from them, so it was a great joy when, towards the end of the five months that they were there, another woman asked to hold the baby, who then screamed for them (just as a six-month old baby will normally cry for its parent whenever anyone else picks it up).

Eric and Lois's main emotion during their long drawn out stay in Peru was anxiety as to whether the adoption was going to work out. I can sympathize, having had similar fears while our son was in first the maternity hospital and then a foster home, but we were fortunate in having only a two-week wait. In Eric and Lois's case the legal red tape seemed endless, and at one point they had to advertise Lourdes in the local paper to see whether anyone made a claim on the baby. Finally the full adoption was made under Peruvian law but, even after the three of them had arrived back in England, they were sidelined at Birmingham airport because they were lacking some vital piece of paper!

Eventually, however, to their great relief, they were allowed through customs and were able to introduce the beautiful baby to their excited, waiting family. Once back in England they had to re-adopt the child, which took another full year, but they were fortunate in having a social worker who was very cooperative and positive. During this year of waiting for ratification under English law the bonding, which had already started in Peru, became firmly cemented into an indestructible parent-child relationship.

Although their joy in having a child has been unbounded, Eric and Lois have not found bringing Rachael up entirely easy. She was very clingy when she was small, never enjoyed playgroup, and even in her last year at school was still not very sociable. A certain insecurity, too, has sometimes revealed itself through Rachael's fear of the implications of not being very well off: when Lois has said that they could not afford something, it has often provoked the question, "Will you give me away?"

Rachael has always worked hard, however, and – particularly after moving from primary to secondary school – did extremely well in English. When we talked she was at the local college preparing to take her Advanced Level exams with a view to going on to university, and Eric and Lois were very proud of her achievements, which they said were entirely her own since they had never pushed her. She was studying English Language, Psychology and Health and Social Care, and they told me that it was Health and Social Care that she would like to do at university. This sounded to be the ideal choice, since Rachael shows a great affinity with disadvantaged people. For instance, Lois told me, she was friendly with the Polish bus drivers who took her to college and she regularly took coffee to a street musician who frequented her neighborhood.

Rachael has a half-brother one year older than herself, who was adopted by an American couple. She also has another brother, five years older, who lives in Lima, and a younger sister called Grace. Rachael does not attempt to hide the huge hurt she feels about her birth mother having given her up whilst keeping other siblings. Her birth mother, however, died within a week of giving birth to Grace, when Rachael was four.

When they made their second visit to Peru, a brief but

emotional meeting was held in the lawyer's office with Grace and the aunt who has been bringing her up. The aunt broke down and hugged Rachael, hugely relieved to see that she was being well looked after. The meeting was also reassuring for this aunt because she herself had had a child adopted in Italy. Although Rachael clearly did not feel that she would have liked to stay in Peru, she enjoyed the holiday and was able to relax when they were on a beach in the north of the country, and in Arequipa. Eric and Lois also greatly enjoyed their second visit to Peru, where they found enormous changes to have taken place in the seventeen years that had elapsed since their first one. For one thing, guerrilla warfare had been raging the first time and there had been bombs every night in Lima!

Eric and Lois's only regret about the adoption is that Rachael has had to be an only child. There was a possibility of a second child being found for them, but they could not afford to prolong their stay in Peru any further. She has, however, had close cousins throughout her life, which has been a blessing. One of them (Lois's niece) was born on the very day that they returned from Peru with baby Rachael. There is now a possibility of Rachael being able to have some contact with her brother in America, and her parents are doing all they can to facilitate that as they feel sure that it would be valuable for her.

But nothing has as yet helped Rachael to overcome her feelings of rejection. As I, as well as other authors, have already mentioned, this is alas something that all adopted people have to live with, though the intensity of the feelings will vary in different circumstances and through different phases of life. And, unless someone is successful in resolving the issues through, for instance, therapy and/or reconciliation with their birth mother or parents, it is likely that they will surface repeatedly throughout a lifetime, particularly during difficult patches. My psychotherapist friend Barbara, whose second daughter is adopted, comments that the impact of adoption on the child is "so much more than rejection." She points out that it is abandonment at a time when he or she has no defenses or support with which to deal with it, and she says, "Of course all the damage we receive as children plays itself out in our later relationships. So adopted people will often in a relationship drive the other person away in order to get over and done with the inevitable pain of being left again." The fact that this is all unconscious makes it much more difficult to overcome.

When we met at my house, Lois said that she did not find it easy talking about what had been an emotional time for them. A very important time too, since she and Eric had felt for so long that they both wanted and needed the experience of rearing a child and the love and responsibility that that entailed. Although she does not believe in reincarnation – and Eric added that pressure of work precludes their having time to "think outside the box" – Lois commented that she was very aware that the human brain has huge abilities that we cannot know about. She quoted as examples Rachael's gift for always picking pairs of cards, and the fact that she often knows exactly what Lois is thinking. The latter is of course to my mind evidence of the bond and understanding between them that stems from having been together in previous lives, but I shall have to wait until we have crossed over to the other side to argue that point fully with this particular couple!

CHAPTER SEVEN

ADOPTING AN ONLY CHILD

Philomena's Story

I saw a garden in Flanders
Amid the red ruin of war,
And the roses were blooming as bravely
As ever they flowered before.
The trees were all shattered and broken
And death in the garden held sway,
But the bloom of the roses gave token
That Peace would return some day…[1]

Philomena, who died in her eighties in October 2009, came from a family of artists and musicians, and one of her deceased uncles was a distinguished musicologist. Her father had, at the age of seventeen, after his father's early death, been 'adopted' by a theosophist, who generously sent him to Cambridge. He absorbed her ideas and interests, yet never made any attempt at all to foist them onto either his Christian wife or their children. After his death, however, Philomena, who had always been an extremely open-minded sort of Christian and taken an interest in Buddhism, inherited his books and read them avidly. One day she went to see a well-known clairvoyant, and while she was with him she suddenly had an intuitive flash that she was the reincarnation of her grandfather who had died ten years before she was born. The clairvoyant confirmed Philomena's intuition. She explained to me that she had always felt very close to that "unknown" grandfather, whose poem, addressed to his beloved daughter from a hilltop in France, affected her deeply, and she also said that she could picture herself on a battlefield. This grandfather had played the bagpipes, and Philomena commented, "Whenever I hear bagpipes, it gets me *here*!" (pointing to her solar plexus).

All this made Philomena very open to the notion that her only son, Roderick, had been with her before. She and I first met in 1997, when I was doing my first training course in regression therapy. We were both members of an organization called Amadea, which had the aim of forming an 'alternative retirement community', and they held a few conferences in Devon, where most of the members were keen to purchase a property (which alas never materialized). Since I lived in the North East of England at the time and Philomena in the Midlands, it was not easy for us to carry on meeting, so, when she expressed a desire to do a regression with me, I kept on bearing it in mind and waiting for the opportunity to arise.

When Philomena talked to me about her adopted son, Roderick, I felt immense empathy with her since he was at the time in prison. I told her about some of the problems that we had had with our adopted son, and also mentioned my long term aim of writing a book on adoption. I felt that it might be of help to her to find out something about her past link(s) with Roderick, and we agreed to keep in touch after the Devon conference and eventually meet up for a regression. We did indeed keep in touch, though sporadically, and I always appreciated the beautiful cards that she sent me of her own tapestries. Distance and my preoccupation with other things, however, prevented the desired regression from taking place and, by the time that I had moved to Shropshire, much closer to where she lived, and found time to visit, she was eighty and noticeably a lot more frail than when we had talked before.

But Philomena's great news when we did finally manage to meet again was that Roderick was no longer in prison, but working happily in Latin America and had recently made her a grandmother. Sadly she had not been able to meet either

Roderick's new partner or her grandson, but she had photographs of the little boy, which she showed me excitedly.

Philomena made art her career for very many years. She did a teacher training course, studying English as well as art, and she married at the age of thirty-eight. After trying unsuccessfully for eighteen months to conceive, she and Oliver decided to adopt, and Roderick came to them at the age of seven weeks through their local church. Janet, his birth mother, was English, his father Indian, and he was conceived in Latin America but born in England, when his father came over to study at a British university. However, Roderick's maternal grandmother was very xenophobic, and Janet was thrown out of the house because of being pregnant. She was reluctant to give Roderick up, but had no choice since his natural father was unable to support them. Later Janet married an Irishman, but that to her mother was "no better than an Indian," and so the couple moved to Dublin. She was still living in Dublin when Roderick traced her, when he was in his twenties, but she eventually moved back to England after getting divorced.

Philomena's family were happy about the adoption, but Oliver's were not, which caused the couple some difficulties. Oliver's father was Persian, his mother English, and the whole family were very anti-Muslim, which offended Philomena's open-mindedness. When, after Oliver's death, his parents cut her and Roderick out of their will, she reverted to using her maiden name.

Oliver sadly died ten years after they were married, when Roderick was only seven. Philomena feels that the main cause of his death was his tendency to overdo things and to strain himself, and she says that this was because of his constant desire to save money. The death no doubt affected the young Roderick profoundly – especially since he had just reached an age when he and his father were beginning really to have fun together, doing such 'manly' things as sport, at which Roderick has always excelled. Never an easy child, his behavior deteriorated still further when he was sent away to boarding school. Philomena appreciated later that he saw this as a "second rejection," but at the time she sincerely believed it to be the right thing to do. Her own brothers had been happy in boarding school, and she wanted to avail herself of an opportunity for further study at a university, which she knew would enhance her teaching career.

Roderick's real problems dated from an unfortunate incident, which took place when he was coming near to the end of his boarding school career. He was in a car belonging to another boy, who was smuggling drugs, and, when they were stopped by the police, the other boy escaped, leaving poor Roderick to get all the blame. (The real culprit eventually got caught some time later and was sentenced to ten years in prison.) Prison of course is rarely the best answer for anyone, and in Roderick's case it led to a slippery slope. He was in and out for about five years in all, and Philomena supported him lovingly throughout that time, visiting him as often as she could, even when it involved a considerable amount of travelling. A gifted linguist, Roderick was given the opportunity from one of the establishments in which he was interned to go out to college and attend classes in Spanish, and I feel sure that it is thanks both to that and to his mother's loving support that he ultimately succeeded in 'making good' in Latin America. She did, however, when we met in 2008, still have worries about him, since the firm that he went to work for had gone bust and had been unable to pay him for three months. So she told me that he was planning to make a change and move into English teaching, for which he was qualified.

Philomena explained to me that she and her son had a lot of zodiac signs in common, and that they got on well because they had many of the same difficulties. (She commented that having Mars in Pisces was difficult.) She said that he had always known exactly what were the best presents to give her and, even though she did not have email, the Atlantic appeared to be no barrier to their communication. They spoke on the phone regularly. When I visited Philomena, as well as proudly showing me the photographs of her gorgeous baby grandson, she was delighted to reminisce about Roderick's former beautiful girlfriends. Philomena's cherished photo albums confirm her statement that he has always been exceptionally good looking and a big hit with the women!

When Roderick traced his birth mother, he tried at the same time to trace his father, but was unsuccessful there. He turned up on Janet's doorstep unannounced, and she recognized him instantly because of his likeness to his father. She had a son (Patrick) by her Irish husband, who was ten years Roderick's junior, and an excellent relationship developed between the three of them. When, some years later, his half-brother tragically killed both himself and his girlfriend, Roderick was able to be a big support to Janet. This tragedy hit the family particularly hard because no one had suspected that Patrick had been suffering from depression. When she and I last met, Philomena was still receiving cards regularly from Janet.

After that meeting, we corresponded some more and she vetted the first draft of this chapter. We also spoke on the phone a few times during 2009, and she urged me to visit again and take a look at some of Roderick's writings about his adoption. It was not, however, an easy drive for me to make, and also I was always busy and she needed to make frequent visits to the hospital and was obviously becoming increasingly frail. When I eventually left a message on her answerphone suggesting a date on which I would be able to come, the reply came not from Philomena herself but from a kind neighbor, who explained that she had had a fall and gone into a nursing home. The neighbor clearly felt that the time was not right for me to visit, but thanks to that conversation I was put on a list of contacts and was naturally most grateful when Philomena's executor phoned to inform me of her demise.

I perform shamanic soul rescue work[2] and shamanic

journeying sometimes gives me the opportunity, among other things, to talk to people I know who have died. I undertook such a journey just twelve days after Philomena's death and found her happily reunited with her beloved husband. She told me that it had been a great relief to her to pass over after having been lingering uncomfortably for quite a while, and that she was watching over Roderick, still with a certain amount of anxiety for him but confident that he was going to be okay. I asked her about any past life links with Roderick that were relevant to their recent life together, and this was obviously her first opportunity to look at that. It was also an interesting new experience for me since, rather than hearing Philomena's words in my head, I saw pictures; it was as though we went to look at her Akashic Records together. So here is what I – or rather we – saw.

Firstly it appeared that Philomena and Roderick had been sculptors together in Egypt. They (both men at the time, as one would expect) were working on temples in Luxor, and they were good friends as well as colleagues and understood one another perfectly. Roderick's expertise in choosing perfect presents for her seemed to date from that distant friendship, and I found it interesting that she had had artistic talent in Egypt as well as this time round.

The second lifetime that we saw had even greater relevance to this one. It was in Ireland in the nineteenth century, when Philomena and Janet (Roderick's birth mother) had been sisters in a large Catholic family. Janet had again become pregnant out of wedlock (probably by the same man as Roderick's father) and was consequently shunned by family and society. Philomena was the only person to show her any compassion, and she took Janet and the child in despite being herself in considerable financial hardship. She did not have any children of her own and became extremely fond of her sister's little boy, who was the same soul as Roderick, and suffered immensely from his death by poisoning at the age of about two. Janet, who wanted to make a fresh start and marry, which would have not have been possible while she had an illegitimate child, killed the child herself by giving him poisonous berries to eat. She pretended that it had been an accident and most people believed her, though Philomena herself did have suspicions about the truth of the story. Janet did indeed marry, though unsuccessfully, and that lifetime left her with a debt to pay to both her son and her sister. Her giving Roderick up for Philomena to adopt this time round means that that debt has now been paid. As for Roderick himself, he needed to forgive his birth mother both for murdering him in Ireland and for giving him up this time, and this he did when he traced her and subsequently supported her through the loss of her younger son.

So the lives of these three brave souls – Philomena, Janet and Roderick– have certainly been characterized by loss. This is something that no one can escape, but the big consolation is that it is only ever temporary. Sometimes we volunteer prior to incarnating to 'do loss' for someone else (viz Loraine in Chapter Nineteen), and sometimes we are aware that it is something we need to experience for ourselves and so bravely volunteer for that. Before doing the above shamanic journey, I believed it to be very likely that Philomena and Janet had made a pact between them before coming in concerning Roderick's upbringing, and so I found it most interesting to have my intuition confirmed. Finally, I asked Philomena whether, since she was no longer on Earth, she would prefer that I use her real name in this chapter. She replied, however, that she thought it would be better for Roderick if I stuck to the pseudonyms, and said that she really liked the name Philomena.

Notes

1. London Scottish Regimental Gazette, London, 1918.
2. See my book *Delayed Departure – A Beginner's Guide to Soul Rescue,* Ann Merivale, 6th Books, 2013.

CHAPTER EIGHT

ADOPTING A FIRST CHILD

Ariadne's Story

An anonymous six-year-old child's reply to the question *"What does adoption mean?" was "It's when you grow in your mummy's heart, not in her tummy."*

I remember from my youth a story that my father used to tell of a Harley Street infertility specialist who, at a couple's first appointment regarding their difficulty in conceiving, would tell them, "I'm afraid I won't be able to do anything for you for six months, so please come and see me again after that." In a very large percentage of his cases they would return with the news that the wife was now pregnant! Anxiety and stress are well known as sources of innumerable problems, and one often hears cases of people conceiving either after adopting their first child or after having been accepted for adoption. Ariadne's case is an example of the former; only after she had adopted her son did she succeed in conceiving a daughter. But before embarking on her story, I should like to mention another very interesting case that I heard about at an Ancestral Fieldwork weekend held with Jen Kershaw and Dr. Roger Woolger in Liverpool in July 2010.

Two of the participants at this useful weekend were a mother and daughter who had come over from Italy. Since they were antiquarian book dealers as well as spiritual seekers, we soon got into conversation about my books and the mother, Letizia, told me that she and her husband had adopted a young Indian orphan boy before having two daughters naturally. A clearer example of someone who was in touch with her Life Plan and the pre-birth contracts that she had made would be hard to find!

Although she married at twenty-three and had no obvious physical reason for not having children naturally, once they had decided to start a family, Letizia felt a strong desire (she explains that it was "almost a need") to start their new family "by opening it to a lonely child." This may seem unusual or strange, but my own desire to adopt our third child rather than getting pregnant again was equally strong, and to anyone who understands about families being planned beforehand on the other side it makes perfect sense. The reason why Damiano should have chosen to come to her by a circuitous route is not clear, but anyone with an understanding of karma will appreciate that it was for a very good reason.

Until 1967, the year in which Letizia married, the law in Italy prevented young couples from being accepted for adoption. When, in the following year, they started their quest for a child to adopt, the necessary institutions, courts and so on had not yet been established, and there were no social workers with the necessary experience. Happily, however, Letizia found a newly born secular center (CIAI, which is still active in Italy and now a landmark). A non-profit organization, it was from the start eager to follow the new law, the idea of which was "to give a lonely child a family, rather than a child to two (by no means young) adults." CIAI was at that time in touch with some orphanages in India and South Korea. The one in India (Belgaum) was run by Catholic nuns, who used to keep the girls and send the boys away by the time they reached the age of five. Letizia and her husband were soon promised a child, but before he arrived (when Letizia was twenty-five), their daughter Lucia was conceived. Many couples in such circumstances would no doubt pull out of the adoption arrangement, but not so this one. Letizia says, "When we found out that I was pregnant, I thought 'They will grow up as twins. That's perfect!'" Damiano is their son's original name and he arrived in June, aged two and a quarter, and Lucia was born in September – just three months later.

Although she has not to date had the opportunity of exploring the karma between them, Letizia shares my view that Damiano was destined for her family. Though, as a mother myself, I wonder how on Earth she coped. After that she obviously needed something of a break, and so Serena, whom I also had the privilege to meet, was born eleven years later.

In Italy it is rather more common than in England or America for whole families to continue living together after the children have grown up, but, since they are all five involved in the family book business, it seems to me that this is an example of a family who are particularly strongly bonded and have probably worked together in numerous previous lifetimes. Their life has not been easy – particularly for Damiano, who started out by having difficulty in walking and has had to have medical intervention – but that may well be one of the reasons why it was better for him to be brought up in Europe than in an Indian orphanage. Socializing is also something of a problem for him, and he has suffered immensely from a broken relationship, but nowadays, in his forties, he is well established in his own, independent bookstore that has close links with the family business. Though none of them would ever push him, Letizia feels that he would do well to look at his adoption issues and, should he ever be ready to do that, he would have the understanding and support of all his family.

It is generally accepted that parents' attitudes inevitably affect a child profoundly, and so being 'ousted' by a sibling must obviously compound the difficulties that an adopted child already has simply because of having been adopted. No two people are alike, however, and, in contrast to the person mentioned above, Letizia told me that she has always loved all her children equally, if in different ways.

This is where karma and the different life plans that people make in accordance with it are such an important ingredient to the whole adoption story. And, as I mentioned in the

Introduction, this is of course also where my perspective differs from that of other writers on this subject. In different lifetimes we choose different challenges according to the learning that we decide upon each time. These varying experiences all contribute to our becoming fully rounded personalities. Since we agree beforehand to what we take on in a lifetime, there is never any question of 'unfairness'. Both Letitizia and her daughter Serena share my perspective and the latter, though she has by no means always found living with her brother easy, told me that she fully appreciates that there are good reasons for their having chosen to be in the same family this time round.

The same is true for Ariadne, whose difficulties with her adopted son, Michael, have been immense. Her ex-husband, Brian, is nine years older than she is, but she married fairly young – at twenty-five. After Ariadne had had various operations, and they had tried in vain for a baby for five years, they decided to go for adoption. Since there were so few babies available in England and they did not want to take on an older child, they readily accepted the offer made by a Brazilian friend to look for a baby for them over there. It did not take this friend long to find Michael, who was born on Ariadne's birthday (September 29th), which she immediately saw as significant. (Remember all the 'coincidences' that Eric and Lois found with Lourdes?!)

Michael's mother was a house servant who already had six other children. His conception was the result of a brief liaison she had with a neighbor after her husband had gone off with some of the other children. She was very poor and felt that she needed to get rid of the baby quickly in case her husband returned. So she put him straight into a children's home but then, since this was so painful for her, took him back briefly. However, in spite of the pain that separation from him gave her, she soon realized that adoption was her only option and liked the idea of him being taken to a rich country.

By the time that Ariadne and Brian managed to get to Brazil

the baby was five months old and they collected him from the children's home. The mother had not given him a name, so Michael was their own choice. Ariadne says that she will never forget the "amazing moment" when she received her son into her arms. "We arrived, jet lagged, into a temperature of eighty degrees and wearing winter clothes. The baby, who seemed to us incredibly beautiful, was in the middle of drinking a bottle of carrot juice, but he was nevertheless thrust straight into my arms." Then she continued in a tone that moved me greatly, "The feeling of having suddenly become a mother was quite overwhelming, but then I had to bear some frustration because our friend's nanny, who had come with us, took the baby straight off me again and I wasn't allowed to do anything more with him until the night time." And she added, "Learning patience and coping with frustration are my life lessons!"

The couple did not need to linger very long with the baby in Brazil. After a twelve-hour flight home they were met by all their relatives, and Ariadne's mother, who lived next door to them, helped out while he was settling in. But the phrase "settling in" is perhaps not very appropriate in this case, since there were so many difficulties right from the start. The fact that Michael was underweight was probably the least of Ariadne's worries; she had a good understanding of nutrition and was able to focus on getting his diet right. The things that troubled her more were that Michael never made eye contact or giggled in the way that babies of his age normally did, and that he never showed any preference for her over anyone else. She says, "It was terrible because I felt like a fraud rather than a real mother. My mother, who had only had girls herself, just thought he was different because he was a boy, and I wondered whether the difficulties were due to his being Brazilian, or adopted, or both. As for Brian, he did his best to help, but felt at something of a loss as to how."

Then, when Michael was fifteen months old, Ariadne had IVF and it was successful. Their daughter, Marianne, was born when

Michael was two. Ariadne says, "I don't believe that blood is that important and I really wanted to treat them the same and love them both equally, but it was incredibly hard because Michael was always so difficult and Marianne was so easy in comparison." It was obvious from fairly early on that Michael was likely to have learning difficulties, but they had to wait over a year for a diagnosis from a psychologist. Finally, when he was five, they were told that he did indeed have learning difficulties, but even then Ariadne had to press really hard for extra help and it was some time before he was given an assistant in school. Marianne, on the other hand, has always been extremely bright; when she left school she went on to do her degree at Cambridge.

When my daughter was young there is no doubt at all that she suffered from having a disruptive brother in the house, but Ariadne says that Marianne seems to have accepted all the problems in the family remarkably well. She did, however, (just like my daughter) spend a great deal of time alone in her room, and Ariadne regrets the fact that Marianne had to be left to her own devices more than her parents would have liked. Michael's behavior also put a great deal of strain on the marital relationship. He was able to behave well when he was out, but was completely impossible at home, and Ariadne says that the family was often split, as the only way they could cope was for the two of them to take turns at dealing with Michael while the other one looked after Marianne.

Michael gave them no joy at all, was always grumpy, kept his room a "total tip," and the couple could never have a proper evening together because of the difficulty in getting him to bed. Also, he would often do really unpleasant things to Marianne, such as whack her hands when they were on the table, and Ariadne believes that the fact that her daughter put up with it all confirms her having agreed to being his sister before incarnating.

It was not until he had reached the age of nine that Michael was finally diagnosed as autistic, and Ariadne is a hundred per cent sure that it was caused by his vaccinations. He used from a very early age to make strange noises. She says that these were not too bad to start with, but that they got progressively worse after each of the vaccinations. Before he came to them at five months he had had all the usual vaccinations, plus what they called "some very strong medication" for a pneumonia-type condition in his lungs. This left his cheeks slightly scarred, as if by acne. Ariadne says, "When I got him home the pediatrician recommended re-vaccinating just in case what he had had in Brazil was "insufficient," and then later he had the MMR vaccine when he was about three." She adds, "It sounds ridiculous knowing what I know now, but I was ignorant in those days and just followed the doctor's advice." Nowadays, in his twenties, Michael is diagnosed as having Asperger's syndrome.

But the most interesting point about this whole story is that Michael's problems proved to be the trigger for Ariadne herself discovering her Life Plan. When he was eleven she got to hear of a woman who did muscle testing for food allergies, and thanks to that she eliminated sugar from the children's diet and substituted sheep's milk for cow's milk. She said that Michael craved attention so much that he always wanted conflict, food became a battleground and she had to put a lock on the pantry door, but that all this had a very good knock on effect. The switch to sheep's milk put an end to Marianne's headaches that had been caused by cow's milk and, Ariadne told me, since sugar can make people short sighted, eliminating that from their diet gave an added benefit. Marianne now has excellent eyesight, and both of them actually prefer to eat healthy food. Also, Ariadne invented her own recipes and started producing leaflets with them, which are still selling today.

The family did occasionally get respite care – usually something like one weekend a month – but this was not sufficient for them to be able to have anything like a normal life. However, when Michael was sixteen an educational tribunal sent him to a special boarding school for language disordered children, which gave Ariadne some respite for a couple of years. Then she discovered Health Kinesiology, which she is now practicing professionally. She comments, "I learnt Kinesiology in order to deal with Michael's allergies, but it turned out to be my salvation! Not only did it remove my stress, causing me to feel washed and cleaned from the inside out, but it gave me a whole new way of life."

When Michael was treated with Kinesiology it gave them a difficult six months at first, but after that there was a wonderful transformation. First, when he was eighteen, the treatment gave him eczema on his hands, which Ariadne explains as "releasing the toxins stored in his body ever since the vaccinations," but then he started improving in various ways. She says that he became "helpful, quiet, considerate and caring." Now he lives not too far from them, in supported living accommodation, which should serve him for life. It is unlikely that he will ever be able to work – partly because being on benefit limits the hours that he could do – and in any case he could only cope with an environment where everyone was very kind. He did for a time try working in a retirement home, but he found the people's moods too difficult to handle.

Michael nowadays is generally happy, enjoys drawing and painting, in which he has his own unique style, but Ariadne says that he could not attend classes in that since he cannot take instruction. They visit him regularly of course, though Marianne finds five minutes now and again about enough to cope with. Ariadne comments that she regards her brother as "a little pet" and, since he is more like a ten- or twelve-year-old than a twenty-six-year-old to talk to, they have nothing to talk about. "Marianne," Ariadne told me, "discovered music while she was at Cambridge and is now doing wonderfully composing and performing her own songs."

Ariadne eventually left Brian and, although he would never

have instigated the separation, she says that they are both a lot happier now as a result of it. "He did a wonderful job of supporting us all financially through difficult times," she told me, "but, since he hasn't changed one iota whereas I'm a totally different person now that I'm working as a therapist, we no longer resonate." They remain on good terms and he built her a website for her work, but, when we met, Ariadne had recently embarked on a new relationship, which was giving her much more happiness and fulfillment.

These days Ariadne feels well able to achieve good mother-daughter bonding with Marianne and she believes that this will improve still further once the latter has "come into her power." Though Marianne is at present – not of course unusually at that age – rebelling somewhat against her mother's interests (she wrote a song titled, "Mum says she can fix me"!), Ariadne says that she was to some extent her leader, in that she started feeling the energies of crystals and becoming obsessed with things such as dolphins when she was only nine. In 1997 the two of them went to visit Ariadne's sister in New Zealand, where they attended a channeling meeting. There Marianne made a beeline for the books and Ariadne bought Dolores Cannon's *Between Life and Death* because Marianne told her that it had "given her an electric shock."

This book proved to be one of many that have been influential on Ariadne, who was brought up nominally Catholic. Though her mother was Church of England and she attended a Baptist Sunday School as a child, the family moved to Gibraltar when she was thirteen and there she went to a convent school. But she gave up practicing any religion when she was twenty-one and this left her quite open-minded spiritually.

It would be easy to imagine someone finding that they had an autistic child to be resentful and/or angry, but Ariadne is able to see a purpose in her son's problems even though they gave her family a hard time. She says, "I know that Michael has an amazing spirit inside his difficult body, and I thank him and I honor him because I know that without that 'thorn' I would never have started the investigations that led me into becoming a healer." And she adds, "Without having had Michael I would no doubt have had a rather boring life, just going to coffee mornings and so on. As it is, my life nowadays is really rewarding and interesting, and I can empathize with others because of all the difficulties that I went through myself."

So Ariadne feels quite sure that she knows what her son came for, and this is what to my mind makes her story such an intriguing one. We all come to Earth to learn, and over the eons of this learning many 'errors' are made. One of these 'errors', sadly for the victims of it, is infant vaccination. I would urge anyone doubting this statement either to consult a homoeopath or to study the research findings of the American Alan Phillips[1]. Conventional medicine is of course in good faith with its belief that immunization is responsible for the great decrease in childhood illness and death, but there is in fact much evidence that improved hygiene was already reducing these before any sort of vaccination was introduced. The homoeopathic thesis is that immunization weakens the body's natural immune system, and that the best way for children to overcome childhood diseases is by having them. Alan Phillips' research shows that death or other problems are much less frequently caused by the disease itself than by immunization against it.

Whereas Sweden abolished vaccination against pertussis (whooping cough) in 1979, nowadays, unfortunately, child immunization is compulsory in the US, and in Britain there is a great deal of pressure put on parents to get their children to have it. I sincerely hope that campaigns such as that of Alan Phillips will spread rapidly and become truly effective. We need to learn from the experience of people like Michael and Ariadne, and I look forward to the distant day when everyone has finally done so!

Note

1. Alan Phillips' excellent pamphlet, *Dispelling Vaccination Myths,* is available from pharmacy@helios.co.uk

CHAPTER NINE

ADOPTING SIBLINGS

Jean and Martin's Story

The maternal instinct is very strong in women, and when people monkey with it, it causes trouble – all kinds of trouble.
Betty Jean Lifton, *Lost And Found – The Adoption Experience*

I empathized strongly with Jean when she told me how she hated it when people commenting on her family said such things as "You are good!" We who adopt do it because we want to, not because of a desire to be 'virtuous' and, having often been subjected to the same sort of remark over our having adopted Christopher, I would like to see this better understood by the general population. Jean further said to me, "It's not the way that we originally thought we'd get our family, but it feels the right family for us." And hers and Martin's is as obvious an example as I have ever seen of a family that was planned on the other side before they all incarnated.

Jean came to see me for a regression to increase her self-knowledge and because she wanted to explore the matter of her infertility. She and Martin had had one son (Ron), who was six when I first met her, but he had been conceived following fertility treatment and, when it came to the time for them to think about another child, Jean preferred the thought of adoption to that of going through the treatment again. Martin was also very happy about the adoption procedure because he felt more involved in it than he had been able to be with the fertility treatment. Their son Matthew came to them just before he was three, and at the time when we did the regression there was already a possibility of the couple adopting his younger sister.

Jean and Martin met at university and married when she was twenty-five. She is a teacher by profession, but having children always seemed more important to her than a career, and infertility had been a big issue for her for quite a long time. The past life that she went into with me was clearly relevant to this issue, since in it she found herself forced at much too young an age into marriage with an older, brutish man, who branded her as useless when the daughter that they had lived for only a few days. She died very young, seeing herself as an outcast in her village. Healing came for her, however, in the Bardo, where she had a most moving meeting with a lovely blond-haired little girl called Marigold. I expected Marigold to be her lost daughter in the life she had just re-experienced, but that did not appear to be the case. Rather, she told Jean that she was always with her and that she represented her freedom and her strength. Reviewing this past life enabled Jean to detach from it as no longer applicable, and to move forward into seeing herself as just as fully a woman as she would be if she were more physically fertile.

First of all, when Jean was first pregnant she anticipated having a girl, but then one day she met someone who told her that his name was Ron and she instantly *knew* that this was to be the name of her forthcoming child. Her husband accepted this information without question, and Ron rather than Ronald was the name that they entered on the birth certificate. As for the boy himself, as soon as he was old enough, he started informing people that he had a brother and a sister! This to me is a clear indication of a pre-birth plan that this family made together.

Matthew and his sister Hazel's parents are married but considered unfit for bringing up children. Matthew had already been in a foster home for a while before Jean and Martin were approved for adoption and, since his mother is classed as educationally sub-normal, he was expected to be the same and was consequently given very little stimulus by the foster parents. I mentioned in the Introduction that David and I were not given the opportunity of testing the 'heredity versus environment' question, so it was nice for me to meet someone who has been! Jean is convinced that environment counts for a great deal, and she comments that both the birth parents of their adopted children are victims of circumstances. They are stepsiblings and their wider family has no culture of work; and the birth mother, who has a learning disability, was one of seven children and spent her whole childhood in and out of foster care.

The social worker concerned with his case decided very quickly that Jean and Martin would be the right parents for Matthew, who had not started to talk at all in the foster home, and was also full of phobias and very passive and shut down. When Jean and I met for the regression, Matthew had been with them for two years, his phobias had disappeared, and they had succeeded in getting him to talk and shaken him out of his passivity. Jean was already confident that he would no longer be classified as a child of low ability and, when we met again a couple years later because of my writing this book, she told me that he was doing very well indeed. In order to help him escape from the label of 'special needs' in a school where people had marked him out as different, they had moved him to a smaller village school. The new term had only started two weeks prior to our meeting, but so far he was feeling happier and more confident there. He appears to be at least average or above average academically, despite being younger than most of the class because of having an August birthday, so his only remaining problems are social ones. Jean explained to me that in his previous school the dinner ladies had got into the habit of calling him "Matty babes", which, unfortunately for him, the other children had copied, but now nobody had any reason to think of him as any different than the other children in his new school.

Adoption agencies tend wisely to try to get siblings placed in the same family and so, when Hazel appeared on the scene, the social workers naturally contacted Jean and Martin, who immediately expressed an interest in adopting her as well. Although she and Matthew have similarly shaped faces, Jean says that they are not strikingly alike and that Hazel sometimes looks rather like Ron. The adoption was delayed a little bit because, although both children were taken into foster care as soon as they were born, their parents' lawyer found a loophole, which meant that the assessments as to Jean and Martin's suitability for adoption had to be redone. Hazel nevertheless had considerably less time in a foster home than her brother had, and she came to the family when she was nine months old. Jean says that she and Martin bonded with her more quickly than they had with Matthew, who is more difficult to get to know, and that she and her brother are 'chalk and cheese' in character. Both children are lactose intolerant, which in Matthew was not picked up until he was three, and he suffered from not being fed well during his first three years. Jean comments that he still displays the characteristic common in adopted children of not knowing when he is full. (When she said that I remembered how important food had always been to our son Christopher when he was a child.)

Hazel's foster care was better than Matthew's, although, being the only child in the home concerned, she was babied rather too much and not encouraged to do such things as crawling. The change from being an only child to becoming number three in the family was difficult for her, but now that she is three she is well integrated into the family, and Jean and Martin find that they love all three of their children equally. They have, however, made it clear to the Social Services that, should the parents give birth again, they would not want to adopt another child. (Jean commented that going back to caring for a baby was harder than they had anticipated!)

Ron, who had been so yearning for siblings, described the day his brother arrived as the best day of his life! Jean had prepared a separate bedroom for Matthew, but Ron soon pleaded with her to let him share his room. When Jean and I met for the second time in her hometown, after corresponding on and off by email during the period following her regression, she brought the now nine-year-old Ron with her to the café where we had the rendezvous because he was off school. Fortunately, however, he was not too sick to eat a toasted sandwich, and I was naturally delighted to have the opportunity of making his acquaintance. Jean told me that of her two adopted children, Hazel was the dominant one and made a slave of her brother Matthew. Ron confirmed that she bossed him around too, but admitted that they got on well, and Jean said that Ron was good at playing with her when he was in the mood. (No different from any other family!) She described Hazel as a very girly little girl, while Matthew in contrast has occasionally said that he would rather be a girl than a boy. Hazel also seems to be very bright and quicker at picking things up than Matthew was when he first came to them.

Jean is close to her sister Emma, who has a six-year-old daughter and lives nearby, and so the two families have regular contact. Since I was only able to meet her over lunchtime on my way home from the clinic where I work in Ripon, she had arranged for Emma to pick Hazel up when she finished her morning at pre-school. Jean told me that these first two years with the three children had been tough because of her own teaching commitments with the Open University, so pre-school, which Hazel enjoys, is now a help all round.

Jean and Martin's is described as an 'open adoption', which means that a certain amount of contact is maintained with the birth parents. This consists of a 'letterbox' arranged by Social Services, who once a year forward photographs of the children and a letter to the parents telling them how they are getting on. Since, however, the wider family background is regarded as an unsavory one, Matthew and Hazel are not permitted to appear in public photographs because this would enable the birth parents to trace them. Each child has their 'life story book', and when they are teenagers they will be given more information about their original family. At eighteen they will be permitted to look at their files if they care to do so. When they reach adulthood they will also of course be able to contact the parents if they so wish.

In the meantime Jean and Martin have themselves had one meeting with the birth parents. Betty Jean Lifton, whom I have quoted before (and who campaigned so strongly against closed adoptions!), says in her book *Lost and Found*, "From what I have observed, adoptive parents would benefit from at least one meeting with the birth mother. It would give them a chance to empathize with her and understand their child's heritage." Jean agrees that the meeting they had was indeed useful, though Social Services are not at present recommending another one. Matthew and Hazel have two half-brothers from their mother's previous marriage, one of whom is in long-term foster care and the other is adopted in the south of England. The family have also exchanged a letter with the brother who has been adopted.

Support when one has young children is always important, but it is particularly important for adoptive families because of the special difficulties that can so often occur. Fortunately Jean has one friend who has an adopted child as well as one of her own, but she is hoping to make more such friends. In the meantime the family find attendance at the annual celebration organized by their adoption agency useful and enjoyable.

Jean did not feel a need to have another regression. She did not find any members of her present family in the past life that she went into, but I was intrigued both by the manner in which Ron appeared to have chosen his name himself and by his apparent knowledge about his future younger siblings. I consequently asked some questions about the family using my pendulum. The answers I got were the following:

- Ron and Matthew have been very close friends in previous lives
- Jean and Martin have both been Matthew's parents more than once (though not together)
- Ron and Hazel have been brother and sister before, and Hazel has also been sister to both Jean and Martin when they were siblings
- Jean and Martin, having been siblings before, are now companion soul mates[1]
- The birth parents are paying a karmic debt to both Matthew and Hazel by giving them to Jean and Martin

When I told Jean about my findings, she said that they rang true for her. And I am sure that she shares my feeling that hers is a "family made in Heaven"!

Note

1. See *Souls United – The Power of Divine Connection,* Ann Merivale, Llewellyn, USA, 2009.

CHAPTER TEN

ADOPTING TWO CHILDREN SIMULTANEOUSLY

Ruth's Story (Written by Herself)

> *When you are adopted, perhaps becoming a parent through adoption is just as attractive as the other way. Like something you owe to the next generation of foundlings.*
>
> From *Twice Born – Memoirs of an Adopted Daughter,* Betty Jean Lifton

I doubt if I ever spoke of it, but I wanted twins from the time I was a schoolgirl. Simon, my husband, is actually a surviving twin, and therefore when we realized that we had major fertility problems, and began to look at adoption, we both found the thought of twins an attractive option. It gradually became clear that our best chance of acquiring any baby at all would be from the Third World, and then we quickly came to understand that genuine twins very seldom both survive there – let alone among those available for adoption.

At one time during our fertility investigations, my gynecologist said to me, "If you want babies, get a baby! That often helps, you know." So we did! We ended up fostering a delightful pair of Ashanti twin sisters, aged six months when they came to us, and two years when they were able to return to their parents. To my mind the main disadvantage of fostering twins was emotional: inevitably, a temporary foster home for babies mucks about with their emotions, but we did our utmost to ensure that their primary tie was neither with their natural parents nor with us, but with each other. That, we believe, made the process of moving homes a lot less damaging. We felt no particular guilt about taking them – their parents were desperate anyway and would have most definitely fostered them wherever they could – and we believed that we could provide as good a home as they could hope to get. But our friends were a bit shocked; I had as a social worker inspected private foster homes, and so it looked a bit like 'gamekeeper turned poacher'!

I bought Penelope Leach's book *Baby & Child* and it became my practical bible. Although she has little to say specifically about twins, she is excellent on what is needed at what developmental stage, and we wanted to get it right for them. We did, I believe, get it more or less right, and during that extremely hard-worked eighteen months I learnt to cope, with practiced ease, with the care of two babies as sole adult in the house most waking hours. It really is not difficult, provided that you reckon it is your full-time job. (God knows how 'working mothers' – I was working as hard as I ever have in my life – ever cope with twins!) The main secret of it is to always, always, always be organized enough to keep "one jump ahead," i.e. as soon as a bottle is drunk, it is washed and put into the sterilizer, and the next-but-one is immediately made up and refrigerated, the next bottle of course being already in there; and as soon as one pair of nappies is changed, (we used terries), the next pair is folded and laid out for instant use, etc. Above all, as soon as both babies are asleep you get ready for one or both to wake unexpectedly, and then, and only then, do you use the time to get on with the rest of your life.

These twins were our joy and our delight, which made it much easier all round, of course! Ashanti culture is fierce, seniority goes by age, so the older is always technically 'in charge' of the younger, but equally always, twins must be treated exactly alike – for fear of jealousy – to the point that (their names being Di-Di and Chescha), whenever the Archers theme tune was on and I sang along with it, I had to sing "Di-d'-di di'di d'di – chesca chesca chesca" or they would both become unhappy!

Losing them was hard, but the actual handling of two babies simultaneously is quite an easy skill to develop, even when the children develop at slightly different rates. Chesca was walking well months before Di-di, and I used to proudly toddle her round to the village shops, holding my hand, while Di-di rode in a back-sling, and then swap them over for about ten yards, just to keep them both happy! If Chesca tired on the way home, she just had to straddle my hip, which is not as difficult as it looks, provided one's shopping bag is small enough.

Simon had never previously handled a baby, and he is not a natural at it. He has never learned, for example, the difference between a hungry and a sleepy cry, but he quickly learned the basics of changing and feeding, and really quite enjoyed playing with them. And they always gave him the most tremendous welcome home from work! Because he is our breadwinner, I have always considered it my job to turn out if a child cries in the night – and there was only one single night when both howled at once, and then he got up as well to help. We both missed them dreadfully when they left.

So when, many years later, we came to look at inter-country adoption, we had no particular worries about the practicalities of what was involved. We were, on the other hand, very worried about potential racism. As it happened, that was not a problem in the multicultural city where we were living; but of course we could not know that in advance, and were reliant on the media, which consistently painted unpleasant, sensationalist pictures about it. Therefore we thought it would be unkind to take only one non-white child into a white family, and street. And we felt that, on the whole, two from the same country made sense. We wanted small babies, partly because we knew we enjoyed working with babies, and partly because we did not want, "some poor kid howling its heart out for an elephant-ride in a language we did not understand." Also, since by then we had a born son, we were clear that any adoptee should be a girl. (Anyone who, like Ann, the main author of this book, knew my mother, would appreciate that a boy would have been subject to the most odious comparisons imaginable with Jack – which would have been good for neither of them.) My mother was in fact basically opposed to our adopting at all, at our rather late age, and she was also actually quite racist. (Bizarrely, it was my estranged brother who passionately fought their corner for our mother to include the girls in the small legacies she left to each grandchild. His experiences in Kenya have left him deeply opposed to anything which could be seen as racism in any form.)

Our age, or rather my age, was the third issue, the clincher, once we had found that Sri Lanka was going to be the birth country of our adoptees. Sri Lankan adoption law is basically modelled on British law (so closely that we did not have to re-adopt in the UK, as people with birth countries in e.g. South America do). Sri Lankan law, however, states that fifty is the oldest permissible age for adopters, and my fiftieth birthday fell only a few weeks after we adopted them. Besides, I had had while we were thinking about it what as a theologian I delight to call a 'bat-qol', which is the Jewish term for the voice of God in one's head. I was trying intellectually to weigh up the advantages for one against two, when we knew that if we got two they were very unlikely to be genuine birth-twins. I actually heard a voice (in my head, I think), and it said, "The best gift you can give them is each other." Just that – nothing more! But from that moment we knew neither doubt nor fear about taking on two at once.

We were, as I have already indicated, experienced twin-handlers, so as long as they stayed at about the same developmental stage there were no great problems. Penny was the frailer at first, having been in a poor nursery of some sort, and I think fed largely on rice-water. She consequently had dreadful problems with feeding, although we managed, with a combination of my cunning and our luck, to keep her on exactly the milk we had been recommended as "hers." But we got her through; and once she realized that, to her obvious amazement, whenever she cried only one or other of the same three people ever came to her, she began to flourish. She soon clearly began to love the three senior members of the household, though not her 'twin'/rival.

Penny became mobile long before Dilipa, who was a phlegmatic, placid baby. (We gave them each an English first name and a Sri Lankan second name, but Dilipa later decided that she wanted to change from Mary to her Sri Lankan name.) During the first terrible days with us we are quite sure that she was mourning the mother who had tenderly breast-fed her, and then handed her over with a smile of pure courage. Mary, as she then was, would not take her bottle but, after about twelve hours, when I was beginning to worry about dehydration, and also half laugh because she was refusing the bottle but rooting angrily against my dry t-shirt, Jack suddenly said, "Let me try!" Then – to everyone's amazement, and his deep and permanent satisfaction – she stopped grizzling, lay on his lap, stared into his face, and gulped down the whole bottle! He fed her for the next three or four days almost entirely. After which, gradually and grudgingly, she accepted bottles from me.

Subsequently reconstructing what happened when we were taken by the lawyer intermediary to view the 'possible' babies in her office, this is how I see it. Dilipa was brought by her mother, who breastfed her almost continuously. She had no English but watched closely everything we did, particularly when I told Jack to sit down, and then, carefully, allowed him to hold each of the babies on his lap in turn. I think she was intuitive enough to realize that her daughter would resent me as supplanting herself, and also that it would be good for everyone if a strong bond could be made with the new big brother. So it looks extremely likely that, in the three weeks during which we were allowed no contact while awaiting the Court's verdict, Dilipa's mother deliberately got a young boy to wean her breast-fed baby on to a bottle.

Once we had been back in England for a while, Dilipa's cardiac problems, as yet unknown and undiagnosed, were beginning to slow her development. Penny was a lively little thing, running about while Dilipa was still 'swimming' rather than crawling. My mother, deeply resenting them but still only in the early stages of what was probably Alzheimer's, could not remember their names, but one day she summoned me to the open front door with a shriek of "Oh! Quick! The Yellow One is escaping!" (Penny, in a tiny yellow tracksuit, was attempting to crawl out over the doorstep, and her reluctant grandmother was not sufficiently confident of her own balance to bend over and pick her up.)

Both girls picked up a chest infection at the age of five months, severe enough to land them – with me – in the local hospital for a few days. For some reason the nurses used to giggle when they watched my very easy method of bottle-feeding two at once. I had had to invent it for the Ghanaian twins, and it was considered 'unique', but it works. I lay on my back on a bed with two cot sides, and about two or three pillows behind my head and shoulders (at home we had a 'puppy basket' couch for the purpose). I laid each child along one of my sides, facing me, with her feet more or less in my armpits, and held the bottles so that both could get cuddles and eye contact practically simultaneously – and without having to struggle with her twin to obtain them. I cannot imagine why this technique is not bog-standard, because it works far better than trying to keep both on one's lap simultaneously, and it is also faster than feeding one after the other in the usual way, without significantly reducing contact time. Nor is one baby left crying and hungry while waiting for the other to finish. (I have often wondered whether it would be possible to breast-feed twins with very little essential modification.) If I remembered to spread a clean terry nappy over myself before starting, it was perfectly possible to burp one child by rolling her, face-down, on to my stomach one-handed, without disturbing the other in the least. If I did not remember the nappy, things got very messy for me, but it was still effective! The aim was to treat each child with as much focus as if she had been an only child, and not a twin, genuine or otherwise.

I was often really grateful that they were roughly at the same developmental stage. How anyone manages to bottle-feed one child while an older one – or more – is staggering about and getting into mischief, I cannot imagine! The other basic 'twin-essential' was to have, at all times, a clean playpen, set up with special soft and varied toys, kept only in the playpen. That way, if one child was in big trouble and urgently needed all one's attention, the other could be safely dumped out of harm's way to amuse herself for quite a long time, twenty minutes or so, before she became a problem. Or, if the worst came to the worst, simply be left to howl, in safety, for as long as it took. But cleaning and resetting the playpen had to be done every rest time without fail if things were not to get unacceptably mucky, very fast indeed. For twins, a 'lobster-pot' pen is much easier to manage than the traditional wooden, hinged cage; nobody's fingers get pinched, and it has an integral soft waterproof floor that you can use even in the garden. I have occasionally carried a child under one arm, and the folded pen in the other hand, and set it up almost one-handed, put the child in, and gone back for the pen toys, and only then focused on the child in trouble, all in less than one minute flat (and I am not noted for speed or dexterity). The playpen was a lovely gift, forced on me by the couple from whom we bought the charming village house that we lived in before moving to a city because of Simon changing his job. They had twins themselves and, since it was the era when playpens were considered rather barbarous, I had loftily declined the offer, but they wedged it into the porch anyway when they left the village. Bless them!

We were discharged from hospital in about a week, and after

a couple of follow-up appointments, we were all happy that Penny was considered fit for full discharge. I, however, was not happy about Dilipa, and begged for further follow-ups; all I could say, each time, was that "she does not seem to me to be fully recovered yet." All the professionals, GP, HV, and all the relevant pediatric staff in the hospital were unanimous that she was "fine now."

So began the loneliest battle of my entire life! I knew, I just knew, beyond all doubt, that my daughter was really, really sick and must have professional help. But I was the only human being in the entire universe who could see it and so, for six dreadful months, I had to keep wheedling for more appointments, while lying through my teeth to Simon that it was the hospital which wanted the appointments. He would most certainly have objected strongly to my arrogantly setting myself up against the professionals and making improper use of scarce NHS resources. I did not believe myself capable of fighting both him and them simultaneously, so I neutralized him with lies, which I was, and remain, confident that God forgave.

After six months, the pediatrician said gently but with total firmness, "Look, we can't find anything wrong; I really think this has got to stop now!" I was devastated, but felt I could go no further. So I opened my mouth to agree, thinking that the very best I could hope for was to have been wrong after all, for all these months; and out of my own mouth came a strange little, Cockney, voice – a voice I swear I have heard neither before nor since – and it said, briefly and quietly, "Bu' – Mary's not righ' yet!" Nothing more, but the effect on the specialist was astonishing! He literally jumped, as if a pin had been stuck in him, and replied, "Very well, we'll give her some blood tests." Then he wrote out a chitty for me to take her immediately to the vampires on our way out, and also one for an appointment the following week.

The next week, when I turned up with the twin buggy full as

usual, the pediatrician rose to his feet behind his desk and said, exactly as to a colleague, "I owe you an apology! You were perfectly right, there is something very seriously wrong; serious but I don't think it is dangerous, at any rate not yet. I want you to get her to Great Ormond Street Hospital this afternoon, because there is a new diagnostic machine which is only used once a month and I want her seen on it."

Simon was working out of town that day. I had never driven in London on a weekday, and did not even know where the hospital was (or if I had got there, how to do anything about parking), and I would not be allowed to take Penny with us. Besides Jack, still only nine, would be coming out of school before we could possibly be back, but what are friends for? Mercifully my closest local friend was at home, and she agreed to hold both Penny and the taxi fare so that I could arrange with his school to get Jack met and conveyed to her. (I told his teacher precisely what I had been told – "very serious but not dangerous" – and also to get him to take the taxi I had arranged.) I then left a slightly incoherent message with Simon's secretary, explaining where all his family were, and what to get himself for dinner, thrust poor Penny, two made up bottles, a bag of clean nappies, and the taxi money into my good friend's arms, and raced back to the hospital car park, where an ambulance was awaiting us. But it had no safety equipment for so tiny a patient, so the lads stripped one of the hired baby car seats out of my car (probably invalidating its guarantee!), and away we went. The ambulance crew were, I think, as is often the case, pre-medical students; at any rate they 'sweet-talked' me into asking the technical crew at GOSH to allow them to sit in on the use of this very, very advanced diagnostic machine. I agreed gladly, realizing that that would mean a guaranteed ride home, which had not been promised.

So we met the man who became Dilipa's specialist for all of the next seventeen years; (and because he had a grizzled beard, we never saw his face, like a Muslim lady in hijab). He was surrounded by a gaggle of medical students; and when the machine was on, and little Dilipa was stripped and sedated – but not allowed to sleep, I was instructed to talk or sing to her if she was in danger of dropping off – they began a two-hour, slow, meticulous, investigation. The results on the image-screen could have been the seabed for all I could tell; (it was indeed a kind of echo-sounder, an immensely cruder version of which my late father had had in his last boat!). At one point a medical student whistled sharply, in pure shock, but "Tell you later!" was all the response I got to my question.

Basically, it turned out that Dilipa had been born with no pulmonary artery at all, the function being temporarily filled, with diminishing efficacy, by the ductus, which normally takes fetal blood from the lungs to the heart (i.e. is a temporary vein), and it withers along with the umbilical cord. If the pulmonary artery does not develop, blood flows 'the wrong way' up the ductus for as long as it can, but without surgery such babies cannot live beyond twenty months or so. There is no growth potential in the ductus and so it becomes less and less adequate. Additionally, in Dilipa's case, the upper two chambers of the heart were in reverse position, and she had – as was eventually discovered – no less than eleven 'holes in the heart' (leakages within the system with reverse eddies in the bloodstream etc).

To cut a long story short, our little daughter had a life-saving operation on St. Valentine's Day, 1991. (I went for the traditional walk while she was in theatre and couldn't help noticing that every shop window in London was full of bleeding hearts!) Dilipa had a small post-operative stroke and was hemiplegic for forty-eight hours. The most beautiful sight I have ever seen was her little hand, like a crane-grab, starting to work again, reaching out to a slice of apple! As she lay on my lap, the day before the operation, she looked up at me very, very intently and said, clearly, her first real speech, "Pen-pen? Pen-pen? Pen-pen?" I suddenly realized that "Pen-pen" might be her attempt at "Penny," and if so she was asking for her sister! I thought it could certainly do no harm to respond as if she were. "Penny," I said, very slowly and clearly, "is with Dad-dy. She is all right!" The baby sighed and relaxed, visibly relieved; and after that she never spoke another word for over six months! She was eleven months old at the time of the operation.

We found a day-minder for Penny, and Simon and Jack together looked after her in the evenings. This forged a special bond between Jack and Penny, which was greatly reinforced by the five weeks Dilipa (and I) had to be in hospital for further surgery when the girls were in Reception Year, and Jack was fourteen. That time Penny was taken to school by Simon each morning, but went home with my friend's children from the same school, to our friend (who had held her for the original diagnosis), and Jack also walked there from his school, about an hour later. This good family fed them their evening meal, (and I believe sometimes also fed Simon when he came to collect them at the end of the day). They had been our local referees for the adoption, and were their godparents – truly God-given when we needed them!

After the first operation, Dilipa's development shot ahead in every way. But as for poor Penny, because she was so advanced compared to Dilipa, we never picked up for three years that she, too, had physical problems. It turned out that she had dyslexia, dyspraxia, and hypermobile joints. And all that time we were using Penny as our normal standard of comparison to see how far behind Dilipa was in physical development! When Penny finally did get seen at the Child Development Centre, and what we had thought of as 'sillinesses' were identified as problems, her prayers that night included a spontaneous, heartfelt "Thank you, God, for Miss Iris!" (Her diagnosing therapist.)

Jack is nine years older than his sisters and had taken his status as an 'only child' without any questioning. As with all only children, much maternal time and energy went into finding and arranging playmates. In a village the range of children is small, and one of the excellent side-effects was that his closest friend before he started school was the boy next door – older and larger than he was, by almost three years – but of marginally subnormal intelligence. 'Dave' (let's call him) adored Jack, who had been able to release him from total social isolation (villages can be dreadfully cruel places) and, apart from anything else, Dave was illegitimate, and lived with his mother, her identical twin sister, and their two rather strange parents. But Jack very quickly became the leader – the one who always worked out what they were going to play – and I was quite certain that if three-year-old Jack had said to Dave, "Let's go and lie in the middle of the road," Dave would have said "Great idea, Jack!" and done it. So my first task was to get through to Dave that under NO circumstances were they ever to go outside the garden without an adult; and also that under no circumstances was he to untie the gate for Jack, etc. However, big, thick, but utterly devoted Dave gave Jack a confidence which stood him in good stead all his school days. He never (unlike both his parents!) felt any fear of boys just because they happened to be older and bigger than he was, and when he turned out to be a chess player of some skill, he was never ruffled by playing huge senior boys. As with bigger, so with smaller; he might find a younger child's limitations made them a boring playmate, but if he liked that child he would spend a lot of time ingeniously finding things they could play together, just as he had with Dave.

Jack was seven when we first broached the possibility of adoption with him. He took for granted that any further child in the family would be another boy; and when we said, "actually we were thinking of girls," he was thunderstruck! Then he said, "Well, it would be all right if they were like Flo or Amy (girls he had played with before we moved, but not seen for a couple of years)." Once he had understood that it would be an international adoption, he made, for a seven-year-old, a comment we thought quite brilliant. "About schooling? I have heard that Silver Jubilee is very good for children who can't speak English. Maybe they should go there?" (Silver Jubilee was a state lower school in an immigrant area of the city, about seventy-five per cent of whose pupils had English only as a second language.) His school would have kept him as a temporary boarder while we went to fetch the babies, but we felt very strongly that he would have more problems if we went off on a glorious tropical holiday and brought back a couple of little strangers. We therefore felt that he must come along with us and, if he was really upset and repelled by any baby we were offered, that it would probably be too dangerous to accept it (one advantage over birth!). Fortunately the school agreed that "Jack would learn far more on that journey than we could teach him in as many school days," and let him miss school with their blessing. Their 'price' for the favor was that he had to take one whole lesson with his classmates, talking about Sri Lanka, which he managed very competently, they said.

In the event Jack had to grow up very fast indeed because when we arrived in Sri Lanka Simon suddenly collapsed (nervous strain probably), and was very ill indeed for a few days. The result was that I had to go alone to a meeting with the intermediaries, leaving young Jack to look after Daddy and telephone me if he got any worse and worried him. (Mercifully the meeting was in the hotel.) We had no idea how long the meeting would take and so I was very thankful I did not have to leave Simon alone; but it was really tough on the little boy, who has a huge and sensitive imagination. However, he greeted me when I got back with the manner of a professional nurse: "It's all right, Mummy, he was only sick again once, and I cleaned it up, and he is sleeping now."

We knew the babies would be about ten days old when we went to view them, so I had explained about the reflex by which toes curl out at first but at about ten days, and forever after, curl down if you tickle the soles of the feet. That was all Jack knew that he knew about babies, so, reasonably enough, he quite discreetly tickled their feet, and afterwards reported back to us. "Penny's toes went down, but Dilipa's went out." I had forgotten about it! As mentioned above, each was laid on his lap for about ninety seconds, while they stared quietly at each other.

I think that then, and for many years afterwards, the appeal the girls held for Jack was almost that of puppies. There was one moment, the night before we were due to go to court for the adoption, when I pointed out that this was our last night as a family of three – "from tomorrow we will be five Thompsons" – and Jack went very white. "It honestly does not mean we will love you any less," we were able to reassure him, because it was true and he could sense it. We did not make the disastrous mistake of promising him that they would be playmates because the age gap was too big. There was very little sense of sibling rivalry, their developmental stage and their interests were far too different. Jack was never a greedy child, and he was perfectly happy to hand over those of his outgrown toys which had not already been given away, as they became suitable to their developments. He even took a rather lordly interest in helping them master the intricacies of tricycle riding etc.

Fearing, greatly, the racism of which the media babbled, my first trip into Jack's school with the twins in the buggy was a terrible ordeal for me; but one of Jack's particular friends, Pete, even then an accepted leader and opinion-former, was sincerely, and very publicly, enchanted with them, dropping onto his haunches and cooing over them, more like a baby-mad girl of my generation than I thought possible. He had a little brother of their age, and was (and is) truly 'baby mad', so, thanks to him, "Thompson's sisters" were never an embarrassment to Jack.

Penny was always the more obviously outgoing, chatty, and apparently brighter of the two; and Dilipa's hospitalizations had the side effect of forming a special bond between Jack and Penny. This was later reinforced when, at the age of eleven, because she required special dyslexic and emotional care, Penny was sent away to board weekly at a school not too far away, and travelled home by public transport every Friday evening. Her older schoolmates put her off the London train at Oxford, and then Jack, who by this time was an undergraduate there, faithfully met her from the train, and saw her on to the homebound bus. Sometimes he would proudly escort her round Oxford, to see the dodo in the Ashmolean, or for an ice cream. Huge, fair Jack and tiny, brown Penny habitually walked round Oxford hand in hand on such expeditions, both too utterly innocent to give a thought to the strange looks certain passers-by gave them. (I know because I went on the first couple of these transfers, training both parties to get the pattern reliable.)

Nothing at all would make Penny take her schoolwork seriously, and no teacher ever managed to give her the idea (which Jack had always had from infancy) that learning was fun; but her unused IQ was almost as high as his, and her conversations were, and still are, therefore quite funny at times. They could and did enjoy each other's company, provided they did not have to rely on one another for companionship too much.

Dilipa he found much more difficult when she was a little girl; simultaneously apparently backward, but also far more mature than he, having fought so long for her life. She was almost completely inarticulate at that time. "Marygrams" was family slang for her badly scrambled attempts to express herself verbally (it was well before she had changed to using her Sri Lankan name); usually I could decode them, but the others could not without a lot of help from me. We would sort out the jumble, and I would then say, "What you want to say is…… isn't it?"

"'Esss!" was Dilipa's reply, and she would be delighted at being understood. But if I was defeated she was always sad, but could not usually try any other way. Penny and Jack both had enormous vocabularies for their age (though neither could spell), but Dilipa's was so minuscule she was actually diagnosed ESN and given remedial lessons. Once or twice she got into quite bizarre teenage quarrels, partly conducted electronically. Simon and I were very anxious and very much out of our depths; Simon said, "Boys never behaved like that," so it must be my business to advise – and my memories of my teenage friendships were not in the least like that! She sounded to me like a character from some trashy Angela Brazil story, of the sort I had not even wanted to read in my teens!

Strangely enough, it was Jack who was able to reassure both Dilipa and his parents. His 'girlfriends' are few and far between, and apparently as unusual as he is himself, but since going up to Oxford he has always had many same-age female friends, of whom he is fond but whom he also studies like an anthropologist. So from these insights he was often able to help all the parties involved. As his sisters often remarked, "For a hopeless geek he is really very nice!"

Jack more or less 'wrote Dilipa off' during this phase; he began to take notice of her only when, to the family's astonishment (as well as her own!) she became one of the 'Quartet' of combined prefects and head pupils at the school she went to for her sixth-form years, and obviously made the most enormous developmental progress. At this school she developed artistically, musically and academically as well as revealing unguessed-at managerial talents, and the greatest capacity for sheer hard work of any of us (except possibly Simon).

Part of Dilipa's character appears to be sheer, driving, ambition. She has to excel, and if she cannot excel, she is depressed and miserable. The academic palm of the family was always awarded to Jack – the only one of us to get into Oxbridge – but Dilipa began to flourish when she realized that she could, and did, pass her driving test long before he did. And then, when he ended up getting a lower degree from Oxford than his abilities would have suggested he deserved, she suddenly decided that she had a hope of excelling at university. So she buckled down to get herself a First, with realistic hopes of success, despite the immense difficulties for her of producing academic essays.

Dilipa had fortunately not been subjected to a great deal of racism before a recent incident. While working at a vacation job in a supermarket, a customer ordered her to "go back where you came from." This would be hurtful to anyone, but obviously must be doubly so for a girl who knows that she would not have had a home at all if she had not been brought to England by her loving adoptive parents. Dilipa's immediate reaction was to go and seek solace from a friend of African origin, and I feel that, while Simon and I had always been there to "give sympathy from the outside," it was very good for our daughters to have someone to turn to who could "offer it from the inside." We have also been blessed with a good support network of Sri Lankan families including fellow adopters and adoptees.

Penny, bizarrely, has never had a proper boyfriend, whereas Dilipa has never been without since the age of thirteen, so there has never been any contest there! Dilipa looks on her cardiac history, quite realistically, as a handicap, but one that she is determined to overcome – and a long, painful, hard slog that is proving…*. Recently Jack has been at his least useful visiting her in hospital; he is sympathetic but not really gifted in supporting the very sick. (As he said brusquely, on one occasion many years ago now, "more high-tech than Baby in this cot!")

Nowadays the three of them only meet physically about two or three times a year – always at Christmas, and my July birthday treat is invariably a London theatre and family meal for us all. But they all three routinely text one another, Skype rarely, e-mail, occasionally telephone, never write letters, but have a fairly close shared sibling relationship. Even during the long period of Jack's post-Oxford near breakdown, when he was not communicating with either parent, he was in touch with both girls, and what little we knew of him in those months came via them. Because Simon's parents and my father all died before any of the children knew them, and they only share hazy memories of a senile Granny in a home (Jack remembers a very little about our annual family holidays with her before she became too confused), they have been brought up together in the knowledge that they will share responsibility for either or both of us when we become too enfeebled to help ourselves, and this is something they all appear to accept unquestioningly.

My reply to Ann's question: "Does my claim that you all must have known each other before, ring true for you in any way?" is "I'm afraid not!" I believe that each of us is unique to our time and place in the only ways in which I can now know them. I do nevertheless have, I believe, some vague memories of previous lives, but these are rather like photographic stills – very, very brief sequences of movement. I remember being the son of a Jewish couple who ran a corner shop in Poland, in the very early years of the twentieth, or very late nineteenth, century. I remember the sound of the shop bell, the layout of the shelves, how I had to stack the boxes of groceries, the smell of my mother's cooking from the room behind the counter, the sound and bulk of my parents, and how I had to sweep the shop, and stack the shelves, and clean the windows, and run errands, and I remember a boy who was my friend, from the same shul, but I do not remember any individuals I could identify outside that setting.

I also have a more elaborate sequence, from some dark-age or prehistoric village, which I think may have been in Somerset, and I think two friends of mine, whom I have recognized this time around, and I were women of that village, setting out in late afternoon to do what we could with the aftermath of a local battle fought in the morning. We each had a good knife, and a bag of clean rags and various crushed herbs, and another, big, empty, bag. My older friend I knew would treat anyone she came across, friend or foe, as best she could. I would treat the wounded from our own side, but just quickly, in mercy, stab any surviving enemy I came across; the third of us had robbing the victims as her main purpose, but would help a friend very skillfully if she came across one. I remember my primary purpose was to find my husband. I think I did, but that he was dead, because I remember dragging a body on a broken branch back to the village, for communal burial in a re-opened mound, and the whole village wailing around a few separate bonfires (one for each of our men killed), as night fell.

However, the first time Dilipa was in Great Ormond Street hospital for an operation, there was a Sri Lankan Buddhist nurse, who told me that it was absolutely clear to her that I had done what I had done to repay a debt to Dilipa from a previous life. I have to admit that I like this concept very much indeed, because it frees both parties from any sense either of obligation or pride. I know that Ann (this book's main author) must, when Christopher was being difficult, have had to endure people telling her how "good" she was to take this problem child on. Well, there is a temptation, if the load is heavy, to agree, and consequently to resent it if the load grows any heavier, but the 'karma' or 'debt' concept completely sorts that out! "I am only repaying what I owe her" does not allow room for pride, much less for resentment. Neither does the beneficiary this time around need to feel any sense of obligation – brilliant! Absolutely brilliant! But true? Who but God can say?

*Author's note: Dilipa is at present doing well following a heart transplant, so fingers crossed for her future!

CHAPTER ELEVEN

ADOPTING OLDER CHILDREN

Philip and Wendy's Story

> *Adoptive parents who can be frank about their uncertainties have a better chance of overcoming the problems. For although blood relationships may not be perfect, they do not have to be explained.*
> Betty Jean Lifton, *LOST AND FOUND – The Adoption Experience*

It is my belief that Philip and Wendy are soul mates (very likely twin souls), who came together again this time round, as evolved soul mates often do[1], in order to serve a higher purpose of helping others – in particular the two half-sisters Jane and Sarah, who were born into a very difficult background indeed. Philip and Wendy had both been married before (Wendy twice), and he had two daughters by his first wife and she two sons by her second husband. Though he now runs his own business, Philip was previously in the Army and by the age of thirty-six had lived in forty different places. This necessitated putting his daughters, Jeanette and Sally, into boarding school, and also put an inevitable strain on his marriage. He and his first wife separated when the girls were ten and six and, though he has a good relationship with Jeanette (now forty and married with two children), he is unfortunately not at present in touch with Sally, who found the separation difficult to accept.

Wendy's first marriage, which she explains took place almost against her will, was very short lived. The second one was more successful initially, but she divorced him after fourteen years because his work took him away so much and he played virtually no part in raising the family. However, the two sons, Mark and

David, whom Wendy bore to her second husband, are her pride and joy. (In fact it was through the younger one, who once came to me for a regression, that I met Philip and Wendy, and I found him to be a truly delightful young man.)

Philip and Wendy met through a dating agency, but her previous negative experience with men nevertheless made her wary at first and she ignored the first letter that Philip wrote her. They had several long telephone conversations before she finally agreed to a meeting, and it was no doubt Philip's quick recognition of his soul mate that encouraged his persistence. He was already feeling that the challenge had gone from his army career, as well as being disillusioned with both the army culture and government policy, and so Wendy encouraged him to make a change.

Mark and David were eighteen and fourteen when their mother remarried, and Philip appears to have taken to step fatherhood like a duck to water. They all bonded more or less instantly into a happy family, and Philip now regards the two young men just as he would sons of his own, even though they do still have quite a good relationship with their natural father. This must make up at least a little bit for the lack of contact with his younger daughter.

Philip and Wendy had been talking tentatively about adopting a child (*one* child!) when Wendy, who was working as a counsellor at the time, kept noticing Jane and Sarah in the "Be My Parent" book. When, a whole year after she had first seen them in the book, she found that they were still there, Wendy began seriously to ask questions about them. She soon discovered that they were deemed 'hard to place' because of Jane's supposed ethnic background, which appeared to be "rather less white than snow." In actual fact, since her mother had innumerable different partners, her father's identity is completely unknown, but Jane is strikingly beautiful and looks as though she could well be half Indian or possibly Spanish.

Sarah's father, on the other hand, who is a member of the racist British National Party (formerly known as the National Front), visited Tracey, their mother, for some years, until he went to prison, and he regularly used to beat Jane up because of the fact that to him she looked "black."

Tracey also had three younger children, all by the same man, who, although this was not known to the social workers at the time, was a heroin addict. Jane and Sarah, whom Tracey sometimes used to take to a pedophile as a way of earning money for herself, were on the 'At Risk' register, whereas the younger ones were not there initially because of the apparent 'stability' of Tracey's current relationship. As soon as Wendy expressed an interest, the social workers latched on to the couple saying that they should take both the girls. They were seen as the perfect family for them for various reasons, one being similarity in looks. Photographs show Jane to look extraordinarily like Wendy when young ("with an identical stance and everything"), and Sarah's features bear a striking resemblance to those of Philip and his daughters. One of the social workers picked up on this and commented, "These parents are meant for them."

Unfortunately their experiences have given Philip and Wendy a very low opinion indeed of social workers, "many of whom," Philip comments, "haven't actually had children themselves and so know very little about what bringing them up is like." The thing that shocked me the most when I talked to them was to hear that, prior to taking the girls on, Philip and Wendy were told virtually nothing about their background. It all came out little by little, as their confidence with their new parents grew, and they found, for instance, that Jane was regularly having nightmares about a black guy who abused her while Tracey, her mother, was being abused by another one. Philip and Wendy in due course learned that the girls used to get tied to a bed and had bites all over them, and it was Sarah herself who eventually convinced the social workers that her 'stepfather' was a heroin addict. Sarah did not suffer the abuse that Jane experienced because her father protected her, but she was nevertheless seriously neglected.

Jane and Sarah were aged ten and six when they first came to their new home – 'coincidentally' (if one believed in coincidence, which I do not!) the same ages as Philip's two daughters at the time of his separation from their mother. Another 'coincidence' is that they each have the same initials as one of Philip's daughters. Both Mark and David coped wonderfully with their new sisters; in fact Wendy comments that her sons were the girls' saviors – especially David since Mark went off to university to read medicine soon after their arrival. Philip, however, feels that, although Jeanette has always visited regularly, the adoption may have been more difficult for his daughters since they could well have viewed Jane and Sarah as replacements for them.

Not long after the girls' arrival, Philip and Wendy took them, with Mark and David, on holiday to a villa in Spain, where they all had a wonderful time and the girls learned to swim. The first inkling that they had of anything being wrong was when they were leaving to come home and Sarah suddenly went back into the house and started urinating all over it. Being the sort of people they are, rather than scolding her, Philip and Wendy encouraged both the girls to talk about their problems, and soon they found out, among other things, that Sarah had been abused by a lodger while she had been in a foster home.

Philip says that, although there were two social workers from the girls' home who "hadn't been corrupted by political correctness," he felt that the racism awareness workshop that one social worker recommended for Jane would have been irrelevant to her real needs. The present move towards more open adoption has a great deal to be said for it, but each case should surely be assessed individually. In this family's case one of the biggest problems was the social workers' insistence that the girls write regularly to their mother and send photographs. When they first came to their new home, they did not even like being taken to the local supermarket because it looked just the same as the one near their own home and they were terrified that their family would find them. Keeping contact was the last thing that these two girls wanted, and Jane even at times expressed a desire to go and find her mother in order to knife her!

Important though I believe anti-racist education to be, I found myself agreeing with Philip and Wendy's opinion that 'political correctness' can be taken too far. Another social worker who became involved with the girls after they had begun to open up about their terrible history read their files before meeting Philip and Wendy and came to the conclusion that they should be in a home without a male figure in it. She frequently commented that "girls do not need men in their lives," which was of course most hurtful for Philip, who appreciated the importance of a caring father figure for them and was working so very hard to be that. (Fortunately she did later apologize to Philip, and Wendy thinks that she was biased by the fact of her own daughter not having contact with her father.)

It is hard for an outsider to imagine how difficult and stressful the next few years must have been for Wendy and Philip. Wendy comments meaningfully, "There's adoption and there's adoption" (reminding me how comparatively "easy" it had been for us taking on a young baby); and Philip recounted to me how much he had come to resent the constant intrusion into their home of police, social workers and social security workers. They say that now, when they turn on the news, they understand what is happening to a much greater extent than they ever had before, and Philip is of the opinion that everyone should have a problem child to live with them for six months. This, he comments, would foster greater understanding in our society, and contribute to eradicating prejudice.

Philip and Wendy's own backgrounds are not wealthy ones, but they both come from what one might call 'nice' families, and their daughters' behavior was something completely alien to them. (Whether or not they agreed, I would see it as a huge learning experience that they chose to take on this time round.) The fact that Jane would not talk about anything to anyone but her was very draining for Wendy. Philip explained that to start with he did all he could to control the girls because that was his only way of coping, but that later he came to accept lack of control as an inevitable ingredient of their family situation.

Prior to my visiting them, Philip asked his wife three questions: "Was our adopting these girls a positive experience?", "Would you do it again?", "Would you recommend it to others?" Wendy reluctantly found herself answering all three of these questions negatively. Before I had even a had a chance to voice my admiration for what they had done, Wendy told me that people often say, "You've done something wonderful," but that she herself found it difficult to feel that way. Philip, on the other hand, was more realistic, pointing out that all the other female members of their girls' family had got pregnant at fourteen. They also told me that a fairly recent case reported in the local paper of the murder of a teenage girl had been one of the girls' cousins. Philip says of the adoption, "It is a frustrating experience because they wear you down so much, but eventually you simply have to lower your expectations. Then, when they have reached rock bottom, anything better has to be seen as success!" So, getting both girls through their teens without them becoming either pregnant or drug addicts constitutes "success" for Philip.

While agreeing with the point he made, Wendy still clings a little bit to the feeling that she would have liked to see her daughters do as well as her sons have done. She would also like to be able to say that she loves them as much as she does her two boys, but no doubt most parents would agree that it would be extremely difficult in such circumstances for the bonding to be as strong as with natural children. (It is obviously so very different for a mother like myself, who got her adopted son at two weeks!) Wendy is, however, realistic too about what she describes as the "genetic make-up of a certain group of people in our society." How much is genes and how much is conditioning is of course a subject always open to debate, but here I should like to allude again to my own thesis: that an equally important part of the equation is previous life experiences. By this I mean in this context that a soul with a 'bad history' is more likely to be drawn into an adverse social context than one who is more evolved. Wendy says that she believes in reincarnation – she has often imagined herself as having been hung as a witch – but she has not explored the subject in depth and my suggestion that she, Jane and Sarah had come together because they had known each other before did not ring true for her.

Another of Philip and Wendy's criticisms of the social workers was that, when they took the girls out, it would be to a MacDonald's. "This," they commented, "was taking them back to the culture they had left." In contrast, their adoptive parents took them walking in the woods, to rivers, to the May Fayre and to Brownies and Girl Guides. They also paid for them to have horse riding and music lessons and had them sing in the church choir.

Jane, in spite of the emotional problems caused by her background, was adamant that she did not want to go to a special needs school, preferring to attend the local comprehensive one. Since she had rickets and other physical problems when she was very young, Wendy reckons that she might not even have survived if she had not come to them. The rickets has left Jane with bone problems but, since, as they said to me, "physical development depends upon emotional happiness," Philip and Wendy now see the fact that in adulthood she has grown to five feet two inches as quite an achievement. When Jane reached eighteen, they found a special college in Bristol that they felt would have been good for her, but she would not agree to go there. Having by this time become involved with two local boys who had tried to rape her, she had to move out of Philip and Wendy's house for safety, and she was moved to a home in their nearby city. There the care worker, who is thirty years her senior, fell for her to such an extent that she is now married to him. The situation is more than a little unusual since he has given up his job in order to care for Jane full time, but he apparently has supporting family around and Philip and Wendy are relieved that Jane seems to be happy.

Sarah has also left home and moved in with a family in the same nearby city as Jane first went to. It is a family of people who have never worked and live simply on benefits. Philip told me that, while she was still living with them, she had a job and stayed within the boundaries that he and Wendy set. However, after meeting this other family through a friend, she gave up work and gave them all her savings. Wendy says that Sarah "falls in love with every man she meets within five days," and she unfortunately got pregnant by a Muslim who wanted to be able to stay in England. When I met the couple, the baby was due the following month, and Wendy was afraid that the young man's family was putting pressure on Sarah to marry him. Sarah was, however, looking forward to the baby's arrival, and Wendy told me that she herself planned to do all she could to support the two of them.

Jane, on the other hand, says that she does not want to have children because of both her health and her genetics. She is too afraid of doing some of the things that her birth mother did and says, "I wouldn't be able to keep a child safe." So, even if she can never be for Wendy as 'perfect' a daughter as her sons are 'perfect', at least, thanks to her adoptive parents, she has been able to escape from her disadvantaged background, see it for what it was and that there are better ways of living. This should stand her in good stead for future incarnations. While Philip and Wendy perhaps do not themselves value what they have done as much as can objective outsiders, it is clear to me that firstly they have saved these two girls from what might be described as "a fate worse than death," secondly are continuing to be there for them in a way that their birth parents would be quite unable to be, and thirdly have forged links with them that will continue into the distant future and may well in a future lifetime bring to the relationship a joy that cannot be imagined in their present one.

CHAPTER TWELVE

INTER-RACIAL ADOPTION

Rhiannon and Aisha's Story

There was an old woman who lived in a shoe,
Who had so many children that she didn't know what to do....
English nursery rhyme

My old friend Rhiannon is the quintessence of an archetypal mother. Her former partner, Will, had strong views about not having more than two children for the sake of the planet, so when it came to the second pregnancy she cleverly managed to have twins! This, however, did not satisfy her, and in due course she persuaded Will that they should apply to adopt a fourth child. Social Services in Hull (where we were all living at the time) told the couple that, since they had three children already, they were not eligible for a tiny baby, and they were eventually offered the five-month old Sheila who was deemed "hard to place" because of the fact that she was racially mixed and also because many people in her family background were labelled as educationally sub-normal. Sheila was placed with them as "fostered with a view to adoption," but the whole family bonded with her instantly and so Rhiannon and Will asked to adopt her straight away. Rhiannon, whose own parents' relationship had not been a good example, did not believe in marriage, but agreed to it when it was stipulated as the only requirement for their adopting the baby.

Rhiannon and I had already met at a toddler group with our older children before Sheila came to them, and Will was employed at the same university as my husband. When we got Christopher, who is just six months younger than Rhiannon's adopted daughter, our friendship deepened, and before long we got together with two or three other racially mixed families to form a Hull branch of a national anti-racist organization called 'Harmony'. Thanks to regular daytime meetings and outings that we held with all the families together, the children made friends too, which was a great help to the black ones since we were living in an area that was almost entirely white. Sheila and Christopher were particularly close as young children; in fact when they were about seven they used to say that they would get married. They were both something of a handful, and when they got together in one of our houses, the resulting havoc always seemed to be more than doubled, but I used to feel that it was worth it for the sake of the companionship for Christopher.

Betty Jean Lifton, whose first book[1] I recommended so strongly in the Introduction, talks penetratingly about the problem of "invisibility" when a child is taken into a family as though he or she had been born to the parents, but such invisibility cannot of course exist in the case of inter-racial adoption. There are only two possible ways for a black child to become a member of a white family and, since no mother is likely to want to be thought to have had an extra-marital affair, there will in such cases be an added incentive to explain about the adoption as early as possible. Nowadays this is always strongly recommended by adoption agencies anyway. (In our case the explanation facilitated early sex education for all three of our children.)

Since we and our friends adopted, there has been a widespread change of policy in Britain, which is no doubt also the case in the United States and other Western countries. Because of the fact that racial prejudice – if not discrimination – is still horribly common, despite legislation and increased attempts at education, it is now generally believed that it is better for black children to be placed in black families. I can certainly see strong arguments for that, but this does nothing to change my belief that every child is in the family that was intended for them – a belief that Rhiannon shares. Betty Jean Lifton, in her second book[2], quotes a client of hers: "Now at twenty-five, Amanda thinks of herself as mixed race. 'We are our own race,' she tells her biracial friends. She doesn't think it matters whether a biracial child is adopted by a black or white family as long as there is love."

At the time that we adopted, huge emphasis was placed on the importance of giving such children a strong black identity in order to help them to feel positive about their color in a racist society; and the anti-racist organization to which we belonged gave us a great deal of help in fostering this positivity. We were able, for instance, to buy through 'Harmony' birthday cards and books featuring black children, which were not readily available in ordinary bookshops.

Rhiannon finds racial prejudice as incomprehensible as it is upsetting. While sharing her feelings, I view such prejudice as being caused by ignorance, and nowadays am glad of my knowledge of the fact that everyone learns over time, through very many lifetimes. In my book *Souls United*[3] I discussed various causes of homosexuality, citing as one of them having been homophobic in a previous life. Here an analogy can be drawn with racism, and in my third book, which is about discovering the Life Plan, I talked about the soul's need to redress imbalances, which might at times entail having to suffer something such as racial abuse that one had previously inflicted on others. All real learning comes through experience, and suffering oneself brings understanding of others' suffering.

Living in a multicultural area brings many advantages and, whereas we felt tied to the Hull area by David's job and the children's schools (in which they were happy), Rhiannon soon began to feel more and more strongly that it would benefit her family to move to an area with a much larger black population. Will eventually agreed that the larger northern city of Leeds was not too far for him to commute to Hull University, and another couple in our group, who were both schoolteachers and therefore more flexible work-wise, also decided to move there for the sake of their black adopted son. We were sad about the increased distance between us but determined to carry on with the group activities, and those of us who remained in the Hull area sometimes went over to see our friends in Leeds, for instance at Carnival time (always a major event in predominantly black areas).

Sheila had also become increasingly aware of being 'different' from her white schoolfellows in Hull and her siblings, and in due course she decided to change her name to the more African sounding one of Aïsha. A few years after the family's move to Leeds, Rhiannon and Will separated amicably, and Rhiannon kept the house, which is in a street inhabited almost entirely by black people. For many years now the great majority of her friends have been black, as have Aïsha's, and Aïsha, who is now (like our son) in her thirties, has never had a white boyfriend. Rhiannon reckons that she cannot underestimate the benefits of the move that they made. Lessons in African dance and drumming are just one example of the sort of things that her children have really loved and could not have had in Hull at the time.

As soon as Aïsha was old enough, Rhiannon returned to her profession of teaching to help support the family, and nowadays she works part time with very young children. After her separation from Will, she fell in love with a West African man called Drissa, who was a wonderful drummer and, when Aïsha was sixteen, they had a daughter, whom they named Binta after Drissa's mother. But Drissa, who suffered from kidney failure (and whose treatment had deemed him to be infertile!), sadly died in 1999. This made Rhiannon a single mother twice over, which was of course very hard, but on the other hand she takes to motherhood so naturally that it is difficult to imagine her ever being anything other than surrounded by children. The house (which is infinitely larger than the largest possible of shoes!) has an ever-open door to friends as well as family, and when Rhiannon is not at work there are invariably extra children present. Drissa already had other grown up children from a previous relationship and, when one of his older daughters gave birth to a daughter about a year after her father's death, she called her Rhiannon after her stepmother. Two years later, since this stepdaughter was struggling as a single mother in another city, she gave her little Rhiannon to Rhiannon senior! (She of course qualifies to be in all three of my categories – adoptive mother, stepmother and foster mother – but I am putting her into this section as an excellent example of inter-racial adoption.)

I have found in my life that, when good friends move away, keeping in touch is never as easy as one first imagines. Life moves on, people are busy and, in the case of children, they often grow up in different ways. Christopher and Aïsha did remain friends for a while after her family's move to Leeds, but (like most childhood romances!) the "engagement" did not last. He is more academic than she is and, when he won a basketball scholarship to do his degree in the US, he naturally made a new set of friends to take up his time. We did, one day after he had graduated, manage a reunion at Rhiannon's house of nearly all the families who had originally constituted the Hull anti-racist group, which was tremendous fun. Aïsha had, however, recently suffered the tragedy of losing by cot death a six-month old son, Bayo, and she was naturally in consequence still very depressed. When we talked about it, Rhiannon told me that she believed having a child of their own – a bloodline – to be particularly important for adopted people. (Her words rang particularly true for me after our own granddaughter, Delilah, was born and I witnessed how extraordinarily important she was to Christopher.)

After that enjoyable reunion a few more years passed before I saw Rhiannon again, and in any case she was always too busy to write and our own move to Shropshire further increased the geographical distance between us. Writing this book, however, prompted me to arrange to call one day when I happened to be passing through Leeds, and I greatly welcomed the opportunity of catching up again. It was the summer vacation and so none of the children were at school. As well as the now fourteen-year old Binta and the nine-year old Rhiannon, little Rhiannon's younger sister was visiting in order to give her mother (one of Drissa's older daughters) a break, and Rhiannon senior was also minding a friend's little one for a few hours. Our conversation in the garden was regularly punctuated by a small girl coming out to ask for help with her stitching, which made me feel that in some ways Rhiannon's life had changed less than my own had; but I appreciated her words of wisdom just as much as I always had when we had been in the habit of meeting more regularly.

Although she was still mourning the losses of Drissa and Bayo, Rhiannon was looking forward the following week to her annual visit to California, where Martin, her eldest, now lives with his two children. She was also able to give me the joyous news that Aïsha now had a thriving two-year old son, whose boundless energy kept one or other of them occupied more or less continuously. Aïsha's true love was, her mother explained, still Abdul, the father of the baby she lost, who would have married her if she had been a Muslim. But I was already aware that the majority of relationships failed to survive the loss of a child, and in this case the grief was too great for either of them to be able to give the other the support that they needed. Aïsha subsequently formed a relationship with a man whom she did not initially know to have already fathered a child with someone else.

When she gave birth to Akwasi just three months after her partner's other girlfriend had her child, he took little interest in his new son and, since Aïsha, who has always been good at getting herself a job, was now cooking for people with dementia, Rhiannon was as usual happy to step in with the child minding. At present Aïsha is in a new relationship with someone who is ten years older than herself, but they are not living together.

We talked of course about the past, when our two young ones had so often run completely wild together but, whereas our family had found Christopher difficult in innumerable ways, Rhiannon told me that of her five she had found her twin girl Tara the most difficult. "Aïsha was wild," she said, "but she didn't lie or steal as so many adopted children do and, since I have never valued academia, being more interested in the Arts myself, it never bothered me in the slightest that she was less bright in some ways than our older ones." In any case Aïsha is certainly not educationally subnormal as had been predicted, and what she might lack academically she gains in practicality.

Social Services, through whom Aïsha was placed, never told Rhiannon and Will a great deal about her birth family, but they did know that her background was very racially mixed, and they also know now that, of the five children that her birth mother had, Aïsha was the only one whom she had adopted. This was because she was in a steady relationship when each of the other four was born (one before and three after Aïsha), but obviously this piece of information served to increase Aïsha's feeling of having been rejected. Aïsha was born in Hull, and Rhiannon is quite sure that she once saw her mother in the street. She recognized her from the way she walked, which was identical to the little Aïsha's, and the social worker confirmed that it was indeed the area in which the family still lived.

I have already mentioned that 'acting out' is a healthier way of dealing with problems caused by adoption than suppression and, when she reached puberty, Aïsha went through a phase of writing 'hate letters' to her birth mother, asking her how on earth she could have been so heartless as to give her away. These letters never got posted, but I am sure that the writing of them was very therapeutic. Soon after that phase she expressed a desire to meet her mother but, by the time she had reached sixteen, when that would have been permitted, she no longer wanted to do so. There has consequently never been any contact between the two families.

When little Akwasi was born, Aïsha was naturally terrified of losing him. She would rush him to the hospital whenever he had so much as a sniffle or any other tiny thing wrong with him, until eventually they had to tell her firmly that the child was bursting with health and that she simply had to believe it and take charge of him. I feel sure that any woman who had endured a cot death would naturally suffer from over-anxiety with any subsequent child she had, but Rhiannon says too that of her five children Aïsha is the one to whom family unity is the most important. She is always keen to hold the family together and has been to America to visit Martin and his family several times, sometimes in the company of Will who, being single at present, depends on his children a lot for company. Although Aïsha was jealous when Binta was born and tends nowadays to be "too strict" with her, she is close to all four of her siblings and gets upset if any of them fail to come at her beck and call. (Although both her brothers have moved away, her older sister, Tara, is now working in Leeds.)

Although Rhiannon has always had an excellent relationship with all her children, she says that she and Aïsha argue more now than they used to when she was younger. Often when Rhiannon has been caring for little Akwasi while Aïsha has been at work, she criticizes her mother for something she has done or not done with the child rather than expressing her appreciation. This is surely a hundred per cent normal for any family! (Certainly my daughter, who is not adopted, criticizes me more than does either of my sons.)

Rhiannon, who does not disagree when I comment that she must have had very many previous lives in Africa, has taken

Binta to West Africa several times to visit one of her older half-sisters. She feels her strongest bonds to be with Binta ("because I loved her father so very much") and her youngest grandchild, Akwasi, who came as such a bonus after the cot death of little Bayo. It also made sense to her when I suggested that the reason for this might be the fact that it was with these two that she had the most numerous karmic links. No one who believes in such things has any way of *proving* their existence, but then many scientists will also argue the impossibility of proving the existence of God. When two different clairvoyants who were not even acquainted with one another told me independently about a previous lifetime in which my adopted son and I had been Greek priestesses together, I was convinced as well as astounded. A total skeptic might well manage to think up an alternative explanation for my being given this coincidental information, but this book is not aimed at *total* skeptics. As I have demonstrated in my previous books, discovering karmic links for oneself can be an extremely powerful and healing experience.

Until one has experienced it oneself in a regression, it is hard to understand how anyone can recognize someone of their acquaintance in a previous life, when they were in a totally different body. I had this difficulty myself even after I had started practicing DMP therapy, simply because it was a long time before it happened to me as well. When a client would say to me something such as "Oh, it's the same person as the one who's my husband again now!" I always got a similar reply to my question, "How do you know?" Eyes are said to be 'the window of the soul' and time and again I have heard someone say, "I could tell the moment that I looked into his eyes." Alternatively they might reply, "I don't know how I know. It's just a very strong feeling." And that is something that I can now endorse from my personal experience of past life regressions in workshop settings. Feelings should never be underestimated, and one frequently finds in a therapy session that identifying a person in a previous life explains a lot of their behavior in the present life.

Rhiannon has not to date had reason to explore her past with Aïsha, Akwasi, or any other member of her family, but she says nevertheless that she is convinced that "we come together for a reason and that there's a pattern." She also believes, however, that the move towards "more open adoption," where contact is kept between the child and the birth mother/parents, must be beneficial to all the parties concerned. This is something of which neither of us has personal experience, but no doubt other books will in due course be written by those who have. In the meantime I believe my own family's story to be coming some way towards that.

Notes

1. *Lost And Found – The Adoption Experience,* Betty Jean Lifton, Ph.D., The University of Michigan Press, USA, Third edition 2009.
2. *Journey of the Adopted Self – A Quest for Wholeness,* Betty Jean Lifton, Ph.D., Basic Books (Perseus Books), USA, 1994.
3. *Souls United – The Power of Divine Connection,* Ann Merivale, Llewellyn Worldwide, USA, 2009.

CHAPTER THIRTEEN

ADOPTING A HANDICAPPED CHILD

Desdemona's Story

Spirit of nature, healing and free,
spirit of love, expanding in me,
spirit of life, breathe deeply in me,
inspire me with living energy!
Lyanne Mitchell (from 'Sing Your Faith', a Unitarian hymn book)

Desdemona is very intuitive and has been on a spiritual path all her life. Even at two she appreciated that everything was interconnected. She is grateful to her parents for having left her and her sister to find their own way rather than forcing any sort of religion onto them. This was less common in the 1930s and 40s than it is nowadays. As an adult Desdemona explored various different denominations and eventually settled on Unitarianism as best suited to her personal need for freedom. She has always taken the concept of reincarnation for granted, and Unitarians have no dogma and they welcome varying beliefs among their congregations. Her family were never at all well off and she has always felt an affinity with people who are underprivileged.

At eighteen she married Bill, who was a few years older than she was and ran his own publishing business. Intelligent though she was, she left her own higher education until after having two sons (Michael and Jamie), because, with Bill being older, they preferred not to delay having a family. She then qualified as a Special Needs teacher and, since Bill's business did not bring in a great deal of money, Desdemona somehow managed to work at the same time as rearing their children. After a while she began to feel a desire to adopt a child in need and discussed the idea fully with Michael and Jamie as well as with Bill. They then applied for adoption from Ecuador, expressing a preference for a girl. The process took so long, however, that a third son (Adam) was born to them before little Carmen arrived, and Desdemona then took quite a long maternity leave from her teaching post.

Carmen, who had been abandoned at birth in a poor area of Quito, was reared in a children's home where there was very little stimulus. She had caught polio when she was two and, when she finally arrived in England a good four years later, she had one leg in a caliper. The moment that Desdemona saw the photo sent by the Ecuadorian adoption agency, she knew that she already knew Carmen from a previous life and that she was the daughter destined for their family. Also, the home was always keen to get rid of handicapped children, and so no alternative prospective adoptee was offered to them.

None of the boys showed any jealousy over Carmen becoming part of the family, and the oldest one even made a bed for the doll that Desdemona had already bought for her. As for little Adam, himself barely a toddler, he took her round the house upon her arrival, showing her where the most important things were. Carmen had considerable difficulty walking, but the physiotherapy that Desdemona was able to organize for her did bring some improvement. Also, the fact that Bill had a problem with one of his feet helped Carmen to feel less self-conscious about her leg.

Other problems, however, were inevitably numerous. The Quito home's lack of good care and stimulus made Carmen seem more like a toddler than a six-year-old. Because of her age she had to start going to school straight away, but was naturally far from ready for it. Desdemona would have liked her to go to nursery to start with, but this was not legally permissible for a six-year-old. So instead she persuaded the school that Carmen should be at home in the mornings. Desdemona was obviously eminently qualified to teach the child herself, but Carmen needed a great deal more than instruction in the 'Three Rs'. She had absolutely no sense of danger and needed to have her hand held firmly whenever they went out as she would otherwise have got run over. Nor did she have any idea what to do with toys. In the house she needed watching all the time because she could very easily have unintentionally caused Adam serious harm by, for instance, slamming a door on his hand. She needed very firm handling indeed, as well as a great deal of love and attention, and it was Bill who pointed out that Desdemona's somewhat laid-back attitude with the boys (saying such things as "Shall we put our boots on?" rather than "We need to...") was too casual in dealing with their daughter.

Carmen's serious deprivation resulted in her demanding to be the center of attention *all* the time, and the fact that she was very pretty besides being a gorgeous shade of brown made it very easy for her to get what she wanted from other people. When they were all out together, the boys would be ignored in favor of Carmen. Yet none of them ever complained! This surely indicates that this was a family that had been well planned in advance, and I am personally sure that, like their parents, Michael, Jamie and Adam must all have strong bonds with Carmen from previous lives. Where they were living at the time there was an association for families with adopted children from Latin America, so Desdemona seriously considered joining it. She was, however, completely put off by the first meeting she attended, where a film was shown of children being found in dustbins. This made her feel glad not to have taken Carmen with her.

Desdemona feels that being always the center of attention was understandably Carmen's survival mechanism, but after a few months of educating her at home she was so exhausted by it that she decided she had no choice but to send her to school full time. Carmen's English was by now good enough for her to cope with school, where she did quite well, and she also made friends there without too much difficulty. In fact she stayed at school right up to eighteen and achieved some A Levels, which enabled her to obtain quite a good job in sales. Her leg remained something of a handicap for walking, but Desdemona made sure that she always had plenty of exercise to make it stronger, and in her teens she learnt horse riding, which she greatly enjoyed.

Through her work Carmen met a fellow Ecuadorean, whose family had come to live in England when he was a teenager, and they married and had two children, who are both doing well at school. Sadly, however, Carmen has recently turned against her mother for some reason and is refusing communication. This is particularly hard for Desdemona, who has been a widow for a few years and whose three sons, though close to her emotionally, do not live nearby, but she attributes Carmen's hostility to stem from anger against her birth mother for having abandoned her. This is quite normal in adopted children, and I suffered myself when our son was young from the feelings that were transferred to me rather than to any other member of our family. The difference is that Carmen is doing it considerably later, but hopefully she will in due course come to see things in a better perspective and appreciate all that Desdemona did for her.

Desdemona herself, who is clearly an evolved soul and consequently able to see everything from a long term point of view, is not taking any blame for what has happened in their relationship and remains confident that it will come right again eventually, whether or not this is in their present lifetime. She is a keen gardener and says that she loves to watch things grow naturally with minimal help from herself. She sees this as a good analogy for the whole of life and that nothing should be forced upon anyone who is not ready for it. In the meantime, having reached retirement age, she is happily replacing her teaching by numerous other worthwhile activities and still has a good circle of supportive friends among her fellow Unitarians. At least Carmen is still in touch with her brothers, so they are able to keep their mother in the picture with regard to her and her family. So I hope and pray that she will of her own volition get in touch before too long with the adoptive mother to whom she owes a great deal.

CHAPTER FOURTEEN

THE OTHER WAY ROUND!

Su's Story

> *There is immeasurable strength and great power within us. So…if you develop that power through hard work, you…can accomplish great things. In every being there is complete Divine Power.*
> Sathya Sai Baba

Su and her husband, who are Sri Lankan but have lived in Britain for a long time, have been devotees of Sathya Sai Baba since the 1980s. Having been brought up Buddhist naturally means that Su has always taken reincarnation for granted and – like other people I know who have Baba as their 'guru' – she has for long had the habit of asking Him for answers to the important questions that come into her mind. In her case (again similarly to others of my acquaintance) these answers often come in dreams. So, when they were coming close to retirement and decided to get a house built for that back in Sri Lanka, it seemed perfectly natural to Su to ask Baba to lead her to the 'right' builder for their project. On this occasion she did indeed have a dream in response to the request, and in the dream she very clearly saw coming closer towards her a tall, dark, slim man, whom she did not recognize. Needing to act quickly in order to meet a deadline they had for getting the work started, Su forgot about the dream for a while and, on the recommendation of a friend, she made arrangements with two brothers who worked with a team of between ten and twelve. The older brother, whom we are calling Tony, was a well-qualified builder, while Peter, the younger one, did such things as the electrics and plumbing. When they were a few weeks into the work, Su suddenly remembered about the dream and recognized Tony as the man she had seen so clearly in her dream.

The work progressed both while Su and her husband were able to be in Sri Lanka and when they returned to England, where their only son is well settled in a career, Su found herself not only becoming increasingly fond of Tony and Peter, but also wanting to help them materially by doing such things as buying them tools for the work in addition to paying their fees. This puzzled her and so she again asked Sai Baba the reason for it. She then promptly had a dream which was clearly a past life one. In this dream she knew herself to be childless and she saw two young brothers whom she knew she was about to adopt. The older of the two was rather boisterous, while the younger one, who was much quieter, was clutching a rag doll. On this occasion she instantly recognized these two children as Tony and Peter and so felt that it totally explained her desire to help them.

Su then appreciated that, since they had been orphans in a previous life and she had cared for them, these young men had now returned to her to build the house that she and her husband were needing. This, I think, makes a delightful story, but sadly it also has a less happy twist to it. At one point when they were in Sri Lanka while the house was being built, they had a man come to do some tiling. As soon as they met he told Su that he had had an instant vision of her in a previous life. He said that it took place at the court of the great monarch Ashoka, where he 'saw' her descending a staircase. She obviously had an important position in the household because, quite apart from her dress, which looked like that of a princess, once she had finished the descent, she reprimanded a builder who had just completed a wall. She told him in no uncertain terms that he had not done the job properly and must pull the wall down and start again. The builder had angrily refused to do so and had then cleared off. The tiler was quite sure that this builder was the same man as Tony, and it was for that reason that he felt he should tell Su about his vision.

Fortunately the present-life house was in due course finished to Su and her husband's satisfaction, but, when the final bill arrived, she saw that there was a mistake in the addition and that they had been overcharged. When she asked Tony and Peter to come and see them about it, they failed to do so, which made her feel sure that the 'mistake' had been deliberate. She talked to her accountant about it, and also told the police, but in the end she paid it nevertheless. Her reason for doing this was that, as a very spiritual person and a good Buddhist, she believed it to mean that she had a karmic debt to these builders and it was therefore best to pay out the money and then let it go. She explained to me that her reason for informing the police was simply to avoid the risk of others being similarly overcharged.

When we met, Su told me that she had always had a fear of being regressed to a previous life, but that she really wanted to know whether or not her tiler's vision was accurate. We discussed the matter a bit and I found that what she had been told really rang true for her. For instance, she told me that she had always been fascinated by royalty – particularly by women of that caliber – and that she always looked twice at regal pictures, particularly when they were Eastern ones. But she also said that her fascination with royalty was by no means confined to the East, and that she had been glued to the television throughout the Jubilee celebrations in 2012.

I would of course never dream of pushing anyone into having a regression – such a desire should always come from a person herself – but, since she did not have any real problem that needed dealing with yet very much wanted to know whether or not she had really lived at Ashoka's court, I suggested to her a simple means of verifying it. Su is far from being alone in her apprehension about being regressed, which is a pity because the subconscious is always in charge and will only bring up what the client is ready to deal with. But in any case, as I said, having let go of what she believed to be a karmic debt to her former adopted sons, she did not have a big issue that needed resolution. I therefore, with her agreement, led her into a simple visualization, which worked very well. People often have difficulty in trusting what they see (as I did myself when I started my therapy training), and so I always say to them – just as Roger Woolger used to say to his students, "It must have come from *somewhere*." I have learnt from long personal experience that if something seems to make sense and *feels* right, it is likely to *be* right.

Well, what Su saw in the visualization into which I led her was a young woman who was certainly dressed like a princess because she was wearing gold-colored shoes with curved, upturned toes and a white dress with a gold border. She also described in detail to me the gold drop earrings that she was wearing. The shape of the shoes surprised her, which to my mind is a very strong indication that the picture had not come either from her imagination or a painting that she had seen somewhere, and also she clearly saw herself putting her hand on a three-headed lion at the bottom of the staircase, which accorded with what the man who had done their tiling had told her about his vision. She further told me that she knew that Ashoka's father had had ten wives, and so she felt it very likely that she had been a half-sister to Ashoka himself.

Over our many lifetimes we often get into repeated patterns. This is one of the many things that can be cleared in Deep Memory Process therapy, but in order to do so one needs first to become aware of them. Tony's final words to Su after their house had been completed were, "I'm not going to build your parapet walls," so she sees this as a repetition of what had happened at Ashoka's court when, in a different body, the builder had got angry and refused to rebuild a badly completed wall. So they got another builder for the parapet walls, which are the norm in Sri Lanka, and Su knows that she and Tony have done all they can together for the time being. Who knows what might happen in a future life? Hopefully Tony will soon learn the lessons he needs to learn with respect to honesty and fair dealings; and I am confident that a future relationship between them will be a rather happier one.

PART THREE – BIRTH MOTHERS

> *...the birth mother is forced to live a double life from the moment she surrenders her baby. Advised to go on as if nothing has happened, she keeps secret what is probably the most important and traumatic even of her life.*
>
> Betty Jean Lifton, *Journey of the Adopted Self – A Quest for Wholeness*

Like everything else in this world, birth mothers who give up their children come in all shapes and sizes. The stories I have here (including that of our own son's birth mother, in my own family section) give, I hope, a fairly good representation, since each one is so different from the others, but the subject is much too large to be covered comprehensively in a book such as this one. I should therefore again like to refer anyone with a particular interest in this aspect of the subject to Betty Jean Lifton's *Lost and Found*. Although her counselling practice focuses on adoptees, her book also inevitably refers to several birth mothers with differing histories and attitudes towards their offspring. Her book from which I have quoted above was published in 1994, and hopefully there has since been much improvement in the way that birth mothers are generally treated, but for many people the scars are still there.

One of the most obvious points about this topic is the sea change that has occurred during a single generation. Fortunately we have now come a long way from the attitude towards 'fallen girls' that was prevailing in Ireland in the 1960s, and which was so poignantly depicted in Peter Mullan's 2002 film *The Magdalen Sisters*. (Why is it always the poor girls and their offspring who get stigmatized, while the birth fathers escape unscathed? I suppose the answers are obvious!) Many would no doubt argue that we have gone too far the other way, but that is the nature of the pendulum; now – as with very liberal attitudes towards sexuality – we need to aim for balance. Personally I am convinced that it is almost always better for a child to have two parents and have an overwhelming admiration for mothers who give up their child for adoption for that reason. Whatever one's attitude, however, there is no denying the lasting pain that is caused by such experiences for all those involved, and (as with abortion) anyone who is persuaded that they will be able to "get over it quickly" is sadly deceived.

Those who have either read Martin Sixsmith's book *The Lost Child of Philomena Lee* or seen the recent award winning film *Philomena,* starring Judi Dench and Steve Coogan, is likely to empathize doubly with women who have given up a child, either forcibly or of their own volition. Philomena Lee's case may seem to be a very extreme one, but it is alas only the tip of a very large Irish iceberg which has been kept under water for far too long. The film's appearance is serving the excellent purpose of drawing public attention to the scandal, which, according to a Guardian report, will dwarf even the numbers involved in the Magdalene laundries. This report quotes Susan Lohan, co-founder of the Adoption Rights Alliance, who was herself forcibly taken away from her mother in Ireland in 1965. She says that the issue "also implicates so-called pillars of Irish society such as politicians, public servants, solicitors, nurses, doctors, midwives and social workers. The so-called nice middle-class people who knew about, who arranged, who funded and who were directly involved in forced adoptions." The fact that Martin Sixsmith's search for Philomena's son (Anthony Lee, was alas already deceased before he was traced) took a whole four years is largely due to the deliberate withholding of information by the Irish nuns concerned, and they have not been prosecuted. One must admire Steve Coogan not only for his acting of Sixsmith and co-writing the film, but also because he is now saying, "I will absolutely do anything to help them [i.e. both the bereaved mothers and their lost offspring]. The church reaction has been same old, same old. I am happy to wade in." It is my personal belief that Philomena Lee is a brave soul who, when she was making her Life Plan, willingly took on her suffering because of the ultimate good that would come from bringing this long-standing practice into the public eye. Let us hope that the current campaign will soon be a hundred per cent successful.

Someone else for whom I have unbounded admiration is Margaret Humphreys, a Nottingham social worker, who brought to light the scandal of the thousands of children who were deported to Australia and other Commonwealth countries in order to save on child care costs. When the film 'Oranges and Sunshine' was televised, I was delighted to see that Jim Loach was following in his father's footsteps. It is based on Humphreys' book *Empty Cradles* and gives moving, though heart-breaking, accounts of a number of these children (now adults), many of whom were badly abused by so-called 'Christian' Brothers, and it also documents the enormous amount of research that Margaret Humphreys did after investigating the first case that landed in her lap. Her own children were quite young at the time, but she has a tremendously supportive husband, who encouraged her research even though it involved numerous trips to Australia. She established the Child Migrants Trust, which is still doing invaluable work. Quite apart from the suffering of the children concerned, can you imagine the agonies experienced by so very many of their birth mothers? As often as not their reasons for having to give up their child were financial and, as though that was not bad enough in the first place, many of them who did eventually succeed in getting themselves into a position of being able to reclaim their child were then told that he or she had disappeared without trace. One of the most important aspects of Margaret Humphreys' work has been bringing about reunions between birth mothers and their deported children.

But even less extreme cases, many of which have happier endings than the aforementioned Irish ones, still inevitably entail a great deal of heartache. When a mother gives up a child of her own volition, it must be unusual if her reasons are anything other than what she sincerely believes to be the child's welfare. This, as we have seen, does not alleviate the child's feelings of rejection, but this book is an attempt at putting all sides of the story.

CHAPTER FIFTEEN

VIOLET'S STORY

For all prayer is answered. Don't tell God how to answer it.
Edgar Cayce Reading 4028-1

In my comparatively long life I have known a large number of therapists and I have found them, almost without exception, to be people who have chosen to enter the profession after working through problems of their own and having in consequence a desire to help others. Violet is far from being an exception to this rule. Now well into her fifties, she is an accomplished therapist with numerous strings to her bow and in a happy, stable marriage to a supportive man, but her life as a teenager was very different indeed and her difficult upbringing led to a story which has, alas, not ended happily. However, such stories are far from being unusual and no one can be blamed for the outcome. We come to Earth repeatedly in order to learn, in some lifetimes we learn more than in others, and some people still have further to go in the learning process. Realizing this can sometimes allay the pain a little bit, but pain is also an important tool for our learning.

Violet has never known her father or anything about him, her mother was middle class yet (in Violet's own words) "liked being pissed all day long and was devoted to alcohol, opera and alcohol," and her stepfather, who was an alcoholic, was a danger to her. Neither of her parents could be trusted in any way, and – almost inevitably – her two younger half-sisters grew up with problems as well. Both of them now drink heavily and both have illegitimate children, as does one of Violet's nieces.

It is therefore hardly surprising that by her mid-teens Violet was addicted to cigarettes, alcohol and drugs and in a relationship with a heroin addict. Her boyfriend, John, was the first born of a woman who rejected him but went on to have six other children. He was so small at birth that his grandfather brought him home in a shoebox, and he grew up to be a seriously damaged man, who died of alcohol abuse in a binge drinking session in 2006. Violet says that she realizes now that he was mentally ill and probably bordering on personality disorder, but that at the time she "worshipped him because of his total unsuitability, mystery and drug addictive nature." However, when she got pregnant, before she was sixteen, everything changed.

There was never for Violet any question of not keeping her baby, and she promptly conquered her own addictions. Social services tried in vain to persuade her to have the baby adopted, and she says that she felt very happy through most of the pregnancy. Her son, whom she named James, was born in the morning of June 10th, 1970, after a trouble free pregnancy and rapid birth. He weighed 8lbs 10ozs and was, in Violet's words, "a healthy boy with a long, slim body and a perfect head with light brown hair and such beautiful eyes. The nails on his fingers and toes were like little pearls." She continues the story thus: "I didn't get to hold him at first – I don't know why. I asked for him and I heard him cry, but I didn't remember anything until I woke up in the ward and looked at the bottom of the bed. I saw what I thought was a wasp moving over the cot but it must have been a hand. It was my baby. He was beautiful and I had no idea what to do next. I was sixteen and a half."

However, though James was born healthy, Violet herself suffered severe physical symptoms following the birth. When she found out that her chart said that she had a temperature of 106 or more, she thought she must be dying and just lay back in surrender. But then, after a while, she realized that she must have made a mistake and that she might live after all. She says, "What a day! Neither outcome seemed to matter much as I was still dopey and everything was surreal. The rest of my stay in hospital is a blur. Breastfeeding hurt a lot and I didn't really know what to do with my baby, but the nurses helped me."

After the birth, Violet's relationship, which had already been becoming problematic for her, deteriorated still further because "John was a heroin addict who could not provide for us at all and I didn't want him to be anywhere near to my precious baby." Initially the two of them went back to live with Violet's mother and stepfather, but soon the social worker arranged for her to live and work in a farmhouse nearby in order to help her to stay clean and safe and give stability to the child. She escaped from John and he was not allowed to know where they were. At the farm Violet had two other children to care for and housework to do in return for her little attic room and food. She was paid, as far as she remembers, £2 per week.

Violet says that "James was perfect and I adored him. But looking back now, as a fifty-six-year old woman, I am aware that I was unable to see further than an hour ahead at a time." Then she adds, "Very little mattered to me. I had the mentality of a sixteen-year-old and no idea what being a mother was." This is fully to be expected for someone who was not only very young but had also never been given any proper example of motherhood. However, despite the confusion, which had already been caused by her difficult upbringing, she felt an overwhelming love for her baby. In fact she says that she was more or less completely unaware of anything apart from this. "All my focus went on this wonderful little life that fascinated me, and my sisters loved my son too."

Violet's days at the farm were "long and perfect and full of joy." She says that she found it bliss to be in a stable home for almost the first time in her life. When she was very young she had regularly had pleasant stays with an aunt and uncle, but after she was about thirteen and her behavior had become rather wild, she thinks that she must have done something to embarrass the aunt, whom she describes as a social climber. Violet cannot now remember the details, but she remembers the huge rejection and her great sadness at losing her aunt's love. Unfortunately they never made it up before her aunt's death at a very young age, but Violet has worked through this rejection many times on different levels. The final layer of distress and loss concerning her aunt came up in 2009, when she addressed it in a Dynamic Theatre workshop[1]. That enabled her to make peace with her aunt, and she and her husband have since been to stay with one of her cousins, which she found to be a healing experience.

A little while after the birth James unfortunately developed a problem. He started vomiting, projectile fashion, and the health visitor refused to take Violet seriously when she asked for help. This, she later learned to her fury, was because of her drug history, despite the fact that she was now clean and healthy. But fortunately, when the farmer's wife insisted that there was something wrong, she was listened to and James was then rushed to hospital, where he was treated for a hiatus hernia.

James was very upset and distressed at being in hospital, and each day when Violet visited she found him "purple and shaking with outrage and terror." She says that she had no idea of the implications of this at the time, but vividly remembers not understanding much, being very distressed herself as well, and just wanting her baby back. When he came home they were all happy again and Violet could see no end to the life that they had. She even had a number of suitors, which she now feels to have been "strange, to say the least, for a sixteen-year-old single parent with no prospects."

When James was three months old, the farmer and his wife went away on holiday and she stayed behind with the children and the grandparents. She says that something – she doesn't know what – happened during this time. "Maybe I just grew up, or maybe it was something these older people said or did, but anyway I came to realize that I would perhaps never be much of a mother in terms of money and success and that maybe the best thing I could do for my son would be to give him to a wealthy family for adoption. I had very little self-esteem at the time due to my own shaky upbringing."

So, when James was four months old, he was taken away at Violet's request. She says, "I knew that I would never be good enough for him and I wanted him to have everything that I felt unable to give him myself. It seemed to me to be the only course of action even though I knew it would kill me to lose him." In fact it almost did kill her because she felt quite sure that she would not want to live without him and had already planned her suicide. The social worker's assurance that she would soon get over it did nothing at all to help with the loss!

Fortunately the person who dropped Violet off on the day that James was taken away for adoption had a premonition that something was wrong and returned later to find her nearly dead in a pool of blood. She says that she really did not want to be saved. In fact she so much wanted to die that she went back onto heroin. But she was again saved – this time by a kind, much older man, who took her away to another part of the country. A year later they were married, but she broke his heart not very long afterwards when she fell in love with somebody else and went to live with him instead. That relationship did not last either, but Violet has always been good at supporting herself. After working initially as a secretary, she trained in business and then ran a series of businesses of her own before eventually starting on the healing path in 1993.

Violet says, "For the nigh thirty years that followed James's adoption I can truly say that the thought of him never left me. I couldn't touch or look at my sisters' four babies until they were five or six because it caused me too much pain." Eventually, after doing a lot of therapy training, she became able to look the agony in the face. She began addressing it with a Family Constellations session[3], when somebody played her son and the two of them held each other for "what seemed like a lifetime." Just three months later she received a phone call from James' partner, Jill, saying that he was looking for her! (This is a typical result of Family Constellation work. Violet, however, says that, "though there are brilliant people doing constellations," she does not recommend them in general, since there is often "far too much control and manipulation." Although she has had good experiences with a few groups, she finds Dynamic Theatre[1] to be "much cleaner, clearer and freer and therefore more truthful.")

Violet says that only when she heard that James was looking for her did she become fully aware of the extent of her misery "because of the sheer, immeasurable joy and happiness that the news brought me." "What bliss," she says, "to know not only that he was alive but that he wanted to find me!" They met just a week later, but the happiness, alas, was not to last. Violet had read Verrier's *The Primal Wound* and also other guidelines, all of which advise taking it slowly, but James refused to do anything by the book and so she somewhat reluctantly agreed to the early meeting. Violet's partner at the time was himself adopted and so she explains that she had to be careful of his sensitivity; but despite the care that she took, he came to dislike James intensely very soon after they met.

When they first made contact, in 1999, James was twenty-nine and was living about a four-hour drive away from Violet, with his partner and their two children. He came with a friend, who was a happy, cheerful man, but James himself was anything but that, clearly uncomfortable in his body and unable to sit still. (Sitting still is something with which my own adopted son has always had great difficulty.) Violet found herself "somewhere in between bliss and disbelief" when they met. She says that James stayed for a few hours and then left, and that the next meeting was at his home, when she stayed nearby in the home of one of his friends.

Violet soon discovered that, despite having had the privileged upbringing for which she had hoped – with an older sister –

James had no qualifications, career or stability and was clearly deeply unhappy. It turned out that it had been his adoptive family who had suggested that James trace Violet, to try and explain his dreadful and, to them, inexplicable behavior. He had run completely wild, was a heavy drinker and would regularly disappear on drinking binges with no regard for anybody but himself. Violet has a strong feeling that he was only tolerated because of the fact that his adoptive parents, Ruby and Rod, were powerful in the locality. He had become a parent simply because the girl he had sex with conceived two weeks after their first meeting and he then found himself caught.

At the time they first met, James was trying to get some qualifications at evening classes and to be a good father and partner. He was also trying to conform. Soon after their first meeting he asked if the reason he had been adopted was because she had found his vomiting to be a nuisance and had not wanted a sickly baby. The question came as a huge shock to Violet, who had never dreamed that he would imagine anything like that, but James had read the social work report and it had implied that she had been a drug addict after his birth.

Despite the separation from John after James's birth, he was still living in the same area as Violet, and over the years she had seen him around every now and again. So, after knowing James for about three months, she let his father know about him and arranged for them to meet. They had breakfast together at her house. John had given up drugs but was alcoholic and, in Violet's words, "only needed a sip of booze to be tipped into garble mode." She says that he was at the time "a shaking wreck," but that "he cleaned up to meet James." James liked him and they subsequently met up for drinking and gambling sessions. Violet says that her relationship with James deteriorated very soon after that, as he preferred to go drinking with his father rather than have a sober weekend with her. So she came to regret having introduced them and "that was the start of the argument about messing people around." She says she can see now that it was partially her fault, but that at the time she felt let down when James wanted to be with his father rather than with her.

Despite the efforts that he was supposedly making to sort himself out, around four months after their reunion James's behavior and unreliability reached a level that was beyond Violet's tolerance and she told him that she would not put up with being treated the way he treated everybody else. He was very angry and refused to speak to her again. She also had to endure a lot of flak from her family because of what was going on.

Two whole years passed before Violet suddenly received another call from James. He said that he had sorted himself out. "No more binges. Happy families and – whilst still working at the family business – he had got a hobby and was now a part-time magician." And Violet added that he sounded excited and very much alive and said that he was proud of himself. So they began their acquaintance again, and this time it was a little more on an adult level. Jill wanted to marry him, but it was clear that he never would. The children were happy nevertheless, and there seemed to be a sort of peace. Violet says that she enjoyed getting to know him and them, but that the sense of insecurity and instability was still as much present as ever.

After that, however, there was another long silence. Violet does not remember the reason for it, but she did not have the confidence to contact him first and, although she sent cards and wrote regularly, she never got any reply. When he finally contacted her again, in about 2007, she found that he had finally had the courage to leave his unhappy relationship with Jill and was living with a friend, apparently much more happily. She was then invited to stay with him and had the opportunity to see him working both as a children's entertainer and as a magician for adults at a campsite. She thinks that he wanted her to tell him how okay he was, which she did not yet feel ready to do, but in any case they had a good time together and it felt good because he was so much happier.

A few months later James met a young woman called Jan and fell in love for the first time in his life. The relationship, however, was obsessive on his part and jealous and possessive on Jan's, and Violet says that she does not know which was the more wounded of the two of them. Ultimately James told Violet that, because of Jan's neediness, he felt forced to move to live with her in another location and separate from his children. In fact, Violet learned from Jan later, he had arrived penniless and withdrawing from drugs, with people wanting to break his legs for debt. He was consequently not entirely welcome, but although not happy, Jan was hooked into the relationship. This was a pity because Violet really liked Jan and Jan liked her as well; it was from her that Violet learned that James had a cocaine addiction and a gambling problem as well as being heavily in debt. She says, "It wasn't exactly a surprise, but it was a disappointment."

Another disappointment for Violet was James' lack of willingness to look at his pain or to have anything other than a superficial conversation with her. She says that "Occasionally he would dip into something real, but only for a short while and then the mask would re-surface." She continues, "He had a complete breakdown after the first time his children came to stay and I think he saw the damage he'd done by moving away from them. He'd been stealing and borrowing money from everybody and was welcome nowhere by now. I am sorry to say that he could not be trusted." However, Violet was nevertheless willing to have him come and stay with her, "as everywhere else was devastation for him." She says that "He told many different stories to me, to his girlfriend Jan, to his ex-partner, Jill, to his adoptive parents, to make sure that we didn't compare notes." And – perhaps the worst shock of all for Violet – his partner Jan said that he accused his birth mother of sexual abuse. He was also reported to use untrue facts about his adoption in order to try to gain sympathy. For instance, he told people that he had been born addicted to heroin because of his mother's own early drug abuse.

Unlike Violet, who still wanted him to come to her home – "hopefully to recover" – James's adoptive parents, who subsequently split up acrimoniously, disowned him after finding themselves unable to have a relationship with him anymore. Prior to that, when he was on withdrawal from cocaine and went to stay at his parents', Ruby asked him to leave when she had to go shopping because she could not trust him alone in the house. He was devastated yet never able to see her viewpoint. His sister also gave up speaking to him.

Although Violet says that James had been given the sort of home she had hoped for, it seems to me that it left a lot to be desired despite being comfortable materially. Adoption agencies have for very many years now always stressed the importance of telling the child that they were adopted at a very early age, yet James told Violet that he only found out that he was adopted during a row about his behavior when he was twenty-one. He said that he had always felt different but never previously guessed why, and that all his peers just assumed that he knew that he was adopted. He also told Violet that he was unhappy at being sent to boarding school at the age of seven and that, when he was only fourteen, he had discovered a video recording of his parents' involvement in a 'swinging session' (i.e. a party at which people swap sexual partners).

However – damaging though seeing this video may have been for James – it is not for me to be judgmental about other people's sexual habits, and it seems that his parents did everything they could to try to understand James and even encouraged the meeting with Violet to see if the answers were there. He finally fell apart completely when he fell in love for the first time, having never felt love before that, but many adoptive parents have difficulty in getting their love accepted. Their subconscious feeling of rejection at birth makes it difficult for adoptees to trust in any love that they are subsequently given, which of course makes difficulties for partners as well as for parents.

Though she did on one occasion let Violet make use of a room in her house while she was away, James's adoptive mother, Ruby, was nevertheless not cordial to her when they met, which was always in the company of other people. At their first meeting she made a scathing reference to "girls like you," seemingly oblivious to the pain such a remark would cause. On the other hand, Rod, her husband, was pleasant and friendly to Violet, but he later went off with a younger woman and moved away.

The pattern that made Ruby, and James's ex-partner Jill, seek out his birth parents in the search for answers is, as we have already seen, not untypical for adoptees. James told Violet that he was periodically "overcome by a feeling that comes down on him from nowhere" and that he would then find himself in the pub or the bookies, or doing on line gambling or coke, and that, when he came around a few days later, "Everything has gone."

The saddest thing of all for Violet is that she has now lost touch with James completely. She says, "I was expecting him one afternoon after his breakdown in 2008, when he disappeared for about a week, but he didn't arrive, nor did he call. I have not heard from him since and, because the family believes that I am an abuser, I cannot contact them." She would dearly love to see her grandchildren again, but fears that she cannot do so "without stirring up pain for them." She says now, "I have no idea what I will do if and when he contacts me again. I think I will simply offer him love, but it depends upon the state he is in."

In her second book *Coming Home to Self – The Adopted Child Grows Up*, Nancy Newton Verrier says that "adoptees' responses to that early trauma ... get reenacted over and over in various relationships in the present," and that her book's objectives are "to help adoptees find the authentic Self, a self which has been distorted by living without genetic markers and mirroring (being reflected back) as they grew up in non-biologic families," and "to help them go beyond the victimhood of their beginning of life and come into their own power and sense of responsibility." It would be nice if all those ever involved in an adoption process were to read this book of Verrier's! Violet says that "James is a deeply wounded person but also one who has hurt so many people and never taken responsibility. He has used his betrayal as an excuse to live wildly and with ruthlessness rather than face the pain. I can understand this, but it has not been effective for him. He is very intelligent but misdirected." She also says regretfully that "The way he was last time I saw him, I doubt that I could trust him in my home."

This is particularly hard for Violet, who has done so much work on herself, learned a great deal about behavioral problems, discovered the efficacy of therapy and is now able to use that to help a lot of other people. Yet she is powerless to help her own son. She concludes, "It has not been a happy story for anybody. James's adoptive family, his school friends and the friends in the district he grew up in have all disowned him and, last time I heard, he was being chased by debt collectors and loan sharks relating to the addictions." But she adds, "I have never felt bad about having had James adopted because I felt so awful about myself at the time that I knew he'd have a better chance elsewhere. Of course it is clear now that things didn't turn out for the best but, at the time, it was a good decision."

Violet's own total shift of path was a dramatic one, which began with a serious car crash in 1990. Then, following a three-year illness, she read and studied for about five years before becoming a healer. I said, very truthfully, in the first paragraph that she was an "accomplished therapist," but she actually describes herself as having started out as "the world's most reluctant therapist." She has always had a great love of animals and the first step on her new path was working as a healer with traumatized horses. Initially this was all that she really wanted to do and she became well known locally as an animal healer. When, however, she went out to farms doing demonstrations, these pulled big crowds, and people soon began begging her to do for them what she did for the horses! So she explains that, despite initial resentment about working with people, "in the end I could not refuse and now I really love my work." It was a case of "gradually surrendering to the process somewhere along the line," and, from working about fifty-fifty, she ended up acquiring more and more qualifications and treating people about ninety per cent of the time. She comments "I finally surrendered about ten years ago and now, if I try and get off this path, I can't!"

Since her accident and subsequent healing, Violet has had many counselling sessions and been over and over the question of James' adoption and their later reunion. But she says, "What I have never addressed is how truly wounded and damaged he is, or our last few meetings when I knew he was a junkie (like Mum and Dad!), and all about the dishonesty etc. Nor have I addressed how I would deal with it should he return." She also says that "There is a feeling of a bad penny with him and he is very bad news in every way."

Some people firmly believe that the 'bad penny syndrome' is inherited, and they might well make a comment such as "What would you expect of someone coming from that sort of background?" However, my husband has recently been making a study of genes and would assure me (were I to need such assurance!) that, though there may be genes which give an individual a tendency towards addiction, such addiction, in any case influenced by environmental factors, can in certain circumstances be overruled by conscious control or personal will power. This means that the alcoholic or addictive condition cannot be directly inherited; it is only adverse circumstances that will cause someone with a predisposition to addiction to succumb to it.

Many people have addictive tendencies; I myself could never be alcoholic, but I do find chocolate addictive and it is easier for me not to eat it at all than to eat just a little bit. Violet, however, has not touched a cigarette for very many years, and the drug addiction of her youth was short lived. And, whereas many former alcoholics describe themselves as "recovering alcoholics" rather than "recovered…" Violet told me that it was only in 2010 that she decided to give up drinking all together. For a long time prior to that she did not have a problem with alcohol, but says, "I couldn't understand why I needed to drink at times, so quitting meant I didn't have to think about it again."

Violet is also fascinated by the whole question of genes. She says that, even when James was just a few weeks old, he already had mannerisms similar to his father's, and that as an adult he looks and sounds just like him even though they only ever met a few times. They had each been brought up and still lived in different parts of England, where the local accents are very unalike, yet Violet found it hard to tell them apart on the telephone!

Violet is fortunate in some ways since her learning about Life has given her an understanding of reincarnation and karma, which helps her to appreciate that his present lifetime is not James's only chance and that they may well come together again in more favorable circumstances. She has not as yet found any past life links between the two of them, but she has worked on James's birth in a session with a distinguished Deep Memory Process therapist. Although she remembered nothing about it consciously, she says that in the regression she found herself asking her mother to get a gun and shoot her because the pain of giving birth was so unbearable. She comments, "What a thing to remember! This was what James heard in the birth canal – that he'd hurt his mother enough to make her want to die." Her own therapy training and practice has taught her enough to appreciate the devastating, and possibly lifelong effect that such a sentiment could have on a newborn child. (Babies in the womb may not yet have much language, but they *do* pick up feelings from their mothers and identify with them. [See *The Secret Life of the Unborn Child*[3].])

Another point that interests Violet is what she describes as "The four month syndrome." She says, "James was adopted when he was four months old, we fell out after knowing each other again for four months, and the next time we made friends it lasted about that long too." "Co-incidence?" she wonders. "I don't know." Personally I cannot help feeling that the separation from his mother at four months might be so ingrained into his subconscious that it caused him to re-enact it later on.

Sad though it is, I cannot see Violet's story as a hopeless one. The love that she says she still feels for James in spite of everything must win out in the end and it is doubtless already doing him more good than she realizes. She says that she misses James and that she and her husband have recently been talking about how they could possibly find out where he is. "It is his birthday in June and that is always a time when he thinks of me, but when you have told as many lies as he has, it is hard to come back." She also says, "This may never be possible, but I would like to have a true relationship with him." I myself am sure that this will happen at some point in the future, even if not in their present lifetime.

And who knows what might happen in due course with her grandchildren? A good friend of mine was very sad indeed when he lost touch with his grandson after the boy's mother, who was alienated from my friend's son, moved away without leaving an address. Recently, however, the boy himself, now a teenager, has traced his father via Facebook and they are all enjoying meeting each other. I am in many ways no great lover of the internet, but Google and Facebook have a great deal to be said for them!

Notes

1. See Mark Wentworth's web site: www.colourforlife.com
2. See *Peace Begins with the Soul – Family Constellations in the Service of Reconciliation,* Bert Hellinger and Colleen Beaumont, 2003.
3. *The Secret Life of the Unborn Child,* Verney and Kelly, Warner Books, London, 1999.

CHAPTER SIXTEEN

ASANTE'S STORY (TOLD BY HERSELF)

Your children are not your children.
They are the sons and daughters of Life's longing for itself.
They come through you but not from you,
And though they are with you yet they belong not to you.
You may give them your love but not your thoughts...
Kahlil Gibran

I had been coerced into going to this horrible school that was all about rules and right and wrong, and I was miserable. Most things were wrong; few were right. The Adventist religion that was preached in that sect's many private schools had made me rebel internally even before I was sent to one of them, and I was walking a fine line away from being a juvenile delinquent. Now eighteen and in Grade Twelve, I really had no idea what I wanted to do. I did, however, know for certain what I didn't want to do: to go to school at CUC. A lot had been placed on my head. Most recently I had been called the reason that my father had never joined the Church.

I was angry, hurt, on valium, smoking out the window of my dormitory room and drinking peppermint liqueur – just rebelling in fact. So, depressed and on the edge of being suicidal, I sought comfort. I found it in a one-night encounter with a young man from Lacombe – a Philistine like me, and my school mates jokingly called us non-Adventists.

It took some planning; I had to arrange to go away overnight and get the permissions and make up the story. I don't remember what the story was, but I went to a hotel in downtown Lacombe. Then I got together with – I'll call him Denny – for just one encounter, and I knew when I returned to my hotel room that night that I was pregnant. I knew it for sure and wrote it into my diary. I was soon proved right.

I'll skip all the family stress that arose from this and only say that my parents supported me. They were quite wonderful in an unshakeable kind of way, even though they obviously weren't happy about it. But that was my parents; they were kind and generous people. I was the youngest child in a family of four, and the sister next to me had just given birth to a little boy. Hers was also out of wedlock, but only because her fiancé, who was a deacon in the SDA church, dumped her when she got pregnant.

So we two sisters moved together to Vancouver, BC, in August. She found a job; I went to school to learn how to be a keypunch operator. My pregnancy was unremarkable on the physical level. I was young, healthy and slim, and everything went very smoothly.

Spiritually and emotionally it was also very smooth. In fact it was nothing short of remarkable. I grew up and I learned about love. For as the pregnancy went on and this entity I carried inside of me became a living reality, I loved her. I didn't know it was a female at the time, but I loved her. I talked to her and enjoyed her. The existence of someone who mattered more to me than my selfish self did me a great deal of good.

While attending a class for unmarried expectant mothers, I watched many of them go through great angst and heartbreak over whether or not to keep their child. Their tears, pain, self-blame and many other stresses were part of our weekly meetings. I consider myself very fortunate to have been aware that I was not mature enough to be a single parent. Of course I was also living with my sister who was a single parent, so I had first-hand experience of what it was like. Besides, I felt very strongly that I wanted my child to have both a father and a mother. This was my first choice for the child. I also, however, decided that if my child wasn't adopted immediately, I would not put it into foster care. I felt strongly that it was better to have one consistent parent than possibly more than one set of mothers and fathers, and so I decided that, rather than putting the baby into foster care and not knowing if it ever had a home of its own, I would take it with me and do the best I could.

Both the decision to have the baby adopted, and the decision that if it wasn't adopted immediately I would take it home, were simple. I was clear both emotionally and mentally. The main angst that I had was the decision as to whether or not to see the baby before it was adopted. I was afraid that if I saw it, I would be haunted by that little face. On the other hand, I was afraid that if I didn't see it, I would be haunted by not knowing what this child who had come through me looked like.

Almost equal to that was the concern over the choice of what name to give the child. The name would of course almost certainly be changed by the adoptive parents, but none the less it was important to me. I'd been playing with names for children long before this experience and I loved unusual names. I felt I didn't want to give away one of my favorite names to a child who wouldn't even get to keep the name, but still I wanted the name I chose to be meaningful. Eventually I decided that if it was a girl that I would call her the name of the first best friend I had had and the most recent best friend I had made. I don't even remember what ideas I had if it was a boy.

It wasn't just living with my single parent sister that brought me clarity. I just knew that if I tried to raise this child that I would resent it for robbing me of my youth and my freedom. That was one level of my experience of knowing. It also went beyond that into a deep knowing that this child didn't belong to me. I came across Kahlil Gibran, and his words in the poem *On Children* spoke to me of what I already knew about this child that I carried inside of me. It was a deep, deep knowing. The kind that brings the peace that surpasses understanding. And so I was at peace, knowing that I was clear within myself over the choices I had made regarding this beautiful being that I carried inside of me.

The duration of my pregnancy was one of the best times in my life.

The social worker I was assigned played a very large role in this peaceful time. She was very kind and thorough, and the system as it was set up at that time was really quite humane. I filled out forms that gave me the opportunity to express what kind of a home I would prefer for my daughter. For instance, I got to specify that I would like her to go to a home where music had an important role, as she came from a musical family genetically and music is always helpful in our lives. I wanted her to have the opportunity to develop any musical talent she might have inherited. There were many other specifics on which I had input – religion or no religion, for instance. I stated that I'd like her to be in a home that wasn't necessarily religious but that honored God and had a spiritual nature. I had just begun to try and puzzle my way through the difference between being spiritual and being religious, and I wanted her to have some kind of an environment that would give her awareness and choices. It was incredibly helpful to me to feel that I could play some part in determining what kind of home she would be in. Of course I knew there were no guarantees that my desires would be met, but at least I got to express them.

I was also able to write her a letter explaining to her why I did not keep her. I was told that it would be up to the parents whether or not they gave her the letter, and that this was usually given around the age of eighteen, but again, at least I knew she would have the possibility of having something that might help her through any feelings of rejection or abandonment or not being loved.

Once I was out of the turmoil caused by being in the repressive Adventist school environment, and therefore out of the depression and anger and off the valium, I was able to love the being who was coming into the world, and it was thanks to that that I discovered the philosopher and spiritual guide within myself. I wrote my daughter an honest, straightforward letter, telling her how much I had loved carrying her and that it was my love for her that had allowed me to be honest with myself about the fact that I wasn't mature enough to raise her alone and that I wanted better for her than what I would be capable of giving her myself. I also told her that I felt there was a higher purpose in what was happening, and quoted Kahlil Gibran and told her that I felt she belonged with the people who were raising her. It was wonderful to write that letter, even though I found out many years later that she had never received it.

My parents moved to Vancouver just a few months after my sister and I did. This was a blessing – especially for my sister, who found out that her five-month-old beautiful baby boy had cerebral palsy. She needed help and they gave it most willingly. Also, my paternal grandmother, along with four of my father's seven living siblings, all lived in the Lower Mainland of BC, and so we were surrounded by a large family of aunts and uncles and cousins, headed by a quiet, unassuming matriarch. Everyone was kind to us. As I write this now, at the age of fifty-nine, I'm filled with gratitude at what a huge blessing it was to have this experience in such a positive atmosphere and at how much grace there has been in my life.

When the moment of the birth arrived, my waters broke in the morning. I called the doctor, who told me to go to the hospital, and my parents picked me up and took me there. Labor didn't begin straight away, however; it was induced. This was 1969, and in my world then there was no awareness of natural childbirth. So the first few hours of being in the hospital had some false starts and stops, but eventually real labor began. The doctor came by to see me and announced that I had several hours to go and he was going home to bed. Within an hour or so of his leaving I started to have pushing pains, and the little girl was born five hours after the labor had truly begun. I had an epidural towards the end, and so the nurse and doctors in the delivery room told me when to push because I was feeling very little physically. This was a huge blessing – especially since the effect of the epidural began to wear off before the innumerable stitches I had to have had been completed! She came before I was fully dilated, and so the tear was substantial. When I asked the doctor how many stitches I was having, he replied that I was better off not knowing, and he never told me. Like all babies, however, she knew when the time for the birth was right.

Because of this tear I was kept in the hospital for ten days. This was really perfect because it gave me time to heal, and, more importantly, it was much easier being in the same building with her before she was adopted than it would have been being at home awaiting word.

One day when my father came to visit me, he disappeared for a long time. I still hadn't been able to make the decision about whether or not to see her. I really didn't know what to do about that, but when Dad returned to my room, I asked him where he had been. He said that he had been to see her and this suddenly brought me the clarity I needed: if he had been to see her, it meant that I could see her too. I don't remember precisely what he said when he came back to my room. My father was a man of few words. Whatever he said, however, and the fact that he had cared enough to go, gave me the courage I needed to see her myself.

And so arrangements were made and the baby was brought to my room. She was all legs. She had her father's strawberry blond hair, and she felt healthy and calm while I held her. Though I shed some tears, I was mostly centered in the knowing within myself. We were only together for about twenty minutes, but it was enough. Enough to know she was well, and that I had indeed been on the right track with the decisions I'd made. The social worker broke the rules without me even asking, and took photographs of her. So I am blessed to have a few photos of the child whose life I was granted the privilege of birthing. Almost immediately after she was with me, I got word that she had been adopted. This was a huge relief since it was the penultimate day of my hospital stay and so I could go home knowing that she had a home. The social worker told me what she could about the family. Quite frankly I can't remember what the parents did, but I do remember that they were an ordinary working class family who lived away from Vancouver, and that they had one son who was a couple of years older than her. I was at peace.

Even though the father had played no role in this beyond the first night, I felt it important to tell him that he had a daughter, and so I phoned and gave him the news. I also told him that she'd been adopted and that I didn't want anything from him; it was simply that I thought he might want to know that he had a daughter. And so closed the main chapter in my experience of bearing a child.

The second chapter occurred when the daughter I had named Pamela would have been about twenty years old. I was receiving a massage from a talented woman, and she picked up on the fact that there had been a baby in my past. This massage was given to me in my home, and after the therapist had left and I was still lying on the massage table, I suddenly felt a feeling in my abdomen like a baby kicking. It's such a unique feeling that even all those years later I recognized it immediately. Then I was overcome with the joyful thought, "A baby! Oh a Baby! How beautiful!" This was a very odd thought, because the experience of bringing Pamela into the world had also brought me the clarity that I did not want to have children. To this day I have never wavered in this. So I noted the experience as odd and interesting and went on about my life. A few days later I was cleaning out an old trunk full of stuff, when I came across a brass bookmark that I swear to this day I had never seen before. On it was engraved the word "PAM." Well obviously I took it out and kept it with me for a while as I began to wonder what was going on to cause me to have these experiences. Then I had another experience like the first feeling of how beautiful that a baby was coming. A bit later I had a dream. Most of the truly significant dreams of my life have been snapshots – single frame dreams like a photograph. This one was of me holding a baby. The photo also contained my partner and a child that he had fathered, who had been taken away from him when he was only three. The boy's mother had left my partner and gone to court for sole custody, which she won. In spite of being in a career that could have moved him around, he stayed in the same place for eighteen years to make sure that if that child wanted to reach him, he'd be able to.

I am also fortunate in having a second set of parents in my life. We adopted each other through pure love. They are Don and Jean Daughtry, and they have devoted their lives to doing readings exactly like Edgar Cayce did. It was all the events that I was experiencing regarding a baby that took me to them for a reading to find out what was going on. They told me that my daughter had never been told that she was adopted, but that she was sensing it and was mentally reaching out to see what information she could gather. She had reached me through that God-given telepathic telephone that we all have ingrained in us. And through my experiences, and reconnecting with the blissful feeling of having Pamela, I had answered her call and calmed her mind. How that was for her specifically I have no idea, but it was good to know that she had found solace. As for my partner's part in the photograph, we were told that his son would contact him on his eighteenth birthday, and he did so – on the very day of his birthday!

I was also told that I would eventually meet my daughter when I was in my fifties. I'm now fifty-nine and this hasn't yet occurred, but I'm at peace with that. I also, however, feel okay about meeting her, and I confess that now, as I get older, I have more moments when I feel that I'd like to meet her than I ever did when I was younger. Since I want it to be completely her decision,

I have registered with the adoption services that if she searches for me, she can find me, but I have not activated a search for her.

In the reading with my 'Edgar Cayce-type parents' I told them about a repeated vision that I had had of Pamela many times over the years. I saw her in the attic of her family home. Her parents had died – either together or close together in time – and she was going through the home and cleaning it out. I saw her there in the attic going through old papers and coming across her adoption papers and the letter from me. Her parents never told her she was adopted, but they couldn't bring themselves to get rid of the letters either. In this vision she is on her knees as she reads these papers she has just found. Don and Jean thought that there was a high probability of this being a true vision of the future. So, will she find them, I wonder? Will she locate me? It is in the hands of the great Intelligence of Love that assisted in bringing her and me together in this miraculous way.

PART FOUR – THE PEARSON FAMILY

CHAPTER SEVENTEEN

ANN'S PERSPECTIVE

He is my boy now. My boy.
In the morning we eat porridge together,
he drinks from the yellow cup I bought him.
Jackie Kay – The Adoption Papers

When Christopher was seventeen he wrote this poem:

Adoption

A newborn is greeted by parental light and warmth.
I was born to twin suns.
At times I was blinded, other times I felt cold.
Like insects, children are guided towards their sun.
I was disorientated by the misconception that I was circling an artificial light.
Petrified, expecting the light to darken,
Callously switched off, or exhausted of fuel.
I flew further from the light,
My subconscious testing its integrity.
But the fuel seemed infinite;
The light intensified to lead me home.
I considered it a challenge.
Angered, I flew out further,
Waiting for the love to die, and the light to fade,
Not thinking nor caring of the darkness that would ensue.
At times the light did flicker, but the warmth always remained.

I closed my eyes;
I felt for my sun, and found my way again.

A lot had happened before then, and a lot more has happened since. Some of it was difficult and painful; most of it was good; all of it had a purpose that I now appreciate was for our learning. I was 34, David 35, when we married, and we had already agreed on the names Paul and Alice for the children we wanted to have straight away. Since I had been the eldest of six, and my mother had also had two miscarriages, I had always been convinced that I would have no problem getting pregnant and this proved to be the case. Paul was born just over a month before my 35th birthday, Alice twenty and a half months later. Since David was completely satisfied with our 'pigeon pair', I tried very hard to be as well – even giving away every item of baby stuff immediately Alice had outgrown it – but it did not work: I felt deep down that something (or rather some*one*!) was still missing in my life.

At the time I was a good Catholic, and so the notions of reincarnation and pre-birth Life Plans were as far as they could possibly be from my mind. I attributed my dissatisfaction with 'only' two children to having come from a large family myself. But I had hated being pregnant, and the desire to adopt a child that I had felt in my younger days was revived when some friends of ours who had two young sons adopted a black baby girl. Race relations had for long been a concern of mine, in the Hull area I was missing cosmopolitan Geneva that I had left behind during the sixth month of my first pregnancy, and I felt that completing our family with a black child would in some way combine the work that I had also left behind in Geneva with my new vocation of motherhood. In any case I knew firstly that there would be no chance of a couple like us being offered a white baby for adoption, and secondly that it would be easier for me to persuade David to adopt than to bring another child into our overpopulated world.

When I first mooted the idea to David, he replied, "Give me a month to think about it." What a long month that was for me! However, once my husband makes a decision he never wavers from it and, during the long waiting period, when I frequently became disheartened with the whole process, he always did much to boost my trust and confidence. Once Barnardo's had accepted us for their waiting list, we told Paul and Alice about it straight away, and their excitement and subsequent impatience was not always easy to deal with while I was finding my own patience being severely taxed. The delay was caused not only by the shortage of babies to adopt, but also by David's being invited to work in Geneva for the whole of the summer of 1978 and then in Paris for five months immediately after that. Also, when the first available baby did eventually turn up, Barnardo's rightly gave priority to a couple who had only one son and also a fertility problem.

Until they had moved away and distance made keeping in touch difficult, we were friendly with the above couple, whose adopted son I know gave them even more worries as he was growing up than Christopher did us. Our acquaintance was made possible by the regular meetings that Barnardo's held for their adoptive and prospective adoptive parents. At those meetings we heard many stories from people who had nightmarish experiences with children who had been adopted considerably later in life, and these both filled me with admiration for the adoptive parents and confirmed my own feelings of not being cut out for such a task.

Finally, sometime in September 1979 (probably around the time of Alice's third birthday – I can't quite remember), Barnardo's phoned us with some possible good news. They had been interviewing a young woman I will call Geraldine, whose baby was due towards the end of October. The father was her Sierra Leonean ex-partner, Mansa, whom she still loved deeply, but they had split up because of various problems (caused partly by his having been sent to boarding school in England when he was only five years old). They were both graduates of a nearby university, to which she was planning to return to do a teaching diploma, while he was seeking employment in London prior to returning to Sierra Leone; and when she found out that she was pregnant, she made the well-considered decision to give the baby life. The decision to have the child adopted was partly due to her feeling strongly that she wanted her child to have two parents. She also liked the idea of his having a brother and a sister, since she herself had one of each, and that was her main reason for choosing us rather than the two other prospective adopters that Barnardo's had proposed to her. Other factors in her choice were that her degree subjects had been French and Drama (mine were French and Spanish) and that, like me, she had been brought up Catholic.

At first it seemed too good to be true (very few babies are 'placed' before birth!), and, remembering how I had felt physically during the last month of my pregnancy with Alice, when caring for little Paul had been so very taxing, I felt overwhelmed with gratitude at someone else doing the hardest part for me. This gratitude was, however, mixed with apprehension because, having twice given birth myself, I could not imagine being able to part with a baby after one had set eyes on it. Excited though I was at the prospect of my dream being realized, my thoughts were constantly with Geraldine and the agonies that I knew she must be going through. At one point during the waiting period, the Barnardo's social worker asked us whether, should Geraldine desire it, we would be willing to meet her before the birth. We replied in the affirmative, but in the event were frankly relieved when she declined the offer of a meeting. The thought of confronting her pain so directly seemed almost unbearable to me!

The days of waiting dragged on, and another thing that we

had to think about was a name should the baby be a girl. Alice would have been Christopher (*was* going to be Christopher according to my mother-in-law, who had always claimed that "Pearsons only ever have boys"!) and Barnardo's had put us down for a boy, and so the sudden possibility of a girl put an entirely new perspective on the whole thing. We discussed girls' names at length and were torn between Eleanor and Rosalind ("beautiful rose") but, when the joyful news of a healthy baby boy finally arrived a few days into November, obviously no new decision about a name was necessary. That is, apart from choosing a Sierra Leonean name from a list that Geraldine had kindly obtained from her ex-partner. She herself named her son Thomas, and so we kept that as his first name, adding Kandeh as his third name, despite the fact that our two older children each had only two given names.

In retrospect I think I was wrong not to agree with David's suggestion that we stick with the name Thomas rather than using the name we had previously agreed upon had Alice been a boy. My brother John already had a son named Thomas and I pointed out to my husband that there was an unspoken rule in our family about not duplicating names. This was indeed true, but family rules can always be broken; one of my nephews, Robert Charles, refused to continue the Merivale tradition of using the name Charles for the firstborn son and named his oldest one Cyrus. I have never had any objection to the name Thomas, but preferred Christopher and was reluctant to drop it for the second son for whom I had been yearning. The 'family rule' was really an excuse on my part and I now think that it would have been more respectful to Geraldine not to have overridden her choice of name. I see my subordinating his name of Thomas as an indication of how much I had to learn (and probably still have to learn!) about the 'adoption triad'. In fact Christopher himself has never wanted to own his first name, always signing himself C. K. Pearson; I used to see this as an expression of part of his initial subconscious anger against Geraldine but, when he read this through, he commented, "I think it's more just wanting simplicity."

On the other hand, I do believe that names are of immense significance. For many years now all his friends and acquaintances have called our son "Chris," but there are so many Chrisses (of both sexes!), and, although he himself says that "it's just too pretentious to insist on three syllables," I feel that it is a pity to abbreviate such a nice name. St. Christopher may well have now been proven never to have existed, but that to me is irrelevant: the legend is that he carried the infant Jesus Christ over a river, and the name means 'bearer of Christ'. So what name could be more apt for someone with an important task in the world? And another *very* interesting point about the significance of names is that we learnt when we went to Sierra Leone (over ten years after making the choice) that Kandeh meant 'chief'. What name could be more appropriate for a born leader?

Mothers and babies in those days were kept a bit longer in maternity hospitals than they tend to be now. This meant that, immediately following the birth, Geraldine had several days of being close to Thomas, but also Barnardo's were keen for her to have an even longer opportunity to change her mind about giving him up. So at four days old Thomas was placed for ten days in a foster home not far away from us. We were given permission to visit him there just once during those long ten days, and the love that I felt for "my new baby" from the first second I set eyes on him differed in no way in intensity from the love I had felt from the very beginning for his older brother and sister. What is more, not being exhausted from giving birth myself, I felt even better able to appreciate the wonder and excitement of an addition to our family. I felt *immensely* privileged and again indescribably grateful to Geraldine. Paul and Alice were obviously excited too about the arrival of their baby brother, and the foster parents told us that Mansa, the baby's father, had come for a visit and had clearly been deeply moved by the sight of his beautiful son.

I shall never forget the day when we brought our new baby home. It was Thursday 15 November 1979 and he was exactly two weeks old. It poured torrential rain all day long and, what is more, we still had builders in the house busy completing a now much needed fourth bedroom. I found the first months hard, but they were certainly no more difficult than they must be for any mother coping with three young children. Paul had his fifth birthday exactly two months after Christopher was born, which of course meant that he had to start school. His reluctance to leave his baby brother was touching in the extreme, and when, many years later, the famous clairvoyant Edwin Courtenay told me that they had been blood brothers before, I found it very easy to believe. Alice's karmic relationship with Christopher, however, is very different from Paul's and it is not my business to elaborate on that, but her attitude at the time is well summed up by the reply she made on the eve of our going to the adoption court on 22 April 1980. When I told the two of them, "Tomorrow we're going to see the judge and we're hoping that he'll say we can keep Christopher," she said very firmly, "Yes, but we ALL *won't* cry if he doesn't"! At the time we attributed her different feelings to the fact that she was three and had therefore had longer as the baby of the family; it was only learning about reincarnation and karma much later on that gave me a totally different perspective on the matter.

The five-month wait for the adoption to be made legal was not nearly as tense as the wait for the birth. In theory Geraldine could have changed her mind at any point up until then, but I felt sure that, had she been going to, it would have been at a very early stage. She gave her son up entirely out of love, with what she firmly believed to be his best interests at heart, and I knew that she knew the extent to which he had already become integrated into our family. I was full of admiration for her bravery, thought about her and prayed for her frequently, and was very grateful for the photographs of both her and Mansa that she had supplied and which came together with all the other information about the two of them that Barnardo's gave us. All that, combined with photographs that we took ourselves, provided a very good basis for an album telling Christopher's story. As he was growing up he would often proudly show this to visitors.

Over the next years I thought about Geraldine particularly each time that November 1st came around. I knew that the birthday must still always be a hard time for her – in fact I could not imagine that it would ever get easier – and I often yearned to know what had become of her, hoping that she had by now married and had more children. So, when Christopher was about twelve and we suddenly had a phone call from Barnardo's asking whether we would be willing to exchange letters with Geraldine once a year around the time of his birthday, I was naturally delighted. The social worker concerned explained that she was now having psychotherapy and that her therapist had recommended that she try to trace us and she said that, rather than Geraldine being given our address or us hers, they would act as 'letterbox'. The first letter made it clear that she was still single, but that she was doing well in a teaching career in the area of the country in which she had been brought up. We always wrote back of course, and we always gave Geraldine's letter to Christopher to read as well. It was only many years later that he told us that he had in fact never read them, giving as his very understandable reason that he disliked feeling different from his brother and sister.

When Christopher reached the age of eighteen, Barnardo's told us that they were now handing over to us and that it was up to the three of us to decide whether or not we wished to maintain contact. Geraldine not only replied in the affirmative, as did David and I, but also requested a meeting. This filled me with a mixture of delight and apprehension; Christopher was indifferent and said that he did not wish to be involved, and a lunch date between the three of us was arranged on neutral territory at a time when Geraldine was visiting a university friend of hers who was still living up north. As soon as we met my apprehension vanished: Geraldine, who has her son's wonderful eyes as well as his delightful sense of humor, proved very easy to talk to and we both thoroughly enjoyed her company. It was of course not easy in a restaurant in Harrogate to talk profoundly about emotions or anything comparable, but it was very good for us now to have a proper picture of the woman with whom we intended to continue to correspond indefinitely. Birthday exchanges continued to be the pattern but, once we had all acquired computers and got on to email, our exchanges became easier and more frequent (despite the fact that Geraldine, in complete contrast to her son, has never really taken greatly to email in preference to the handwritten word!).

A few more years on Geraldine gave us the good news of her marriage, and soon after that she expressed a desire to meet us again and introduce us to Kevin. By this time we had recently moved to Ludlow and so I suggested that they come for a weekend. What a weekend it was! Firstly, we really hit it off with Kevin, who was a truly delightful man and clearly a great support to Geraldine, and secondly, being in the relaxed environment of our own home, we were much better able to enter into profound sharing than we had been at the previous, fairly brief, meeting. It was spring and we were able to enjoy a good walk in some of our beautiful countryside, and Geraldine opened herself up to us in a manner that I would never have imagined possible. I had been laboring under the illusion that at the time of Christopher's birth and all the aftermath she had had real support from her family and others, and so it grieved me immensely to learn that this had not been the case at all. Her mother had never been sympathetic to her plight and, what is more, her father had died in the August before her son's birth on

November 1st. Nor had she had any real support from social workers or colleagues, who all seemed to expect her to "just get on with it and get back to normal as though nothing had happened." She had wrestled on her own for several years before going into therapy, but fortunately the therapy that she eventually had proved to be genuinely useful and had also triggered her own interest in training and working as a therapist with children – something that she is now clearly very good at.

The couple came again for a weekend some time later and on this occasion they brought their two 'babies' with them – a pair of delightful and energetic terriers. Life is always full and we have not yet managed another meeting, but I hope that will happen soon. Sadly, following a seven-year battle with cancer, Kevin died in September 2013 at the age of seventy. This is obviously immensely hard for Geraldine, though a recent telephone conversation showed her to be bearing up very courageously, and fortunately she now appears to have better support than she did at the time of her son's birth. Until recently Christopher always said firmly that he did not wish to meet her but, following an email she sent him in March 2014, he invited her to Cremona, where he is at present living, during the week in April that we were to be there. Unfortunately it was too short notice for her to make the necessary arrangements, but the invitation still stands and she is hoping to get over there in the company of her sister at some point in the not too distant future. This eventual meeting between Geraldine and her son is sure to be a very emotional one – at least for her (Christopher at present sees it differently, feeling that he has now worked through his adoption issues) – so it will be good for her to have support from someone very close to her.

Betty Jean Lifton says that "There was a time, not long ago, when many professionals believed that only maladjusted adoptees had a need to search for their origins," and this was indeed what the Barnardo's social worker told us early on (supposedly reassuringly!). She continues, "The implication was that good (and loyal) adoptees did not search. Now therapists are beginning to understand that there are primal stirrings behind the adoptee's need to reconnect in some way with the birth family."[1] I myself changed my mind on the subject, firstly after learning more about the implications of being adopted, and secondly getting to know Geraldine and coming to appreciate how much knowing her son personally would mean to her.

When he was very small Christopher did often speak about his birth parents, but it was always pure fantasy. Conversations would sometimes run something like this: "I've been to Mars!"

"Have you really?"

"Yes, I went with my first mummy and daddy. And we went to some other planets as well."

"That must have been interesting."

At other times we would be compared with them unfavorably. They had been "more generous," "more lenient" and so on. We of course found that amusing rather than painful; the more difficult times were to come later on.

When Geraldine came to visit us in Ludlow we learned from her that Mansa had not in fact returned to Sierra Leone but had remained in London, where he had had both another relationship and another son. She had kept in touch with him for a while and at one point had had his address, but they had lost touch at some point after Mansa split up with his second son's mother, and she believed the address she had to be completely out of date. No doubt if Christopher ever wanted to, he would be able to trace him – Geraldine and I feel that it would be nice if he and his half-brother were to meet – but at the moment there is no prospect of that. (He has, however, had a little bit of email contact with his only blood cousin, Geraldine's nephew, who is considerably younger than Christopher and regards him as something of a role model.)

Christopher has never not known that he was adopted. Betty

Jean Lifton wrote much about the adverse effects of "the secrecy surrounding the closed adoption system," but that never applied to us because Barnardo's were able to give us a lot of information about our son's background, all of which we passed on to him when the timing felt right. Apart from anything else, his color would have made his being adopted impossible to hide, and in any case we were always in agreement with all the social workers about the importance of adopted children learning something about their circumstances as early as possible. Of course when the background is a somewhat unsavory one (such as the child we heard about at a Barnardo's meeting who had witnessed her father kill her mother), it must be much more difficult to give one's child a full picture, but we were lucky in that way, just as we were in many others.

During the first few years the adoption issue was to a large extent in our household supplanted by that of race. Now, however, that I have learned so much more, I see that as a mistake on our part: the two issues should probably be given equal importance. I had myself encountered racism painfully many years previously, particularly while working in London, where I had had a number of black friends; my own father was distinctly racist and it may be a good thing that he did not live to meet his black grandson. But nothing can hit one more severely than when it is one's own child who is made to suffer. Nursery school was not too bad, though I did have to go in and request that they provide brown paint when the children were asked to do self-portraits, but the first primary school that Christopher went to was dreadful in that way. Apart from one Indian boy in his year, Christopher was the only non-white child in the whole school, and we gradually realized that he was being made a victim of verbal racial abuse on a daily basis. It is perhaps fortunate that he has always been exceptionally tall and strong; that may well have saved him from suffering physical abuse as well. Alice was at the same school, but at break times they had to be in separate playgrounds. She was always an absolute brick when her brother fled to her for consolation after having been called "Nigger," "Chocolate drop," or something equally offensive, but then he would be reprimanded by a teacher or dinner lady for being in "the wrong playground."

By this time, thanks to the anti-racist organization in which we were so active, we were very well versed in matters such as anti-racist education, and so, armed with various bits of literature, I made more than one appointment with the school Head in order to complain about what Christopher was enduring and make a few suggestions. But I got absolutely nowhere with her! "They get it from their parents," would be her reply. "There's nothing the school can do." Would she have given the same reply if the children had been stealing from or killing each other? Fortunately, however, when Christopher was seven, a friend and I were organizing a weekend conference in Hull on anti-racist education, and we sent out invitations to all the schools in the vicinity. One of the people who came was the Head of a little Catholic school in the center of the city, and by the end of the following week our son had been transferred to her school! Not only were there a few other black children in that school, but also, this Head assured me, she had a very firm rule against name calling. All the children knew that they would be punished for verbal abuse of any sort, and Christopher was urged to report anything adverse that happened to him to a teacher. His bad experiences at the previous school made him diffident about this at first, but eventually his confidence was built up and so we happily saw the end of problems in that domain. Once he moved on to the secondary school already attended by both Paul and Alice, there were undoubtedly further unpleasant incidents of racism, but by that time he insisted that he could handle it himself, and said that he would prefer it if I did not go into the school to make complaints.

Before it was time for him to go to secondary school, however, we had a family holiday in West Africa. Even before Christopher came to us, we had told the Barnardo's social worker that we would one day all go to Sierra Leone, and the idea that it would be useful for his black identity grew ever stronger during these early years. The whole thesis of 'Harmony', the anti-racist organization in which we were active, was that pride in one's color was a vital weapon in our society, and fortunately we got to know a mature student from Sierra Leone who was studying for a Master's degree in Education at Hull University. He and his family lived in Freetown, where he and his wife both worked, but he had built a house for his retirement in his own village, Waterloo, just twenty miles from Freetown, and he kindly offered to lend it to us when we came. Also, my old friend Peter Sarpong, now Archbishop Emeritus of Kumasi, wrote that he would never forgive me if we did not include a visit to Ghana in the trip.

Thinking that at the age of ten Christopher would be old enough to remember the trip for the rest of his life and still young enough for it to be formative for him, we decided on the Christmas vacation of 1990. We flew first to Accra, where the bishop's (as he then was) driver met us and drove us to Kumasi for nine days, and then we flew on to Freetown, where Jonathan and his wife Mary looked after us wonderfully. Apart from the Catholic priest, whom we met when we went to mass, we were the only white people in Waterloo and therefore evoked much interest and curiosity. It was our first visit to any developing nation, and the whole month was most memorable. In both countries we were taken on numerous excursions, and in Waterloo Christopher played football with some of the village boys. Curiously, with the one exception of a schoolboy in Peter Sarpong's own village, who, pointing at Christopher, said to the bishop, "That one must have been here longer than the rest of them," nobody noticed that he was not white! I shall never forget Christopher saying ruefully, "In England I'm black, here I'm white. I don't fit in anywhere." Many years later, though, he told us that, though he had got certain good things out of it, for him the visit to Africa had had the adverse effect of emphasizing the difference between him and his brother and sister. I can now understand that perfectly, but at the time we sincerely believed the trip to be for his good.

It isn't always easy to keep abreast with new ideas, especially when one's own main preoccupations and activities have changed. When we first got involved in anti-racism thirty plus years ago, Harmony, the organization of which we were members, was campaigning for schools to adopt overtly 'Anti-racist policies' and I know that at that time a number (probably mainly in London) had already done so. Recently I asked a local teacher friend, whose Kenyan wife is also a teacher, whether he knew much about the current situation in this respect. He had not himself heard of any school with a declared anti-racist policy, but replied that all schools were now expected to have clear policies against bullying. Certainly one of these 'crimes' leads to the other, but is a clampdown on bullying always sufficient? Since (as our son's first primary school Head used to say!) "Children learn racism from their parents," they often need to unlearn it, and therefore education of this nature should be an important ingredient of any school curriculum. Certainly too, when last year our Choral Society was giving a concert jointly with a Birmingham choir and held a rehearsal in a school in that city, I was impressed by some anti-bullying posters written by children which were adorning one of the walls. Whether this indicates a lot of progress since our day may be open to debate.

The question of 'color terminology' is something else that has for long been discussed. In the national association named Harmony, we were taught that the terms 'colored' and 'half-caste' were both frowned upon and that, since our racist society grouped all non-white people together, the term 'black' was the one that should be universally used. The term 'mixed race' was considered permissible as an accurate description in many cases, though such children should be described as 'black', while simultaneously being encouraged to be proud of their color. Well, 'half-caste' clearly sounds derogatory, and 'colored' is nonsensical since everyone on Earth has a color of some sort, but I know that Asians sometimes object to being classed as 'black'. And nowadays the rule/norm in America is to call people 'African American' rather than 'black'. Also, our son now says that being mixed race has on occasion made him feel not totally accepted by people who are "more black" than he is, and he says that the only two women with whom he has ever fallen in love were both mixed race like him. A complete and final solution to all this will presumably only be found when racism has been entirely eliminated and the whole world has learnt to value everybody equally.

Turning now to Christopher's childhood behavioral problems, they have become for me so distant and irrelevant as to be hardly worth a mention. I will say, however, that our difficulties were compounded by our son's being exceptionally tall for his age. When he was two he looked four, and so everyone expected him to behave like a four-year-old. I have one very vivid memory of being accused of lying about his age; it was in Mexico when David was working there for a term and Christopher had committed a particularly 'heinous crime' at a railway station. Everything undesirable that he did in childhood – lying, stealing, being generally uncontrollable – is listed in, for instance, Nancy Newton Verrier's first book (*The Primal Wound*) as completely normal for adopted children, but the trouble was that at the time we were totally ignorant of these facts and still laboring under the illusion that, having been given our child at such an early age, it should be "no different from having a child naturally." We got accused by white people of "treating him more leniently than the other two because of being adopted," and simultaneously we were told by black people that "all the problems stem from his being black in a white family." The former was patently untrue – in actual fact we were always much firmer with Christopher than with Paul and Alice because he needed a lot more control than they ever did – but the comments nevertheless greatly undermined our confidence as parents. I got the brunt of it because, as I learned later, it is completely normal and natural for a child who feels, subconsciously at least, rejected by his birth mother, to take it out on the adoptive mother. Alice, who was always a particularly reserved and tidy child, also had a great deal to endure when her books got borrowed and returned tattered (they are both of them to this day enormous book worms), her toys broken, and so on.

On the plus side, though he would regularly pinch sweets or pocket money from his brother and sister and raid the larder when no one was looking, Christopher was always phenomenally generous. If he was given, say, a box of chocolates for his birthday, he would promptly share it with the whole family. Also – unlike many adopted children I know or I know about – he was (and still is) always very demonstrably loving and affectionate. I have always loved all three of my children equally, though differently (because each is so different from the other), but Christopher has always been the one with whom it is easiest to express feelings of affection. Furthermore, even when he was in one of his very worst moods, he was never aggressive physically.

Therapy was another huge plus in our family history. Over several years we saw several different therapists, both together as a family and separately, and I can truthfully say that if it had not been for that I would never have become a therapist myself. Lawrence, our homoeopath, to whom I first took Christopher when he was seven because of his asthma, is the one who helped the most, but since his clinic was sixty miles away, when things were very bad, he encouraged us to seek additional therapy closer to home. All of the therapists we met were helpful in one way or another, but nevertheless, by the time Christopher was about twelve, I had reached breaking point.

It was then that a friend suggested boarding school and, since we were both against private schooling on principle, she gave me the brochure about a State school in the Lake District that took boarders. At the same time my sister Philippa, who was going through a difficult marriage break up, recommended an astrologer she had found in London, who had already helped her immensely. It was my first experience of astrology and, when Christopher's chart and tape came back to me, I was knocked for six. Every minute detail of his very complex and talented character was described on the tape, and the astrologer also said that, since he would not accept discipline from us, it needed to be imposed from outside the family and that boarding school would therefore be advantageous. Though David took a lot of persuading and Paul was very upset at the idea, I was relieved to obtain support in this way, and I knew that Alice would also benefit from Christopher being away from home a lot of the time.

He was never happy at boarding school, and looking back I can now see that he would have naturally taken it as a second rejection, but not only was it at the time my personal salvation, but it also gave him an introduction to basketball, which he would not have had at the school in Hull. Hence the Lake District schooling was clearly in his Life Plan! Furthermore, after a misdemeanor at the first school had caused him to be excluded in his third year and sent to a second one for the final three years prior to university, he got noticed playing basketball and was invited to play for Cumbria. This proved to be Christopher's making because, thanks to the Cumbria coach knowing about these things, he was awarded a basketball scholarship to do his degree in the States. Going to America had for long been his dream, and we shall never forget the Christmas day when, at just eighteen, he made at the dinner table a formal apology to the whole family for his previous bad behavior!

Nor shall I ever forget the proud day in North Carolina when we attended Christopher's degree ceremony. It had been so hard sending him off to the other side of the Atlantic (the other two had gone respectively to Warwick and Lancaster universities – so much closer), but at least, having met the basketball coach when he had come over to watch Christopher play in a match, we knew that he was going to be well looked after. And his obvious happiness and industry throughout the four years did much to compensate us for the separation. He excelled academically at his college as well as at the basketball, and after the degree ceremony we were invited to a cocktail party at the house of one of his professors. When this kind man made flattering comments about our son and I replied appropriately, Christopher, who was standing nearby, said, "She wouldn't have said that a few years ago!" I replied, "It's true, he was a rather difficult child to bring up," to which the professor exclaimed, "I *can't* believe THAT!"

Throughout his school career all the teachers with whom he came into contact either loved or hated Christopher. With him there was never any middle way! Being so very bright and quick witted, he always had (and still always has) an instantaneous response to everything that is said. Some of the teachers could not help admiring this and also appreciated his amazingly special character, while others were irritated by it and unable to cope with him. The Head at the first of his boarding schools came into the former category and, seeing him as potential 'Oxbridge material', was really reluctant to exclude him from his school. But, since Christopher had already been given a warning about what would happen "the next time" and his wife also wanted him gone, he had no choice. It was this Head who suggested the second school and telephoned its Head about the possibility of taking him on even before telling us about it. This was an absolute godsend because it was before the days of the internet and we had no idea that there was another comprehensive school in the country that took boarders. Also, I was appalled at the thought of having him back at home full time. When I phoned

David at work with the news of Christopher's exclusion, I prefaced it by saying, "The worst possible thing has happened." A foolish thing to say – David promptly imagined that Christopher was dead – but it gives an indication of how desperate I was feeling. As for the second Headmaster, he complained to us quite a while later that he had not been given the full picture about our son's behavior, but fortunately – and probably very much thanks to the basketball – Christopher made it through the three years and secured three As and a B in his A Levels.

I am not sure which came first: my sister's giving me *The Primal Wound* to read or my conversion to belief in reincarnation. But it does not matter; both were equally valuable. When I attended my first Edgar Cayce Association conference, in May 1992, I was convinced that I must be paying a huge karmic debt to Christopher and wondered what terrible things I must have done to him in the past that caused him now to be treating me so badly. Thanks to people I met that weekend I secured a past life reading from the American clairvoyant Aron Abrahamsen[2]. It was a relief when he told me that, rather than owing him something, I had tried to help Christopher in the past and was continuing to do so in my present life. He told me about two past-life connections that he had with our family, and I have since myself found other connections, one of which, when he was my natural son, I wrote about in my first book (*Karmic Release*). Furthermore, the famous clairvoyant Edwin Courtenay told me about a lifetime I had as a healer in Atlantis when Christopher, who had died before I started on my career, had been a renowned teacher whose methods I used and continued to promote. This all explains to me why we have always been so close even through the most difficult times.

Christopher's life since he graduated has been far from being a bed of roses. He had a very successful career as a professional basketball player, both in France and in Italy, but being forced by back injury to give up playing was a dreadful blow to him, and marrying the wrong woman because of a sense of obligation obviously did nothing to increase his happiness. However, the fruit of that failed marriage is our wonderful first granddaughter, Delilah, now aged ten, with whom he has an immensely strong bond. He has told us that, whereas he used to think that "blood ties were not that significant," having a daughter of his own has made him change his mind.

Nowadays he is doing well making a living in basketball recruitment. He bristles with innovative ideas and his clients love and respect him enormously. He has neither job security nor pension fund, but that is true of many of the young nowadays. Also, he would love to make professional use of his Psychology degree, but who knows what the future holds? He is something of a workaholic, and himself admits the reason for this to be the need to "fill the hole" that being adopted left in him. He has in recent years often had good reason for feeling depressed, and at such times I have always wanted him to have therapy, but living abroad has never made this possible. However, he invariably pulls himself through these bad patches, and everyone around him always finds him tremendous fun to be with. Recently he has been working really hard on his adoption issues and, interestingly, has entirely off his own bat reached similar conclusions to those I have acquired through my reading and my interaction with therapy clients who were adoptees. Our only real regret these days is being unable to see Christopher more often, but many people whose children live abroad have the same problem.

When I phoned Geraldine after learning the sad news of her husband's death, we had been hoping that we would see him over Christmas, but his work was keeping him in Italy and he was also keen to get back to the US to see Delilah. I found myself saying to Geraldine at one point, "Well, I don't know when we're next going to be seeing our son." As this remark left my mouth of its own accord, the word "our" struck me with immense poignancy. Reflecting on it afterwards, it occurred to me how very deeply I felt the reality of her being his mother just as much as I am. Yet, rather than diminishing my own motherhood in any way, it seemed to be an enrichment of it. All three of our 'children' are equally part of a strong family – and just the same is true of all three of our grandchildren now that Paul and his wife Becky have two wonderful little ones – but Christopher's being part of this three-generational family has given us all different experiences and ideas, many of which would never have come from our genes.

So to what would I attribute our 'success' – a story so much happier than that of so many adoptions? Well, I sum it up thus: firstly, Christopher has much goodness and talent in his genes. We know his birth mother well, and in fact I regard her as a very good friend. We have not met his father, but we know that, as well as getting a good degree, he enjoyed playing basketball at university. (Christopher would never have acquired that talent in our unsporting family!) Secondly, he was brought up in a loving and secure home, which always accounts for a great deal. However, having said that, I must also say that he did *not* have perfect parenting. David was a wonderful and devoted father, but I feel that I was very far from being a wonderful mother. Hopefully I did all right with Paul and Alice, but they were extremely easy to bring up. (Paul did a little of the 'terrible teen' thing only after he had left home and graduated, while Alice, who is now thirty-eight, has yet to do it! Lawrence, our homoeopath, reckons that Christopher did it for both of them – that they had to be "good" because he was so "bad.") In view of our past-life connections, I firmly believe that I was the mother he chose for his present life, but that does not mean that (although Christopher says that he disagrees!) I was the best mother he could have had. When I felt I could no longer cope with him at home, I sent him off to boarding school, which did not make him happy. (Maybe if he had been happier at school, he would have behaved better.) When I was completely at the end of my tether, I occasionally resorted to smacking (now rightly illegal of course and it never did the trick anyway!). At other times I probably shouted and screamed at him and made awful threats – it's hard to remember now that it was all so long ago and that our relationship is so wonderful and so rewarding!

Thirdly – and I will argue with anyone to my dying day that this is the most important factor of all – Christopher is who he is (one of the most unusual and also most popular people I have ever known) because of his *innate* character built upon countless numbers of lives. He says that, since he feels himself to be "like everyone else, a mix of nature and nurture," I can add him to the list of people who would argue the point, but for me he is, as I believe his poem indicates, a very evolved as well as a very gifted soul, and I feel our family to be immensely privileged to have him in it. Certainly it has over the years – especially when he was growing up – given us all many challenges, but challenges are what we all need for our growth, and easy lives must often be boring. People whose adopted children have not turned out very well, should blame neither themselves nor 'bad genes'. Many souls in our world are still young, many have taken seriously wrong turnings in the past which may take several lifetimes to rectify. People may argue that families are "simply the luck of the draw," but my many years of in-depth research into these matters leave me firmly convinced that our good fortune with Christopher is not due to "luck" but rather part of a divine plan, and for that I shall be eternally grateful.

Betty Jean Lifton, whom I have previously mentioned as an adoption counsellor and writer that I greatly admire, comments in her book *Journey of the Adopted Self – A Quest for Wholeness*, that adoptees are perceived by some people as part of a divine plan. She quotes a Kabbalah scholar as saying, "Adopted people are a special breed. Every soul has a purpose. Adoptees are beautiful souls. Old souls. They have a special fate – a special karma – to redesign the earth." I could not agree more – at least in our own son's case!

Notes

1. *Journey of the Adopted Self – A Quest for Wholeness,* Betty Jean Lifton,
2. It was Aron Abrahamsen who told me also that I had come into my present life "partly as a writer," and the 'life seal' that he gave me is on the cover of my third book, *Discovering The Life Plan – Eleven Steps to your Destiny,* 6th Books, 2012.

DAVID'S PERSPECTIVE

Many adoptees recall stealing from their parents' wallets when they were young because they felt they had been stolen from their mothers and ripped off by the adoption system.

Betty Jean Lifton, *Journey of the Adopted Self – A Quest for Wholeness*

You will find a number of family photographs adorning the walls of our house in Ludlow. There are pictures of our children, taken at various stages, ranging from babyhood to childhood to adulthood. Several are enlargements of photos taken on some of our numerous trips abroad (either for my work or for leisure). There, in the kitchen, to the right of the fridge, is Christopher, roughly at age five, standing next to Paul and Alice, the picture taken in a park in Geneva. All three look happy, and Christopher has a glint in his eye as though he was about to embark on some mischievous exploit. You can see that at that age he was already taller than Alice. Then, to the left of the fridge, there is a photograph taken in Cluny of Christopher at the age of two, sitting on Ann's lap. She had just allowed him a sip of her beer. Never having drunk beer before, he found the taste bitter and tried to hide this reaction, which nevertheless shows up in the shape of his mouth. To this day he maintains that he drank the whole glass himself!

Those trips to Geneva and other exotic locations with the children were wonderful times and bring back good memories. Christopher was always such a combination of being a joy to be with and being very awkward and undisciplined. We have a picture of him in Spain, leaping, in full flight with arms outstretched, from the beach wall on to the sand below – a typical expression of energy and exuberance. But we remember also having to leave a tourist camp site in Brittany, in darkness and torrential rain, knowing that Christopher had largely destroyed the site's pool table. Not all of this (the dark, the rain) was Christopher's fault, and he claimed – rightly or wrongly – that the table had already been partially damaged when he started to use it.

Both at home and abroad, when I was at work, Ann was left to cope with Christopher's behavior for long periods on her own. She and Alice certainly took the brunt of his more difficult moods. (His relationship with Paul was always easier.) Ann and I differed to some degree in our approach to the problems involved. She was for setting clear boundaries to Christopher's behavior, and insisting that he keep within these boundaries. I was always looking for even small signs of improvement that could be encouraged. I tended to feel that, if I talked seriously to Christopher, and presented him with rational arguments as to why his behavior had to improve, then he would be bound to respond positively. But, despite having two different approaches, something that the textbooks usually deplore, we did get together and agree and act decisively whenever decisive action was required. Such a moment came, for example, when we decided that Christopher should be transferred to a State boarding school in the Lake District. I remember, so well, sitting on the grass with Ann outside the Jack Lyons Concert Hall in York during a concert interval, the day before Christopher's last day at his Hull school. I felt so sad about his departing for an uncertain future. But after his departure his links with the family were still to remain strong. An early sign of this was apparent when I took him over for his first sight of his new school, some weeks before the start of the first term. When we arrived near the school, he insisted on leaving the car to go into a few of the local shops, where he bought small presents for his mother, brother and sister. I think it was his way of saying, "I may be spending more of my time away from you, but family links will *never* be broken." (This has indeed remained true ever since.)

It is some indication of the contrasting aspects of Christopher's personality that, though excluded from his new school after three years, he was welcomed into a second State boarding school in the Lake District on the strong recommendation of his previous headmaster! Even at the height of his most 'difficult' stage, there were always other sides to his personality that shone through, and helped us to be optimistic and confident that the more positive side would eventually dominate. Two more framed photographs in our house illustrate well the extent to which our hopes have been realized.

The first of these shows Christopher in full academic dress receiving his degree from Davidson College in North Carolina. He looks proud and confident, as well he might have. He had succeeded with a strong double major in Economics and Psychology, playing at the same time an important role in the College basketball team, and supported by a basketball scholarship. The second of these two photos shows Christopher at Paul and Becky's wedding, where he gave an excellent speech as best man. The photo shows not only Christopher, but all five members of the family, and we are clearly depicted here as a family unit with strong bonds.

Christopher, then, has managed to transform himself from an awkward, uncooperative, rebellious (but also loved and loving) child into the wonderful energetic, imaginative adult that he is today. In doing so, he has had to overcome many obstacles. He was born in 1979, the same year as Margaret Thatcher became Prime Minister, and a period when racism in Britain was even stronger than it is today. He has coped with racism, not through a submissive approach, but through the strength of his personality. He has succeeded as a professional basketball player despite a number of setbacks, including an injury that finally ended his playing career. He has managed to extricate himself from a disastrous marriage, but there is a strong loving bond between himself and his wonderful daughter. He is at the time of my writing establishing a business as an agent for other basketball players.

Christopher's life has been, so far, something of a roller coaster, with many ups and downs, and there are still problems to be overcome. He has thought deeply about some of the questions relating to his adoption, and has had contact by email with his birth mother. In all his struggles Ann has been a source of great strength to him, and I hope we have both been able to give him good support when he needed it. What is sure is that he is now moving in a good direction, and this is marvelous to see.

PAUL'S PERSPECTIVE

What always seemed [more] difficult to explain was Paul's remarkable tolerance of Christopher's undesirable behavior, but the famous clairvoyant Edwin Courtenay told me that they had very strong links as blood brothers.

Ann Merivale, *KARMIC RELEASE – Journeying Back to the Self*

In life I often try to remind myself of the following simple philosophy: "Everyone's different." I feel that if people acknowledged and accepted this fact more often, there would be a lot less conflict in the world. I think it is through Christopher becoming part of our family that I have grown to see the importance of this acknowledgement. By "different" I mean that we all have different ways of looking at things, different things that are important to us, and different tolerances. We often argue with people because we expect them to behave in the same way that we do in a given situation. It is very difficult to imagine ourselves in other people's shoes, partly because we have little knowledge of the experiences that person has been through to shape their way of thinking and behavior.

In a family many differences between the members still exist, but, particularly for siblings growing up together, we have a natural expectation that the differences will be less pronounced. Many experiences are shared, and shared genetics contribute to the 'nature' side of the 'nature/nurture' shaping of our personalities. When someone joins a family who doesn't have this genetic link, however, our initial expectations are confounded. When you add to this the fact that an adopted child has the additional traumatic experience of having been removed from their birth mother, which is an experience most of us can't imagine, I think the similarities we might have expected are even less apparent.

Growing up, while I didn't consciously think about the effect that Christopher's start in life would have had on him or his relationship with others, I like to think that I learnt to accept at least some of the differences between him and myself, and between him and Alice. I think it used to annoy me when others in our family didn't seem so accepting of this. Of course, thinking about it now, this was just an example of my expectation that they would behave the same way as I did.

I distinctly remember feeling the need to *protect* Christopher. I actually felt, in a lot of situations, that he was treated more harshly than myself or Alice. I understand that Alice feels the opposite, but, well, everyone's different. On one particular occasion we were staying at our uncle and aunt's house. I imagine that I was around twelve at the time. We had been told that there would be ice cream for dessert. Christopher, however, was deemed not to have finished enough of his main course to deserve ice cream. I remember that he was quite upset by this, as most seven-year-olds would be. I decided that this was very unfair; I think I thought that the no-dessert-without-finishing-main-course policy ought to (and would normally) be waived while staying at relatives' houses, and I was sure that my parents were only enforcing this because it was Christopher. I became very upset too, even more so than Christopher I think, and while, being naturally shy, I would usually have kept my feelings to myself in situations like that, I launched into a tantrum on this occasion. I was absolutely determined that Christopher should get his ice cream. Of course I lost, and I think I even remember his portion being washed down the sink.

There were two very significant periods, I feel, in Christopher's upbringing, which I think also had a profound impact on our whole family, and relationships between us, and hence should be mentioned here. The first was when my parents agreed to look after Naphtali, a Namibian boy whose father was studying at the University of Hull and was unable to have Naphtali live with him during his studies. I don't remember how long he stayed; I remember it felt like a long time, but in actual fact was probably just a few months. My initial feelings towards Naphtali were ones of resentment. I always felt at my most comfortable when our whole family, and no one else, was together. To introduce someone new, and to be expected to treat them like a sibling, did not feel right to me. Thinking about it now, it was almost in my mind as if Naphtali had not earned the right to be there. In contrast, these were never feelings I had towards Christopher. Of course I was much younger when Christopher was introduced to us, but I think this is only part of the explanation. He had always felt like a sibling to me. This was never questioned; I knew this fact from the outset. But also, Christopher had earned his place in our family. Our "differences" were diminished by the shared experiences of his first few years of life. Of course none of this was Naphtali's fault, and now I feel a sense of guilt towards the way he was treated by the rest of us children, particularly as he was already coping with living in an unfamiliar country and setting, as a young child.

On one particular occasion Naphtali took Christopher's bicycle without asking permission. He cycled up our street on it, and I was either sent, or took it upon myself (I don't remember which now), to try and retrieve it. I was quite happy to do this, partly due to the responsibility I felt to protect Christopher, and maybe also because of the resentful feelings I had towards Naphtali. Catching up with him as he was turning round, I placed my own bike in his path so that he would be forced to stop. However, he was not used to cycling, or used to using this particular bike, and he didn't manage to find and reach the brakes in time. Instead, he rode straight into my bike and fell over the handlebars, landing on the ground with some force, ending up with cuts and bruises. I had only intended to stop him, and certainly didn't intend for him to be hurt, but somehow this event seems representative of Naphtali's time with us, literally and metaphorically.

Having mentioned the difference between my relationship with Christopher and with Naphtali, the similarity between their situations should also be stated. They were both placed, through no choice of their own, in a family who they were not only genetically unrelated to, but were also of a different skin color. Both of them had behavioral issues, and it is very easy to imagine why this was. I think it would have been incredible and unnatural if either of them had joined our family and behaved exactly as Alice and I did.

I am, and I think I was at the time, able to forgive much of Christopher's behavior. Not only did he have the reasons to misbehave already mentioned, but also Alice and I were always particularly shy. I can't speak for Alice, but I know that my own shyness contributed in large part to my "good" behavior, particularly at school; I was always frightened of being told off. Had I not had this restriction, I think I would have been a lot less of a model student than I was. Christopher, on the other hand, was outgoing from a young age. Consequently, he would have been much more able to act the way he wanted to act, or say the things he wanted to say, in the face of authority. Instead, I would have only fantasized about acting the way Christopher did. I think it's fair to say that I was actually fascinated by Christopher's behavior when, as I see it, he was only acting in a way that his personality allowed him to. After all, everyone's different.

The other significant period in our family life was the time when Christopher was sent to boarding school. This was the cause of much disagreement and argument, and I remember having a huge issue with this decision at the time. To me it felt like the 'problem' of Christopher's difficult behavior was being pushed away. It seemed to me that we as a family had agreed to take on the huge responsibility of looking after another child, and sending him away would be a failing in this responsibility. I felt that it was a huge rejection of Christopher, and again I felt the need to protect him from this. I appreciate that I may have found him easier to live with than, say, Alice or Mum did. I think because I didn't have a strong resentment of his behavior I was less of a target for his "naughtiness." I imagine that, because he often elicited a strong reaction from them, this fuelled his behavior more. I don't ever remember him, for example, taking my possessions without permission, whereas there was more than one occasion when he took toys or sweets of Alice's. Maybe because of this there was an element of selfishness in my own feelings. I wanted Christopher to live with us; at this time we had many similar interests. We used to play computer games together, or play snooker on the miniature table in the garage. I didn't want this to stop. I would miss him.

As things turned out, I (and Christopher) lost the argument, and he went to boarding school in the Lake District. I can see now that there were many positive things that came from this, such as the experiences of stronger discipline he received, and his discovery of basketball. Of course, Mum's reasons for sending him were mostly for his benefit; and although she may not have predicted the interest in basketball that would develop, it would have been clear to her (and Dad) that there would be many things he would gain from. As to whether or not it was the right thing to do, given the positive outcomes we now know of, I think only Christopher can say now.

Nowadays I still feel very close to Christopher, despite the fact that we rarely see each other during this period in our lives. He was the best man at my wedding, and when he travelled from abroad to be with us for the event, it was like we had never been apart. I look forward to a time when we can see each other regularly, but due to the nature of his work, this may not be any time soon. I am very pleased to hear that he is enjoying and appreciating his time in Cremona, including the beautiful scenery and architecture. For most of his life this is something that I could have imagined anyone else in our family saying if they were to live there, but would not have expected from Christopher. Everyone's different but, in many ways, everyone's the same.

ALICE'S PERSPECTIVE

Alice's and Christopher's friendship took some time to develop. Paul was almost five and she was three…and at the time I attributed their very different attitudes to him to the fact that Alice was used to being the baby. But that was before I knew anything about karma.
Ann Merivale, *KARMIC RELEASE – Journeying Back to the Self*

Alice, who didn't want to write her own piece (partly because of being reticent by nature and partly because she disagrees with my spiritual views), has always been the 'perfect daughter'. As a baby she sat happily playing with the toys in which her older brother had never taken any interest. As a child she never knew boredom, being always able, if the rest of us were busy, to keep herself entertained with books and her imagination. As a teenager she never rebelled and never got into drugs or alcohol. She excelled academically both at school and university. A typical Virgo, she has always been neat, tidy, efficient and well organized. And now, as a mature, working woman, she is a great (if sometimes critical!) support to her ageing parents.

So it is no wonder that her bombastic younger brother was frequently a trial to her as they were growing up, and that he still tends on occasion to meet with her disapproval. Being 'chalk and cheese' has not, however, prevented the two of them from being intensely loyal to one another. I recounted earlier how at primary school she would on occasion have to defend him against racial abuse, and nowadays they are both extremely good at buying each other ideal Christmas and birthday presents. This is helped by their having similar tastes in literature and film, and the fact that they are both very imaginative when it comes to shopping for other people.

When I asked Alice about her earliest memories of her younger brother, she replied that she remembered the day when we picked him up from the foster home, "sitting in the car in the pouring rain." It is always interesting to notice how people's memories differ. Paul, who is twenty months older than she is and was coming up to five at the time, says that he *doesn't* remember that big day, whereas he remembers a number of things that I don't. Alice also remembers Christopher recounting stories of the things he had done with his "first mummy and daddy," and feeling annoyed at how we "humored him" because she knew that none of it was true! But of course she was very young then. Looking back now, she can appreciate that these tales were analogous to her own stories about the games she had been playing with her own friends whose names were Box and House.

Although psychology was one of her ancillary subjects at university, and although she has much theoretical understanding of problems related to the human condition, Alice sometimes has difficulty in appreciating other people's reasons for being unable to live as straightforwardly and 'sensibly' as she herself does. Having a brother like Christopher is consequently a huge learning experience for her in this lifetime, and that is one reason why I believe them to have come together this time round.

CHRISTOPHER'S PERSPECTIVE

Biracial children are considered black in this country, even though one of their parents is white. The uniqueness of their identity in belonging to both races, which makes them both black and white, has not been recognised.
Betty Jean Lifton, *Journey of the Adopted Self – A Quest for Wholeness*

...her adoptive parents had taken her when she was helpless and raised her with the innocent hope that she would never look back. The unspoken debt was to be paid with acquiescence and silence: It is a form of emotional indenture even though it is made in the name of love.
Betty Jean Lifton, *Twice Born – Memoirs of an Adopted Daughter*

In 2013 I wrote a long email to a colleague who is also adopted and, since during the process I found myself writing quite a lot about my own feelings and experiences, I thought I would quote some of it for my mother's book:

"I understand you completely because I've felt that same way myself sometimes. Losing a girlfriend is hard for anyone, and for an adoptee it might be even harder because on some level I think we are missing the comfort and security that other people take for granted. It's hard to admit it to yourself, and even harder to admit it to other people, because it seems so ungrateful when we've had wonderful parents and lives full of privilege. BUT, in my opinion that is the very heart of the issue. We feel that we should be thankful for all this kindness, and grateful for everything our parents did for us. Maybe that is true, but it's not the natural way for people to feel – especially not from the very beginning of their lives. That gratitude comes with an obligation to prove *deserving* of the love that these wonderful people gave us. That is a huge burden to carry, and you might not ever realize it because it has always been on your back. I had to go through some pretty rough times to gain an understanding of these parts of myself, and that did not happen until I was older than you are now. Before then, if someone had said these things to me I would not have listened. Now I know it's real because just writing those words has brought a lump to my throat and tears to my eyes.

It's crazy to complain about our good fortune and in fact I am not going to complain about it. I love my family and I wouldn't change them for anything, but still *I am going to grant myself the kindness* of acknowledging how heavy that burden can be and grant myself the release of admitting that in some ways, despite my biological mother's good intentions, my adoptive family's love and my socio-economic good fortune, despite all of that, in some ways I am still a victim and it's OK that it hurts and it's OK for me to feel sorry for myself sometimes and I should not feel that I always have to be perfect just to prove that I'm worthy of my good fortune not to have been aborted and to be chosen by such a wonderful family.

The families of adopted children will typically do their best to make the child feel loved. They might even tell him or her that they are even more special than other kids because they were "chosen." The intentions behind this are good, but in fact it might make the child feel under even more pressure to show that he or she *is in fact special*. That was a burden for me, and I am lucky enough to be as intelligent as the rest of my family and also to have talents in other areas of life such as sports which nobody else in my family even really considers to be a real thing. (When I was growing up, if one of us had turned on a soccer or basketball game to watch on TV, the other four would have looked at that person like he/she was crazy!)

I believe that the most loving thing a parent of an adopted child can do is to make him feel *needed*; that is to repeat over and over again how complete the child has made your life not because of any one quality he has or any accomplishment, but by the simple fact of being there to love and be loved. I'm crying again writing this sentence because there is still a deep down need for that inside me. I am sure my parents would have done it willingly if they had known to. They made such a big effort to demonstrate their love for me, even taking the whole family to Sierra Leone and Ghana for a month to allow me a chance to "get in touch with my heritage." That was a wonderful experience, but it did also emphasize how different I was from everyone else in the family, and I think at that age the most important thing is to show the child *gratitude* just simply for being there; for filling a void and allowing the parents the opportunity to express their love. Not to add to the gratitude towards his or her 'saviors' that an adopted child is already carrying.

I think my parents would have done this if they had known to, but they didn't know and there was no way that I could tell them what I needed because I didn't know either. The saddest part of it all is that a lot of this pain and stress is avoidable because it is only on our side. Our parents do love us the same as if we were biologically related and they don't know that their kindness can actually create a burden. I think that often the parents of an adopted child who is struggling to find his way will try everything except the one thing that could help. They will give more love, or more discipline or pay for counsellors or medication to 'fix' the child. All of this is done from love, but the result is just a heavier weight on the child because he was already overburdened by a sense of gratitude to these wonderful people; now he feels that he is throwing the kindness back in their faces, causing distress and forcing them to make even more of an effort. The intentions of the parents are good, but the effect is more pressure, and maybe that's enough to make the child hold himself in line, but it's not the way for him to be at peace.

The real solution might be to tell the child that no matter what he does they are grateful that he is in their lives and that they would love nothing more than to have him stay with them until he is sixty years old. Of course he has to go to school and study like any child, but that is for his own wellbeing; as far as his parents are concerned he could sit at home watching TV all day and they would be thankful just to have him there. In my opinion this is the way to let an adopted child grow into himself, and this is another issue that we adoptees face. A biological child has a blueprint for life from his two parents. Genetic similarity will often mean that they have several traits in common with the child so he can look at their lives and have at least a road map of possibilities for his own. Even if he goes in a completely opposite direction, at least his parents' lives serve as a point of reference. The adopted child doesn't have that. We can see the road that our parents took, but there is absolutely no reason to believe that the paths they chose will be the right ones for us, or even be relevant at all. We have to create our own path and that can be daunting, but if our parents can allow us the space and support to do it (mine truly, truly did), it's possible that we might bring them along with us on a ride along paths that no one else in the family even knew existed. I did! I'm sure that my parents never expected to be watching one of their kids playing basketball in front of thousands of people in the USA, and this is when we can celebrate the diversity that an adopted child brings to the family instead of shrinking from it out of fear that it might pull us apart.

I started writing this for you, but obviously it's become equally or even more important for me. I figured some of these things out about myself in theory, but that doesn't mean that I am magically fixed. That pressure to prove myself worthy of the love I received since being adopted at two weeks old is constant, and it's only by forcing myself to stop and think about it that I realize how heavy a weight it is. I have tears burning my eyes and rolling down my face just from writing these words. It's weird because the tears are very real and yet I feel completely in control of myself. I could easily be sitting and editing a video while the tears pour from my eyes completely ignored. That's not normal. If tears are there, it means that pain and emotion is there, but being adopted means that we have been training ourselves to quiet those emotions and lock them away since the very beginning of our lives.

I should be taking time to think about this stuff every day. I should also be taking time to enjoy the sunshine and read a book and talk to my daughter and develop a real relationship with a woman, but instead I spend almost every waking hour working away on my computer. Here's the crazy part: at least thirty per cent of that work is completely pointless *and I know it*. My emails don't all have to be perfectly worded English. I don't have to be the best in the world at every single aspect of this job, even aspects that I invented myself and other people still haven't even thought of! I also don't have to make this email a masterpiece of creative writing, but still I am trying to!

Where does all this need for perfection come from? To the point that I literally cannot stop working until you force my hand with your concerns and give me an excuse to sit out here in the sun, ignore all these basketball players, drink a cappuccino, cry these tears and let these words out. That being said, even writing this email is working in a way because at the same time as I am genuinely trying to share my thoughts with you, I am basically showing off at the same time, and that's pretty much what all of it comes down to: showing off.

When you carry the burden of a self-imposed obligation to be grateful to your parents for their love, it's going to lead you in one of two directions. Either you will rebel against it and find every way possible to sabotage your life so you don't have anything to feel grateful for, or you will become insanely driven in an attempt to feel worthy of a love which to any child raised by their biological parents (even poor or single or drug-addled parents) is taken completely for granted. I have another perspective on this now because I have Delilah, my biological daughter. She drives me crazy with how much she takes everything her mother does for granted, but at the same time I love watching it and I love that she won't have to deal with the issues that you and I do. Even though I'm away from her way too much and don't call her when I'm away like I should, I don't worry about her because every time I come back I see her obnoxious sense of entitlement regarding everything her mum does for her every day and her lists of demands for me. I see it, shake my head, smile...and I love it! That's how things should be. You should feel that the only debt between yourself and your parents is owed from *them to you*.

Delilah is the continuation of my genes, of me, so anything I do for her, I am also doing for myself. One day (I hope) she'll have her own children who will carry my genes forward again and whom I'll be able to watch develop and keep carrying part of me forward. I don't care how many diapers I changed (actually it wasn't that many), how many designer clothes or fancy cars I couldn't buy because of my financial obligation to her. None of that comes close to her gift to me of being her and being a part of me. This is the natural way things should be and I don't think she can ever feel indebted to me no matter what I do for her. Anything I do for her, she will accept without thinking twice and still feel unfairly treated about whichever requests I don't grant. *That's how it should be*. With my parents I always felt a slight apprehension whenever asking for anything (especially if it was financially significant) and if they gave me it, on some level I would think, "Wow, I got another freebie. I wonder how long this luck is going to hold." That's how everyone feels in relationships outside their family. Non familial-relationships are based on give and take so that both sides have to feel fairly treated, or the relationship falls out of balance. I believe that we adoptees feel the same way about our relationships with our parents, the problem is that there is not much giving back you can do from the age of nought, and so if you apply the typical non-familial relationship accounting rules, then you find yourself seriously in debt and under a lot of stress trying to compensate from the moment that you realize that you were adopted and what adoption means.

The absolute biggest mistakes of my life were made by being too hard on myself, and I think this stress from a non-existent but very heavy debt is the reason why. I probably would have made twice as much money in my basketball career if I had worked a little less hard and allowed myself to rest and relax. Instead I spent hours of extra time in the gym and in the weight room until I exhausted my body and ended up with a herniated disc in my back. Even after that I didn't slow down. I took between eight and ten Ibuprofen a day, never missed a practice and kept pushing harder and harder to make up for the fact that I didn't have the chance to develop my skills as a basketball player until I went to Davidson because of the fact that I had grown up in a part of England where basketball was not taken as seriously as cricket. I pushed myself to the point that I did not play one single professional season without chronic pain, was forced to retire before I was ready, and with a half dead foot from sciatic nerve damage to carry around for the rest of my life as a reminder.

The deep depression I suffered for two years after I finished playing was due in large part to regret over that stupidity and a heart-wrenching desire to go back in time, be less obsessive and have the basketball career I should have had: pushing myself less but making more money and having more fun. I was lucky enough not only to be adopted by a wonderful family. I also got this big athletic body, which should have allowed me a privileged and enjoyable life, but I ruined it and cannot even play sports for fun now because any impact makes my back feel uncomfortable and the numbness in my foot gets worse. I tortured myself over that to the point where there were days when I would abstractly consider the appeals of suicide because I couldn't see how any life with my slightly damaged body could compare to the life I would have had if I hadn't ruined my body through my own stupidity.

I was never truly suicidal, though. There were many days when I didn't want to live, but I discovered that I also did not want to die, and when I realized that, I realized that if I was going to stick it out on this world I might as well make the best of it. Even if I could not be a professional athlete any more, I have more good fortune than just an extra-long body. I also have a good brain, some money in the bank and wonderful parents who actually gave me more money so I wouldn't have to dig into my own savings immediately when I started my career as a full-time agent. I also had my own agent who took a chance on me when I asked him for a job, even though I hadn't done much to prove that I would be an asset to him. Still he invested a substantial amount of money and time (which is always in very short supply for a successful agent) to let me try.

Eventually I forgave myself. How can I really be self-critical for working too hard when everywhere you look there are commercials and motivational messages telling you to push through the pain, turn it up a notch and outwork everyone else in the world? No one told me that my engine was already in overdrive, my work ethic was unhealthily excessive and I really needed to just slow down. There are no Nike commercials saying "Whoooaaa, don't overdo it," but that's because nearly everybody else on this planet will stop and let themselves rest way before the point that their body is in danger of breaking down. This means that for most people working harder is a surefire way to be more successful.

In contrast, I have spent a good part of my life as a certifiable workaholic who would do better by slacking off a little bit. This is not something I'm bragging about or for me to feel proud of. I wasn't fighting temptations and exercising self-discipline. There isn't much temptation for me to do anything except work because I cannot relax when I'm not working. The funny thing is that I haven't always been this way. Up until age sixteen I was always in trouble and doing the bare minimum of schoolwork, but I was smart so I slid by. When I was sixteen, I discovered basketball, which gave me better focus for my energy but even more importantly, I developed very strong feelings for a girl at my boarding school. We were very good friends but she had a boyfriend she did not want to leave and so the relationship was just a daily dose of heartbreak for me. My workaholism blossomed then as a response to her rejection and I think that's very significant. Ever since that time I have been very, very driven. I also didn't have such strong feelings for another human being until I met my ex-girlfriend in Nantes when I was twenty-nine. That's significant too. The focus on work (as a basketball player and part-time agent) was anaesthetizing me from feeling any emotions and having to do something with so much potential for hurt as becoming attached to another human being, even my baby daughter. (It was easy to justify that to myself, and it still is – by claiming that the work is for her too. It's true but that's only part of the story.)

Skip forward to today with all the experience and wisdom I gained and how am I spending my days? I'm staying up all night obsessing over minute details on projects that no one else will notice and making you miserable by setting a completely impossible example for you to follow. There is no way you should be working anywhere near the hours I do and I would not want you to. I should not be doing it myself, but just because you diagnose an illness doesn't mean that you immediately have the cure.

There is only one major difference between myself now and myself five years ago and that is that today I am *self-aware*. That's the one thing I would like to help you to learn because it changes everything. Now I might spend two hours writing an essay about Daniel Hackett being a hero and posting it on Facebook just to receive some praise when I have way more important and urgent things I should be doing (like sleeping for one). That's pretty stupid, but the reason I feel OK about it now is that at this point in my life I know what I am doing and why. I might still have a hard time relaxing away from work, and I might be way too obsessive and detail-oriented, but now when I do those things, I do them for myself and for the pleasure I feel looking at what I have done and being proud of it, rather than for receiving praise from other people. I know it's silly, but it's my life and it's what I choose to do with it."

Since I have all my life wanted to help people, I hope that my personal insights might be helpful to adoptees who read my mum's book, who might still be struggling with fully understanding the issues and burdens that being adopted has meant for them. I felt rejected by the woman who was supposed to love me the most and care for me and nurture me and help me understand the world – the woman who carried me. Deep down there has always been a conviction lurking in me that I must be worthless because of that. She didn't just 'reject' me though. She chose a family for me, and she chose two people with the kindest hearts I have ever known. They raised me and protected me and supported me. There were bad times, when I was just too out of control and they sent me to boarding school. Maybe that re-aggravated my wound, but they never abandoned me. They showed me the goodness of people and the value of kindness, and it's because of those things that I believe that aspiring to be kind and good and help people instead of hurting them should be a person's highest aspiration. It has been a hard road sometimes because I've been trying to prove that I am worthy of the love they showed me and I never felt entitled to it. Deep down part of me still thinks I'm not, but my parents never ever made me feel that way. They loved me unconditionally and so even during my darkest days I've been able to move forward. I have spent too much of my life obsessively moving forward and not enough of it enjoying the ride. Sometimes that's even hurt my chances for success, but I've never lost my optimism and I have never been afraid to trust or take a risk, because I've never felt that I would be completely on my own, even if I failed and lost everything. Maybe I do give too much and for sure that comes out of insecurity, but it's not such a bad thing and I also receive a lot back. I believe I have also made some people's lives better, and I can see sometimes that having me around makes people happy because I know them and value them and see the good in them. That's a good feeling too.

I married for the wrong reasons, but strange as this may sound, the extent to which my ex-wife and I were incompatible was actually fortunate. It was so glaringly obvious almost from the beginning that we did not have a future as husband as wife that the period in which I could deny the inevitability of a split was much shorter than is often the case. Our separation and divorce were acrimonious and painful, but at least we did not spend valuable years of our lives holding on to impossible hopes for happiness with the wrong partner as many well-intentioned people do. At the time, neither my ex-wife nor I had any idea of the way that being adopted impacted my capacity to form attachments or make decisions, and we both suffered as a result. I regret that for both of us, but I do not regret the relationship because I don't ever, not even for a second, regret the existence of the person whom I treasure most in this world, my daughter.

When my mother asked if I could write something about my feelings with regard to interracial adoption, I told her that they would not leave much room for anything else in her book and would probably require two separate volumes of their own. Maybe I will write those books one day, but until then I want to thank her both for her intentions in writing this one and for the love with which it is filled. That love and those same good intentions are the reason that I'm the man I am today. A man who is very far from perfect, but whatever is good within me is borne from her love and the love of my father, my brother and my sister and the years that we shared growing up together as a family.

It's not unusual that I feel grateful for having these wonderful people in my life, but the manner in which so much love was bestowed upon me is exceptional. I would love to express the appreciation I feel towards my mother for making this possible, but I'll resist for now...because doing so would be enough to fill volume III.

PART FIVE – ADOPTEES

> *The adopted child, who must grow up as if dead to his mother, has the need to believe that the woman who carried him in her body still carries him in her heart; just as he needs to believe that the woman who did not carry him in her body, but who cares for his daily needs, carries him in her heart. The task of adopted children is to reconcile these two mothers within them – the birth mother who made them motherless and the psychological mother who mothered them.*
>
> From *Journey of the Adopted Self – A Quest for Wholeness*, Betty Jean Lifton

Roots have always had great importance for us members of the human race. The ancient Polynesians were skilled navigators and were knowledgeable about astronomy as well as the migratory habits of birds and animals. Guided by their fellow creatures as well as by the stars, they journeyed in their 'wakas' (canoes with outriggers) and discovered to their north as early as AD 300-750 a group of beautiful islands, which they named Hawai'i, and they made them their home. Between 750 and a thousand years ago they travelled southwest to Aotearoa (otherwise known as New Zealand), and there their descendants are known as the Maori. In 1893 Queen Liliuokalani surrendered the kingdom of Hawai'i to the United States, and in 1900 it officially became US territory, but none of this happened without protest. On 6 February1840 some of the Maori tribal chiefs refused to sign the Treaty of Waitangi, which was the prelude to the proclamation of British Sovereignty over New Zealand three and a half months later. No doubt the dissenters, though a minority, had a very clear idea of what it would entail in loss of lands and rights. This book is not the place for a treatise on the racism of which the Maori in Aotearoa, the Polynesians in Hawai'i or the aboriginals in Australia have long been victims, but, on a visit to all three, I was happy to observe how much is now being done to rectify the mistakes of the past. (Witness, for instance, *Te Whare Runanga*, the beautiful Maori meeting house in the impressive Waitangi Treaty grounds. Or the fact that, thanks to what she had learnt in school, my Australian cousin's twelve-year-old granddaughter was able to explain to us something about the wonderful Aboriginal art in the National Museum in Canberra.)

For the Maori, although the community always takes precedence over the individual, knowledge of their own lineage is of paramount importance. At meetings amongst each other or with members of other tribes, everyone introduces him or herself by reciting the names of all his or her forebears. (It must take an incredibly long time, but the Maoris' use of time is very different from ours!) And, as for other tribal peoples throughout the world, their connection to the land is of great importance as well. So, when Maoris meet, they also introduce themselves as coming from a certain town or village, adjacent to a certain river, hill or mountain, and, on returning to their own home, they greet their own (for instance) mountain by giving it the name of the person they have met together with a greeting from that person's mountain, river or whatever it may be.

In the North and West we have largely lost this close connection with both our lands and our forebears, yet how many people do *you* know who are busy researching their family trees? Personally I have met a very large number of them, which surely reinforces my point about the importance of roots in the human psyche.

For people who have never felt accepted by, or at one with, their blood family, an awareness of these roots may be much more difficult. I myself needed to break completely free from my family in order to be able to find my path in life, and I have rebelled by refusing to take any interest in my ancestors and little in my relatives. I eventually compensated for that when, at the age of fifty-two, I became converted to belief in reincarnation and began to explore my own past-life connections with people who are no longer connected to me by blood. An alternative reaction to not feeling fully part of one's blood family is to become obsessive about it, regaling everyone with whom one has contact by recounting one's most recent findings about anything to do with one's family!

Neither of these reactions is particularly to be recommended and, in an ideal society where everyone was valued for his or her special gifts and individuality, neither would be necessary. But the adopted person has none of these options; the adopted person is cut off from his or her roots either at birth or at an age when it will later be difficult for them to remember anything about their birth mother or family. As my friend Barbara, whose second daughter was adopted as a baby, says, "However much you love your baby – and it is easy to fall in love with the baby who is put into your arms when you have all this love to give – yet from her point of view you have the wrong heartbeat, wrong smell and wrong sound to your voice, and so on and so on. It's a really massive adjustment for the young child to have to make. They always know that they don't quite fit in. My daughter sometimes used to tell me that she felt as though she came from Mars!" And Barbara, who at that stage did not have the full appreciation of the difficulties that she has now, would reply jokingly, "I expect if I pricked you we'd find that your blood was green!" She says, "Josie would laugh and yet later I realized she was trying to tell me that she felt different. We told her bedtime stories that let her know she was adopted. I know she loves me so very much and I her, and I did in later life apologize to her for not being able to carry her and told her how much I wished that I could have done that."

It was after training as a psychotherapist that Barbara's understanding deepened, and she also came to appreciate that the four of them who had come together as a family all had varying abandonment issues, which supports my belief that families are planned in advance on the other side. Mary, the older daughter, was born six weeks prematurely and put straight into an incubator "so," as Barbara says, "no loving mother's arms for her, for quite some weeks," and Barbara and Fred adopted Josie after being told that having another child naturally would be too great a risk. However, Barbara thinks that Josie's abandonment issues "are the worst because she was given away the day she was born and of course had nothing with which to meet that devastating experience." She says, "I remember a time when Josie was in her teens and I found her rather distressed. We were standing alone in the living room and I was trying to console her, when I suddenly heard my voice saying, very clearly and tenderly, that there was nothing she could ever do that would make us turn against her, that the door to our home would always be open to her, no matter where she went, no matter what she did. I would always love her and there would always be a place here for her. I realized much later, when I had come to understand much more about the abandonment aspect, that my heart had reached out to her, from my own sense of loss as a child, and I had said the words that I had longed to hear from my own mother." Here Barbara could be echoing me, though I also did not see it that way when Christopher was very young. Interestingly, Barbara added, "As an adult she doesn't remember this conversation, but she was less troubled afterwards and more settled again."

Barbara, as I mentioned earlier, went on to stress that the impact of adoption on the child is "so much more than rejection – it's abandonment when they have no defenses or support with which to meet it." She further comments that "adoption isn't the only way one can collect abandonment issues. I have watched myself do this so many times. I am able to stop it once I catch on. Awareness is such a powerful saving tool."

Awareness is something that we have been watching develop in our own, now thirty-five-year-old son, and three of the people in the ensuing stories have, just like him, done amazing things for themselves. Josie, Barbara and Fred's adopted daughter, who has been into therapy to deal with her abandonment issues, is now happily married with two children of her own. Her mother says, "We are very proud of both of our children." So, if you are an adoptee and still struggling with all or some of the issues surrounding it, I am sure that you could achieve amazing things too, so please take heart!

CHAPTER EIGHTEEN

ATHENE'S STORY

O Lord, Remember not only the men and women of good will, but also those of ill will. But do not remember all the suffering they have inflicted on us; remember the fruits we have brought, thanks to this suffering - our courage, our generosity, the greatness of heart which has grown out of this. And when they come to judgment, let all the fruits which we have borne be their forgiveness.
Written on a scrap of brown paper and found at the side of a dead child at Ravensbruck.

Raju and Nanda (who were fostered rather than adopted), and Blanca, who was adopted into a different culture from the one in which she was born, all see themselves as having benefited from their moves. Athene's, on the other hand, is from our contemporary Western point of view a more 'normal' type of adoption, and she regards her present life as a challenge that she took on for her growth and learning. (As I explained in my book about the Life Plan that is of course something that most of us do sometimes, but I doubt whether there are very many brave souls who choose the particular difficulties that Athene did.)

Athene's birth mother, Elizabeth, and her father, Peter, had had a very brief affair, and Elizabeth, who was only twenty at the time, decided to give the baby up for adoption because Peter did not want to have any more to do with her. Athene was adopted at six weeks by Connie and Edgar, since Connie was unable to conceive because of being anorexic. Athene explains that her adoptive grandmother had died when Connie was only twenty-one – "a critical age, when the ego comes in in a more profound way" – and she believes her mother's anorexia to date from that premature loss.

Edgar was a completely devoted husband and father, and it would appear that her parents' marriage must have been karmic, because he was such a rock for Connie when, Athene feels, most men would have walked out on her. She was always in total denial about her anorexia, despite the fact that she never weighed more than five stone (seventy pounds) and was only four stone (sixty-six pounds) when she died in her eighties. Athene realized at quite an early age that it was she who was going to have to look after her mother, rather than the other way around. Connie ate very little indeed, drank nothing but a tiny bit of water, and Athene reckons that it was only her incredibly strong will that kept her alive for so long. She also tells me that common characteristics of anorexics are that they are exceptionally good cooks, and that they hardly sleep. Athene was fully aware of her mother's problem from the age of about seven, and she used to feel guilty when her plate got filled with wonderful food while her mother herself never ate, if at all, any more than a small child's portion. Connie never slept for more than three or four hours, and her sleep was often interrupted by nightmares.

Edgar, on the other hand, was an ideal father, and Athene says that she loved him more than anyone else in the world. He was totally steady and always there for her. Athene was devastated when he died in 1993, but still values their closeness. She thinks it possible that he has also been her father in a previous life, and is quite certain that they already knew each other well before deciding to come in as father and daughter this time round. He was a very spiritual man and used to attend a little communion service every Thursday. Athene always used to pass the spiritual books that she read on to him – books such as Yogananda's autobiography (*Autobiography of a Yogi*), which she first read when she was only nineteen.

Connie and Edgar had started out with the idea of adopting a second child, but they changed their minds when Athene was about five and they were finding her so difficult to deal with.

"We adopted children," she explains, "live in a state of hypervigilance all the time," and her mother, she says, was unable to impose the boundaries that are particularly important for such children's security. It was only after she had grown up, and read things such as Nancy Newton Verrier's *The Primal Wound,* that Athene came to understand what had been going on in her childhood, and this helped her to become the mature, rational woman that she is now. She has also attended a couple of Nancy Newton Verrier's workshops.

As is completely natural for a child who feels that she has been rejected by her first mother – and here it is important to look at things from the child's point of view even while empathizing with the difficult circumstances of a birth mother – Athene never allowed herself to get close to her adoptive mother. This was of course hard for Connie, who used to say, "My mother and I were so close; it's such a pity that you and I can't be." And Athene says that Connie really could not cope with her when she was going through the 'difficult teenage' stage (which, as I myself experienced personally and as Verrier explains so well, tends to be accentuated among adopted children).

Athene does not remember a time when she was not aware of having been adopted. Although she now realizes that it was not strictly true, she has always loved the story that her mother told her about her adoption, and whenever she was ill as a child, she used to ask Connie to tell it to her again. What Connie said was that she and Athene's father had been to a nursery, where they had looked at all the cots with babies in them, and that as soon as they had seen her, they *knew* that she was the one for them.

On leaving school Athene did a secretarial training and she worked in that field for a while until the birth of her eldest son. Then, while he was growing up, she worked as a nursery nurse. Her relationship with her first son's father was short lived, but she later married and had another three children. I have often heard it said that having children of their own is particularly special for adopted people, and Athene is very close indeed to all four of her children, and a wonderful mother. However, the relationship with her husband, whom she still loves, was a difficult one because of his tendency to suppress his emotions (she comments, "I always had to do the emotions for both of us"), and they separated when she was fifty-seven.

About nine years before her separation, Athene decided to trace her birth parents. She found that Elizabeth had emigrated to Canada, married, had four more daughters, and then got divorced. Peter, who unfortunately inherited his father's drink problem, became a doctor and married twice – much more happily the second time. He had three children by his first wife, who divorced him rather acrimoniously, and two daughters by the second one, to whom he had been married for over thirty years by the time he died in his mid-seventies.

Elizabeth agreed to meet Athene when the latter happened to be visiting North America, but it was far from being an easy day for Athene as Elizabeth insisted on spending the whole time doing things, thus leaving no time to talk. She comments that one of the many things that are hard for an adopted person is that they miss out on 'genetic mirroring' (something that she now appreciates having with her own children). Tears came to Athene's eyes when she told me about the moment when she and Elizabeth had gone to a baker's together. Athene chose her favorite – a mocha cake – and Elizabeth then told her that she had always made her other children coffee cakes for their birthdays. "That was the only thing that we ever had a chance to share!" she said to me sadly.

Peter, on the other hand, was much more welcoming and, until he died, Athene managed to develop quite a good relationship with him. She and Elizabeth had met in the spring, and the following September Elizabeth came to England on a three-week visit. When she stayed overnight with Athene, she talked non-stop about Peter, and it was clear that she had never got over that heartbreak. When she wrote and asked him to meet up with them in Cornwall, Elizabeth could not understand when he failed to reply. She appeared to be insensitive to his difficulty, as a happily married man, in meeting her again, but Athene says that she pretended not to mind.

Although Athene had been guarded initially when she embarked on making contact with Elizabeth, she now feels very sad that her birth mother did not want to open up to a relationship. They corresponded regularly to start with, but when Athene took her to the station at the end of her visit to England, Elizabeth said that she did not feel that they had a sufficiently strong relationship to carry on writing to each other.

Through our many lifetimes we often repeat patterns, and the feeling that mothers do not support one is something that Athene has brought through from a previous life in Africa. When we first made friends, she was seeking a regression because of her horror of torture. (Horror of torture is of course a hundred per cent normal – or should be! – but Athene felt hers to be excessive, and she wanted to do some Deep Memory Process therapy prior to going on a protest visit to a Trident base in Scotland.) She felt very passionately indeed about all issues connected with such things as human rights, and it was she who gave me the moving quotation from one of the death camps.

When we worked together, she went into a short life as a young African girl who suffered horrendous rape from a group of three men. Her father, who was violent, had already played around with her when she was very young indeed, and her mother was no good at all at defending her. After the rape, another woman found her and took her in because she did not want to go home. Later they all had to flee the village when it was attacked by another tribe and she died at about that time.

Despite this painful past life, Athene has a tremendous interest in Africa and a great love of African music and dance. At the end of the regression, when I took her (as we always do in

Deep Memory Process sessions) into the Bardo (the inter-life), Athene had a useful discussion with her guides, from which she came to appreciate that her lesson for her present life is to become committed to herself. Her subsequent visit to Scotland was, she felt, very well worthwhile, and she told me afterwards that she now felt a bit less "raw" when thinking about the issue of torture.

Since Athene is a natural healer, and since one of her sons is dyslexic, she worked for some time as a dyslexia facilitator, but now she feels that the time has come for her to move on. When we did the regression she was completing a Barbara Brennan healing course, and she says that this is one of the things that has helped her the most in recent years. She was content at the time with her part-time job in a health food shop, but wanted in due course to give that up in favor of setting herself up as a healer. Thanks to her experience with her mother, she was recently able to help a friend whom she recognized as becoming anorexic even before she had admitted the problem to herself.

One of the occasions on which Athene and I met was immediately after Mother's Day, and she told me that it had for the first time in her life been a really good Mother's Day for her. This was not only because of the fact that her daughter, who was living with her at the time, had spoilt her, but also because she recognized that she had finally come to terms with her adoption issues and felt completely at peace with herself. It is obvious that both Mother's Days and birthdays will tend to be particularly poignant days for adopted people, with all the negative subconscious memories that are stirred up at such times, and Athene recounted her childhood memories of nearly always being ill on her birthday. She explained how difficult it had been for her adoptive mother, who always did her very best to organize lovely birthday parties for her and then had to cancel them when at the last moment Athene was not well enough, in spite of having got very excited about the party beforehand. Even when she was coming up to fifty, Athene told people that she did not want anything, and she knew that that was for fear of not being recognized. However, her husband organized a party and, with his insistence carrying it for her, she found that she enjoyed it. And she believed that her sixtieth birthday, which was coming up shortly, would be better still: she was herself planning a really good party with music and dancing!

CHAPTER NINETEEN

LORAINE'S STORY

Every thought-seed sown or allowed to fall into the mind, and to take root there, produces its own, blossoming sooner or later into act, and bearing its own fruitage of opportunity and circumstances. Good thoughts bear good fruit, bad thoughts bad fruit.
From *As a Man Thinketh*, James Allen

Emily stood, trembling, in front of a huge linen cupboard with white doors. She was absolutely terrified because she had been sent to fetch the sheets and did not know which were the right ones. She did not know how long she had been there, and all she could think was "She's so strong and I'm scared." Suddenly her ruminations were interrupted by hands around her throat and a cry of "You stupid girl!" Why was she always so cross? Emily simply could not understand what it was that she had against her.

The house where Emily worked was enormous, with very large grounds, but she lived behind the back stairs, slept in a dormitory with a low ceiling, and only got occasional glimpses of the beautiful parts of the estate. She had been working there since she was only nine, shortly after her parents had died. Her older sister, who had taken her there, had assured her that she would be treated well so long as she worked hard, and that she would be able to go home occasionally.

Emily did work hard. She had worked incredibly hard for a long time now, was often tired, and yet she had still not been home again. Quite apart from missing her parents, she often thought nostalgically about her home life, wondering how her brother was getting on working on the nearby farm, and whether her sister was courting yet. But right now her big problem was how to select the sheets from the cupboard without incurring the wrath of the woman who had sent her for them.

"She" soon turned out to be a large, red-faced woman, who was the cook in the big house, Emily was now my client Loraine, and this dreadful bully of a woman was in her present life Loraine's adoptive mother. When in the same regression I took Emily forward to the age of fourteen, we found that by then she had learnt which sheets were which and was good at mending and cleaning them. She liked working in the laundry, some of the women there made her laugh, and she had got better at keeping out of the cook's way. Her older sister had by then got married and had children, but Emily was still unable to see her family nearly as often as she would have liked.

In a subsequent scene, when Emily was about seventeen, the cook appeared to have gone completely mad. Someone had to go upstairs and report that she was hurling things about in the kitchen, and then she been taken away in a cart with a cage. This was a huge relief for all the staff in the house, and the new cook who was appointed treated them well. Yet Emily was never able to forget her earlier ordeals, and never stopped wondering what it was that the red-faced cook had had against her.

A couple of years later, when there was a servants' ball, Bob became Emily's sweetheart. The landowners then moved both of them to a smaller house, but before long Bob was moved to yet another post and she never saw him again. The smaller house was a happier place, with only about eight workers. Emily, who now had her own bedroom, was content when she was put in charge and respected by her juniors. By the time she was about thirty-five to forty we found, however, that she was less content, as she would have so liked to have married; but she still worked hard and tried always to do everything right. Death came when she was about sixty and very tired and breathless. Her sister was already dead and, though people looked after her well, Emily was lonely.

In the Bardo (the inter-life state), Emily met her sister, whom she immediately recognized as her (Loraine's) present older daughter, Issabella. Emily also recognized her brother as Loraine's present son, Ben, but she was still too scared to meet the cook. I thought that she might have been all right with her brother and sister there to protect her, but she said "No," that she had to protect *them* from the cook! When I summoned a power animal, the wolf that Loraine sees in meditation came, but she was still unable to get to the cook, who was in "a dark and scary place." She asked the wolf the reason, and he simply looked at the moon, implying that the cook was a lunatic. Emily was further told in the Bardo that the purpose of that life had been "to see the madness," and that she herself had in comparison behaved very differently and preferably.

All the traits that were apparent in that earlier life are still apparent now. While Loraine has retained all Emily's good qualities – service, compassion, trying hard to please and so on – her present mother, whom I will call Madge, is still full of bitter, bad energy, even if it has been watered down a little bit. And, interestingly, in her present life, Madge has always hated cooking, whereas Loraine learnt to cook at an early age and has always enjoyed and been good at it. When she was a child, the food in their house was never good, and nowadays Madge has little interest in food apart from cakes. This regression also explained why Loraine has always felt particularly strongly bonded to her older daughter and her son. (At the very first session we did, Loraine had found another lifetime in which she had left an unhappy marriage, and Issabella had also been her daughter then. In that previous lifetime she had later returned to the place and been absolutely heartbroken at not being able to locate her daughter.)

Loraine, who was adopted as a small baby, was an only child, and her entire childhood was plagued by her inability to please her mother. She is very artistic and creative (for a while her profession was making wedding dresses), and she used to love making presents for everyone. Yet she never enjoyed making anything for her mother because she knew that whatever she did would be criticized. Fortunately she had a bolt hole in the form of 'Auntie Honey' – a grandmother figure who understood what her mother was like and was always sympathetic to Loraine – and she was also close to her best friend's mother. When, much later on, Loraine traced her birth mother, Gina, she did not dare to tell Madge, who had always been jealous of 'Auntie Honey'. In fact, when she first mentioned her idea of trying to trace her birth mother, Madge was extremely negative and discouraging about it, and nowadays, although Loraine is in touch and good friends with Gina's family, she still never mentions them to Madge for fear of her hostility about it.

Loraine, for whom Gina is a friend rather than a mother, does not appear to feel any anger with her for having had her adopted, but rather compassion for the difficult situation she was in. Gina had a tough life because five years before giving birth to Loraine, she had a son (Will) whose father abandoned her and, when she got pregnant the second time, her family sent her away because they could not take another illegitimate pregnancy. Peter, Loraine's birth father (whom she has not traced) promised to marry Gina and only told her after she had got pregnant with Loraine that he was married already! Gina later married the father of her third child, Tamsin, who is five years younger than Loraine, but he left her when Tamsin was only twelve.

Loraine met her husband John at Art College, they married when she was twenty-four and had two daughters followed by a son. It was the huge burden of caring for her ageing mother at the same time as bringing up her family, combined with her inability to say "No" to her that first sent Loraine to me for therapy. She was one of the "best" clients that I have ever had, in that she was always so determined to overcome her difficulties, so reliable in turning up for all her appointments, and so faithful about doing her 'homework' in between sessions.

When Loraine read *The Primal Wound* early on in our acquaintance, she realized that she had avoided things in order to avoid rejection, and that she had built walls around herself to stop the unhappiness from getting through. With me she began gradually taking the walls down brick by brick. Soon we were able to put a lot of the bricks into a sack, row out into the middle of a lake and drop them in, but she still needed the security of the wall behind her. Gradually Loraine started experimenting with stepping away from the wall, and in due course it became safe to say that she had left it behind completely.

The burden on Loraine had greatly increased in 1998 with the illness and subsequent death of her father. She had had a good relationship with him, and the two of them had always collaborated to avoid upsetting Madge. In the many past life regressions that we did, Loraine found one in which her adoptive father in her present life was her natural father. This of course explained at least in part the strong emotional bond between them.

The trigger for that session was the sad remark, "I've never had a mother," and we found that the mother in that lifetime had died when the baby was only ten days old. Her childhood that time was difficult because, though her father was caring, they had to flee from France because of being Huguenots, and she was put into one home and then another while her father went to Holland to find work and buy a house for the two of them. She spent a bit of time in England before being reunited with him, and they lived in a small house until she married a well to do Dutchman when she was in her late twenties. They had three sons and then a daughter, whom they lost as a baby, and so when her eldest son married, she was happy to gain a daughter-in-law. Since her children were young when her father was dying, she sent a servant to look after him, so this time round it was good for Loraine to have the opportunity of looking after that same father herself. Unlike many past lives, that one was a full and happy one but, despite reunion with her mother in the Bardo, the sadness returned to Loraine with the question, "Why do I never have a mother?" The recognition of that previous mother as her present younger daughter, Louisa, helped somewhat, but the only answer given to her question at that point was "You'll find out when the time is right."

Normally in DMP therapy the lifetimes that surface are traumatic ones, the reason being that those are the ones that we need to deal with. Sometimes, however, the therapist feels that it would be helpful for a client who has been through a great deal of trauma to find a happy past life. But when I suggested to Loraine that she look for a life with a loving mother, she was unable at that point to find one. There was no doubt good reason for this, and she was already aware that one of her present challenges was to give herself the mothering and love that everyone needs. 'Inner child work'[1] is often recommended by a therapist for the wonderful results it can bring, and with Loraine we once reframed an incident when she was ten, when she was out with the dog and stopped to pick some flowers for her mother, who, on her return, scolded her for being late and threw the flowers away. She then performed a tie-cutting with Madge and found that the ties were only in her lower chakras. This is an indication that her mother's relationship with Loraine is about power rather than love – a sentiment of which Madge alas appears to be incapable.

Being able to see her mother as "the mad woman," combined with all the work that Loraine was doing on herself, greatly helped her self-confidence and made her better able to voice her feelings. She realized too that her mother was also very aware subconsciously of "the mad woman," since she was always extremely wary of being considered mad. Madge is now suffering increasingly from Alzheimer's, and Loraine told me that she holds on to her sanity at all cost, often saying that she does not want people "to get their claws on me." Loraine still, however, wanted an answer to her question, "What is it that she has against me?" It took a long time for another previous relationship between them to surface, but eventually Loraine found a male lifetime in which she had (again!) lost her mother. In fact that time both her parents had left Loraine, then a boy of only about eleven, when they had had to go off and work elsewhere. They promised to return but never did, leaving the young boy to look after his younger sister, and he found the pain of separation so intolerable that he cut off from his feelings – a coping mechanism commonly used by most of us at one time or another. When he was twenty this boy went off to look for his parents at some quarry or mine and, having no luck in finding them, he then worked there himself for a while before being enlisted with some friends to go and fight skirmishes for a Lord. When that job came to an end, he worked on a farm, eventually returning to his own 'village', which consisted of some huts on a cliff face, where he worked with metal. His younger sister, who by then had her own family, never forgave him for having cleared off and, when he was in his forties and had a fatal accident at work, she resented having to care for him during his last three weeks while he lingered on in pain.

In the Bardo after that life the man who was now Loraine regained his feelings and was overjoyed at seeing his parents again. His mother explained that they had been unable to return because of having been moved around a lot, and that she had then fallen sick and died in her thirties. Loraine was rather less pleased with the discovery that the younger sister was now Madge! In my book *Discovering the Life Plan*, I recounted a case of another client of mine with a difficult, over-demanding, mother to whom he felt sure that he must have a big karmic debt, but whose mother we eventually found had in her subconscious greatly exaggerated the debt her son had to her. It seemed to Loraine and myself that the same was true with Madge, although she was told by her guides in a subsequent session that there had been another lifetime in which she had been annoyed by Madge, who was at the time about twelve years old, and had pushed her into a river or over a cliff. The guide told Loraine that because of that she needed to learn patience and compassion with Madge, but personally I feel that she has more than done that a thousand times over!

One of Loraine's most significant past lives was one in which she was a woman who lived as a weaver in a simple village and was married to a wheelwright. They were happy initially, but she was the only real thinker in the whole village and, after she had started speaking her mind about how to improve things locally, her husband threw her out and married someone who he said could be a "proper wife" to him. They had two children, and she moved into a nearby shack, which had no room for a loom. She made a living by dying cloth for people, and also made use of herbs for healing, but all the villagers were against her. When they burnt down her shack, she found it a relief to leave, and she walked and walked, begging for food on the way, eventually ending up in a busy town and getting a job in a convent. There she cooked and wove, and the nuns talked to her and respected her for thinking. It was a long life, which ended probably at the Reformation, because soldiers invaded the convent, running in the garden and wrecking it. Since she could no longer walk, the nuns stuffed her into a cupboard to hide until the soldiers had gone, but she died inside the cupboard.

In the Bardo this time the word 'respect' appeared as important, and Loraine realized that in that lifetime she had eventually gained respect after a difficult start. In her present life Loraine's mother has never respected her and she has consequently had to work hard to gain the respect that she deserves – particularly from herself. After many months of therapy she was doing very well in that domain. Her ex-husband in the weaver's life turned out to be Loraine's present husband, John, and it seems that he is now paying her his debt from that lifetime very well, and that this past life also explains why he is so tolerant of Loraine always putting her mother before him. Following that session she realized that she needed to start giving John more time.

It was coming up to Christmas, which was the first anniversary of when Loraine's father had died, when she told me that, since her mother was determined to be miserable, she was refusing to spend it with them, saying that she would stay on her own in her bungalow up the road. When Loraine told me that this would mean her spending part of Christmas day with her mother rather than her own family, I pointed out that, since it was impossible for her ever to do the right thing for Madge, it might be a good idea to put her family first. So she then gained the strength to give her mother an ultimatum: "Either you come to us or you stay on your own," and in the end Madge went to Loraine's family for about five hours – five hours in which she did nothing but complain.

Relief from the constant worry and burden of caring for her mother eventually came to Loraine in a rather drastic way: she developed breast cancer and had to have a mastectomy. Madge, who had always balked violently at the suggestion of going into a home, consequently had finally no choice but to agree. Owing to my living a long way from the clinic in which I work, Loraine and I were then unable to meet for about ten months. Once she had recovered sufficiently to come for another session, I could hardly believe how well and cheerful she looked following all her treatment! She had had her hair cut and was wearing it in an even more attractive style, her cheeks looked rosy, and all together she seemed to be blooming.

Madge was still as discontent as ever, but the freedom of not having constantly to go to her house and do things for her was giving Loraine the opportunity of having much more life for herself. Issabella was now away at university, her younger daughter Louisa was on a Foundation course and travelling daily to Leeds, which left only her son Ben (who is clearly a very evolved soul) at home. She was consequently finding time for activities with friends, and also doing artistic things again, such as making clothes for Ben, who was unable to find the unusual type of clothes that he liked in the stores. She had also had a lot of help from a therapist who practiced Emotional Freedom Technique, as well as from some hypnotherapy, and had had some muscle testing for deeply held beliefs from a Theta DNA healer.

Loraine was keen to deal with both fear and guilt and, three days after the first session with this Theta DNA healer, Madge had phoned to say that she wanted to apologize for certain things she had done which she now realized were wrong! She even wanted to change her will to favor Loraine more than it did before, but that proved to be impossible since it was then Loraine herself who had the power of attorney. Since then Madge had returned to the "poor me" mode and been increasingly confused and less articulate, but Loraine was really enjoying her freedom from worry, knowing that her mother was being properly cared for in the home. Madge was still telephoning twice a day, but Loraine now felt that she had the choice whether or not to answer. Above all, she felt that she had woken up and begun really to discover herself. Working with a healer on some shoulder pain, she had been given an image of a rusty bolt that would not move. So she had oiled it and knew that the door could theoretically be opened, but was scared of letting in too much light.

When we embarked on the next regression, Loraine wanted to find out how long she had been 'asleep'. I took her gradually back to the womb and she saw that at about twelve or thirteen she had been on the verge of waking up but had not done so because it was too scary. Once she was back in the womb, she felt her intense love for her birth mother, knew that it was mutual and was consequently unable to understand why she was to be given up. So then I took her back a little further, to before she came into her present life, when plans were being made for it, and she saw the circle of people involved very clearly. It was really fascinating!

Loraine's close friend, Eve, who also has an impossible mother, was very much in the center of the circle, and she was the one who suggested the main task for this life: to connect to the universe. Loraine could see that sometimes one chooses a difficult life because such a choice forces one to go inside oneself. She then saw that she and her adoptive father had made the decision to cope with her mother *together*. Her son Ben bounced in full of energy, very strong and powerful, and adamant that he needed Loraine for his mother because of her patience and openness. Eve took Loraine's side, saying that it would be tough for her, but Ben's overwhelming strength won the day, saying also that he needed Madge as his grandmother in order to learn humility and that the struggle would teach him what could be done with difficult people.

Gina, Loraine's birth mother was standing to the side rather than fully in the circle and, when she said that she needed to "do loss" this time round, Loraine volunteered for that. She saw that their past life connection was not particularly strong, but that she did have a strong link with her younger half-sister, Tamsin, with whom she is now close. Her natural father, Peter, was also off to the side, and it was clear that he had strong karma with Gina, to whom he owed a debt. (A debt he has probably yet to pay, in view of how he treated Gina in their present life.) Issabella was very much in the circle, whereas John and Louisa were further out. Madge was not there at all, so the plans were presumably made without her participation. This may well be an indication that she is very much less evolved than the rest of them.

Loraine felt strong in the circle initially, but after being given her assignment she began to feel weak and found that falling asleep was the easiest way of coping. From being in a beautiful sunny field before entering the womb, tiredness gradually overwhelmed her. Once inside, part of her was saying, "Hey, get me out!" but another part was too overwhelmed with lethargy to fight it. When her friend Jane appeared at her side as a man volunteering to help since she knew the real Loraine from when the two of them had been brothers, she asked how to keep awake and was told to "keep trying to open the door." She was also told that there was something "bigger" in store for her to do, but not to worry about it now and to just go with the flow.

Discussing whether she still needed another session, Loraine told me that she was still keen to find out the reason(s) for her cancer. People who suppress their emotions and who put other people before themselves often tend to be cancer victims, but Loraine is someone who always likes to get to the bottom of things, and she thought that another regression might throw further light on what had happened.

However, when we had our next session about three months later, that question no longer seemed to be so important. After all, Loraine now realized, her illness had given her the freedom from caring continually for her mother that she had craved for so long, it had taught her more about healing, and it had helped her to put things into perspective. Issabella was going through a difficult patch and was deferring her university course until the following autumn, and it had been wonderful for Loraine to be free to go and spend a few days with her and give her support with the practical things she was needing to do while seeking temporary work. Loraine said too that she was much less worried about her older daughter than she would have been a few years previously.

There had also been another big development in Loraine's relationship with Madge, who had started questioning why she was in such a bad way "when I've been so good all my life." Loraine felt that the Alzheimer's was taking her mother's ego away to some extent and allowing her soul to come through. She had even – though it did evoke denial – been able to review

Madge's life with her and point out that she had always been a depressed person and consequently not easy to live with. And when Madge was having a big moan about the home she was in, Loraine had told her the truth about the effect that her moaning had on her, explaining that it made her come away depressed and tired. Madge expressed total surprise at this revelation, but she was at least mildly apologetic when Loraine went on to recall how unpleasant it had been for her when, after her father's death, Madge had been really horrible to her. Madge had replied, "Well, you're the only person I can let it out to," which could not make up for the ill treatment Loraine had always received from her mother, but it indicated huge progress for Loraine, who had never previously been able to speak her mind to her mother. My hope is that helping her finally to face facts about the way she has lived her life will go at least a little way towards Madge's recovery for future lifetimes, and I would even venture to suggest that Loraine, as an advanced soul, actually volunteered before she came in this time to be Madge's daughter partly to help her.

Another advance was that, in her meditations, Loraine had finally opened the door! She has to be still and upright for an hour after taking her bone pill, and so uses that time for meditation and healing (visualizing her body rejecting the cancer cells). She has found that there is the most wonderful light the other side of the door. At first it was difficult for her to cope with its intensity, but then it gradually became less intense with more and more things coming into focus.

This progress led to Loraine and myself agreeing that she did not need another session, and it was interesting that with the last regression that we did she came full circle! Right at the beginning of her treatment she had found herself in a past life in which she was being chased by vicious dogs, but her fear that time was so intense that she found herself unable to proceed with it. So over the next months we moved on to other things, but now her subconscious had obviously decided that she was ready to deal with that particular trauma. In Deep Memory Process therapy we work as often as not from the body, and on this occasion the trigger for the regression was a pain in Loraine's back that went round to her side and front as well. The lifetime turned out to be that of a slave (probably in America), whose death was caused by dogs when he attempted to escape. Loraine saw herself being chased by a white slave master as well as by his dogs, who grabbed and mauled her (then him) severely in the exact spots where she had recently been getting the pain. This pain subsided following that regression.

When I took her back to an earlier point in that lifetime, Loraine found herself as a young boy playing happily in a village by the sea in Africa. When she went home, she saw that the family included a baby and three older siblings, and she felt a very strong love for her mother. So at last here was a lifetime in which – at least for some years – she had had a mother! When I took her into the Bardo after the slave's death and she was able to meet that mother again, Loraine recognized her as an old friend from Art College in her present life. She then felt the strength of mother love and appreciated that this had helped her with the bonding with her own children. One can also say that Madge has given her a very good example of how *not* to be a mother, so that is no doubt another aspect of Loraine's learning this time round.

Loraine says too that, following all the therapy she has had, her mother no longer has the same power over her. When we first met, she always felt compelled to answer every telephone call that Madge made, but now that compulsion has gone. Also, now that Madge is becoming increasingly confused and Loraine has become stronger, Madge is more open to Loraine's point of view and she feels that they are at last beginning to find one another. Interestingly, whenever Loraine has felt a shift in herself, she has also noticed a slight change for the better in her mother. She told me that she now at times actually sees a *person* underneath the ego and that this is helping her to like her. Loraine also feels that she has "DONE IT with it her now and is into ME TIME."

The last time that we met Gina was coming up to eighty and they were planning a celebration with the whole family – the first since all of Loraine's children had come to know who she was. (Loraine had told them one by one, once each one was old enough for her to feel confident that they would not spill the beans to Madge.) Tamsin and Loraine are, as I said previously, very close, and Tamsin, who married in her thirties and is very career minded, has no children. Her half-brother Will, who is happily married with two teenage sons, and Loraine are also close.

I have no fears at all for Loraine, and I hope and pray that Madge will be able to see things from a higher perspective once her life has ended, and come to appreciate what her adopted daughter endured and all that she did for her as both carer and teacher.

Note

1. I particularly recommend the books of John Bradshaw, for instance *Home Coming – Reclaiming and Championing your Inner Child*, 1990, USA and Canada, Bantam Books.

CHAPTER TWENTY

NATALIE'S STORY

A threefold cord shall not be broken.
Ecclesiastes 4:9 - 12

Natalie is American and an email friend of mine, having got in touch through taking an interest in my previous books, especially the one on twin souls. (She has been interested in spiritual matters for many years and believes her parents to have been twin souls.) Here is most of her story in her own words:

I was an only child. My parents had married later in life than is usual, in terms of starting a family, especially in the 1950s. It was my father Richard's second marriage, and he already had another daughter, who was eleven when I was born. He was South African, and my mother was from Texas originally, but had moved to California by the time she met my father. In the meantime, my father had moved to East Africa, but he traveled all over the world for his work. He did not get to see his daughter often, due to his work, and her mother and stepfather raising her, but he was conscientious in contributing to her upbringing and helping to pay for the boarding school where her mother sent her.

My parents' relationship had a very romantic and unlikely beginning. They met in 1952 on a Pan American Airlines Stratocruiser [she even sent me a picture of the plane, which later became obsolete because of being so expensive!]. My father noticed her at the New York airport while they were waiting for their flight to Rio de Janeiro, Brazil. This luxurious flight was not a pleasure trip for either of them, but was work-related and paid for by their bosses at their individual companies. My father was a mining engineer who worked for R.G. Letourneau (later merged with Westinghouse), and Vivian, my mother, worked as an administrative assistant for Encyclopedia Britannica. They had both been told by their bosses that they were to sleep all night in the sleeping berths reserved for them, so that they could hit the ground running when they got to Brazil and begin work immediately.

This was my mother's first flight, whereas my father had flown many times for his work. She was seated on the outside, next to someone who had a large newspaper in the window opening, and she kept craning her neck to get a look out of the window. My father was behind her, and he offered her his seat, but she said thank you, but no. A bit later he went to the smoking lounge, and so she took advantage of the empty seat to go to his window and look out. When he came back, he said, "Look, I've flown many times, and I really would appreciate it if you kept the window seat so you can see out." This time she agreed, and they ended up talking all night. Each time that the steward came and asked, "Madam, Sir, are you ready for your berth to be prepared?" they replied, "A bit later, thank you," and kept on talking. When they got to Rio de Janeiro, my mother felt shy about giving him the name of her hotel and so my father ended up calling every hotel that seemed likely until he finally located her and was able to leave a message. In the meantime, my mother could not forget him, and was wishing she could find him again. She went out for dinner with her boss and his wife, and when she came back, there were nine written messages left for her from my father. The rest of their trip, between their work, they spent every night together, dancing on the beach to the big bands that played at the different hotels. They became engaged within a year, and were married in 1955.

The first three years of their married life they lived in East Africa together, then my father's work territory was changed from East and West Africa to South and Central America. They tried to have a child, but my mother miscarried and was very ill, and it was clear that she was going to be unable to have a child biologically. This was around 1958 and by 1959, when they were living Buenos Aires, they had decided to adopt. They thought about adopting through the States, but at that time American Social Services discriminated against older parents for adoption. They did not want to adopt in Argentina, because they had just changed their adoption laws so that the biological parents had complete rights of accessibility and the adoptive parents had very few. In other words, biological parents could try to reclaim their child, or come back into their child's life without the adoptive parents having much choice or rights.

My parents then began looking into other countries, and in one case were turned away for not being Catholics. They engaged an attorney and began looking into adopting from Costa Rica, but then a good friend through my father's work, Edward, who was Chilean, suggested that they try Chile, as their laws were more protective of adoptive parents than Argentina's. My father had a lot of intuition, and all his life he followed what he called his "tummy feelings." This got him out of danger several times, and probably saved his life on several occasions when he was in countries with political unrest. He was in the midst of one or two revolutions and had some wonderful stories to tell as I was growing up. So on this occasion he got a strong sense that his friend's suggestion needed to be acted on. My mother told me that the night when they were talking over dinner and he said that he really felt they should pursue finding a child in Chile rather than continuing with Costa Rica, she looked at him and thought to herself, "You're so handsome. I love you so much, I'll do whatever you want with this."

My "Uncle Edward," as I called him, found out through his secretary Adela, about a young woman who was pregnant and needed to find a good adoptive home for her baby, as the father had abandoned her and they were not married. Mercedes, my biological mother, went to live in a convent in Santiago, and was taken care of by nuns there. My adoptive mother went to visit the convent and talk to the nuns. She did not meet my birth mother directly, but she did learn more about her, and she provided things that Mercedes needed such as clothes. The nuns had met my biological father, as apparently he had visited my birth mother there, and they said he was *"muy guapo"* (very handsome). There was another American family waiting to adopt a Chilean baby, and the agreement was that if I was a boy, this other family would adopt me, and if I was a girl, my parents would. Paperwork was done in readiness for when I was born, and my "Uncle Edward" told my parents he would make all the arrangements for my care, and contact them as soon as the birth took place.

I was born at dusk, *"l'heure bleue,"* which to this time remains my favorite time of day. At that time in Chile there was a very big storm sweeping through the Andes, and the telephone lines were down. Uncle Edward could not get through to my parents for a whole week. When he was finally able to call them, my father was in the US on a work trip, but my mother was home. He said to her, "Hello, Mama!" and that is how she knew that I was born, and that I was a girl. My father was in the United States at the company headquarters, and was very excited when she called him with the news. My mother told me that on the day she got the news, her maid showed her a potted plant that was outside on the windowsill, exclaiming ecstatically, "Look, Señora." In spite of the weather being very cold and wintry, the plant had unexpectedly blossomed with one little white flower. My mother said she felt it was a sign and a miracle."

A few days after the birth, "Uncle Edward" set up a hotel suite in Santiago, with a hired nurse, until Vivian could come from Buenos Aires and get Natalie. When the call came, Richard was in the United States for work, and it took Vivian another week to arrange the flight and get some supplies rounded up, so by the time she arrived in Santiago Natalie was two weeks old.

Then Richard flew to the hotel in Santiago to join his wife and new daughter, and the couple stayed there for about a month. When they took Natalie back to Buenos Aires, the airline company spread a red carpet on the stairs of the plane in celebration, and gave Natalie a brooch in the shape of wings! Uncle Edward's secretary, Adela, was asked to be the baby's godmother and she kept in touch with the birth mother. Mercedes was told when Natalie was born that she could still change her mind about giving the child up, and she had two or three days with Natalie in the convent after she was born, but they heard through Adela that Mercedes had said that she could not give her daughter a good life and wanted her to have the opportunity of a better one.

Natalie has told me that she never felt any desire to trace her birth parents. She says, "I have the name of my mother in a family bible, but not my father's. As I was so small when I left South America and grew up mostly overseas in Europe and Turkey, I have not felt much connection with my birth parents. Also, I have wondered if they survived those very hard years when Pinochet was in power, as so many people died during that time. I pray that my mother did not suffer, and am grateful to her that she made a loving and selfless gesture to give me a new life with my parents."

Natalie further told me that her biological mother was from the South of Chile where they had recently suffered severe earthquakes and famine and she had consequently moved to Santiago. She says, "My understanding is that my father was Chilean also, but I do not know his name. They seem to have been a couple, but when my mother got pregnant I think he abandoned her and did not take responsibility. I don't know anything about either of their lives since Mercedes' time in the convent. Adela, my godmother, knew of my birth mother's situation, and visited her subsequently and took her clothes and gifts that my adoptive mother sent, but then we did not hear back from Adela after the late 1960s and we were afraid that something might have happened to her during Pinochet's regime."

Natalie has a friend called Maria, who runs a wellness center and teaches Reiki classes (www.inwellso.com), and a few years ago Natalie had an interesting experience. One of Maria's students at the time was a lady from Chile and, she says, "Maria said I had to meet her because she was 'ultraperceptive', so I came one day and did so. The lady took one look at me and gave me a big hug and clasped me to her with a volley of Spanish, and Maria, who is of Puerto Rican ancestry, translated for her. The lady said that my people were from the South of Chile from a certain region, and that they were of Germanic and Spanish heritage. I had told her nothing at all and Maria had only shared that I was born in Chile and adopted. Since she knew nothing else about me, I have always remembered that remarkable experience.

When I asked Natalie about childhood problems that she had worked through, she replied, "I would say the main thing that I dealt with was some abandonment issues that I've struggled with at times. It's been very hard to let go of those I've loved, and release them, and say goodbye. Even though I know rationally that I was loved by both my birth mother and my adoptive parents, those two weeks in transition I feel had an effect, that time during which my adoptive mother was unable to get to me. I am sure I was well taken care of by the nurse, but I think it may have impacted me emotionally. Now that I am myself a therapist for children and have studied child development extensively, I know those first few weeks of development to be extremely important."

Natalie married when she was in her twenties, and it lasted until she was in her forties, when she became more absorbed both in her work and in her spiritual path. She completely shares my view that being adopted by Richard and Vivian was in her Life Plan, and she also believes herself to have stronger spiritual links with them than with her birth parents. She says, "My father and mother (who have both died) were of my soul group. I did not know this growing up, but when I was an adult, after my father died, it all began coming together for me. What became clear early on was that there was a pattern and a destiny, and both my parents and I felt that we were meant to be together." Natalie explained to me that she feels herself and her parents to be "spiritually connected as a soul group" rather than having a karmic attachment. She says, "The experience that brought this most strongly to my understanding was a type of 'vision' I had within a few minutes of my mother passing. I had gotten the call and then shortly after that, it was as though I 'saw' (I'm still not sure if it was inner eye or with full eyes) the spirit figures of my parents before me. They were in spirit form and tall golden beings, with faces and somewhat human-like forms but much more long and tall. Although they did not have their earthly features to identify them, I somehow knew that it was the two of them. I was then told, "You are the last of the Clan of Three," and they told me that it had been agreed and decided upon that we would all come together and that I would be the final one to stay behind and continue the work, and that they would be watching over me."

In conclusion Natalie comments that it was her father who was largely instrumental in her adoption, since her mother had wanted to pursue a different avenue through Costa Rica, and they were already working with an attorney there. Despite that, when her father heard from his friend and co-worker, Edward, about Chile being a possible option, he went with this inner guidance to pursue that. She says, "So I know for certain that my life was planned beforehand and, though I now miss my parents greatly, I am grateful for the life that we had together and know that we shall meet again eventually."

CHAPTER TWENTY-ONE

MARK'S STORY

They fuck you up, your mum and dad.
They do not mean to, but they do.
They fill you with the faults they had
And add some extra, just for you…

Man hands on misery to man,
It deepens like a coastal shelf.
Get out as early as you can,
And don't have any kids yourself.
Philip Larkin – 'This Be The Verse'

Mark had in his behavior always been what I now regard as a 'typical adoptee': a very angry young man – fairly young anyway, being in his thirties when he came to me for therapy in Hull some years ago. He had been adopted as a baby, and his older brother, Peter, who was also adopted, was two years old when Mark joined the family, and very protective of him right from the outset. (His mother told Mark later how she had on occasion found Peter dragging the carrycot into his own room!) Mark was the brighter of the two and had, after leaving school at sixteen and running wild for some time, obtained a First Class degree in Psychology, while Peter, whose marriage had recently failed, was struggling both to hold down manual jobs and to maintain a relationship with his two children. This was a big change from their school days, when Peter had been labelled the "good one" and Mark the "bad one," but Mark, who had made a special study of adoption issues while doing his degree, now appreciated that he had always acted out his problems while Peter had suppressed them, which Mark now saw as even more of a problem.

Mark's parents were oddly matched – he described it as "two railway tracks running along side by side but never meeting" – and they ultimately divorced when Mark was in his twenties, following his father's three-year affair with another woman. Before that he went through the classic 'adoption pattern' of lying, stealing, failing to concentrate on school work and being seemingly incapable of realizing his potential. After failing most of his exams, he did odd jobs and got on to soft drugs "because of being in with a crowd where I felt I belonged simply because none of them knew who they were or what they were supposed to be doing." He then travelled the world for a year or two, but decided to come back to England when he realized that he couldn't run away from himself – a realization that some, perhaps less intelligent people, never make! When we met he was in a teaching job, but not finding it at all fulfilling.

Mark was initially the only other member of the family who knew about his father's affair, which was very hard for him. However, despite never having got on with his mother throughout his childhood, he was able to be a good support to her after she was left shattered by his father's departure. He explained that he empathized with her feelings of rejection and that this had brought the two of them a lot closer. Both his parents were teachers, his mother working in the primary school that he and Peter went to, so that when young he had felt himself "to be at school twenty-four hours a day." He said that when he was a child his father was always buried behind a newspaper, but that now that he had a new wife, who was a much better match than his mother had ever been, he got on with him a great deal better. In his childhood the person to whom he was closest was his grandmother who had been widowed when his mother was only eight months old and had subsequently never looked at another man. She lived to 97 and Mark still missed her.

In our first session we endeavored to trace the root of Mark's anger, which he believed himself to have been born with. I took him back to the womb step by step and on the way we paused for a while at age nine, when he and his family were having his first holiday abroad, in Norway. Of this he had mainly happy memories, as it was an unthreatening situation, with his parents being good friends, and he loved the scenery and cleanness of the atmosphere, the new experiences and playing with two other children as well as his brother. Yet even here he soon began to voice a sense of fear – a fear that had "always been there," through all his bones, and was also "intertwined with sadness." When I asked him what the fear would say if it could speak, the reply was "It's stronger than you are." He realized at that point that he was angry about life and that, because of that he could make himself "as remote as the Norwegian mountains."

A few steps further back and Mark was in the womb. There the sense of "something awful being about to happen" was very strong indeed. He knew that his mother had decided to give him up but could not understand why, and the baby's voice found adult words: "I'm about to be separated from my environment. I don't want to be left!" Then I asked him to go back to a previous life in which he had had those same feelings of abandonment and isolation, and he found himself being wounded at an early age in the First World War, furious at "the futility of it all" and at being himself cheated of life. His friends had all been killed already, he himself died from his wounds not long afterwards, and he had brought his anger through into this life as Mark.

To help him let go of the anger, I got him after crossing over into the Bardo to look for his soldier friends who had been killed before he was. They were by now without exception much less angry than Mark was and coming to an understanding of the reasons for their having had short lives. We then asked for the people who were going to be the most important in his forthcoming life as Mark to gather round so that he could look into his Life Plan. From this he quickly identified his beloved grandmother as one of the friends who had been killed before him in the First World War. Both his parents were also old friends, and he found that he and his mother were agreeing to come together "to resolve animosities between us." (Mark had incidentally never yet wanted to try to trace his birth parents.) In the Bardo he had good feelings about his father, with whom he saw that he was planning to get closer, though his purpose this time round was to be less dependent on his father than he had been in previous incarnations. It looked likely that he and his brother had been brothers before, and it appeared that the Plan was for Peter to look after him when he was young and for the roles to be reversed when they got older. Though the profession at which he would be best was not made clear at this point, he was told that his life purpose was "to be a shining light."

It seemed likely that Mark's anger went back further than the First World War and, when we did another regression, he found himself in the dungeon of a Spanish castle. Again he had (as in the womb in his present life) a sensation of being "in the wrong place" and not quite knowing why. Further exploration revealed him to have been a medieval soldier, previously much in the favor of the lord of the castle and engaged to be married to the lord's daughter. He had obviously been thrown into the dungeon when "something went wrong," and he had good cause for being angry. When we explored what had gone wrong, it transpired that he had been caught in bed with his fiancée, which to her father, the lord of the castle, was unforgivable. Again my research shows this to be a typical scenario for an adoptee; he or she has good reason for feeling rejected and angry in their present life, but the anger stems in addition from experiences in previous lives.

The Spanish life had an interesting twist to it because Mark recognized the lord of the castle as a man with whom he had been very good friends, but who had recently turned against him after moving away into an unsuccessful marriage. This friend now felt himself to be stuck, unable to buy himself a new home of his own, yet when Mark, who had foreseen the disaster, encouraged him to leave anyway, they had a big row, which dug deep into Mark's feelings of rejection, emphasizing these still further.

In another session we did some 'soul retrieval' – something from which I am sure many adopted people could benefit. It is important to note that there is a big difference between 'soul retrieval' and 'soul rescue' work. I practice the latter on my own at home and it consists of helping souls who are stuck on the Earth's plane to cross over. This is well explained in one of my previous books, *Delayed Departure – A Beginner's Guide to Soul Rescue.* 'Soul retrieval', on the other hand, is completely different from 'soul rescue' since it consists of retrieving *part(s)* of a client's soul that split off when some trauma occurred, either in their present or a previous life. The big name in this work is Sandra Ingerman, but I know that many therapists now incorporate it into their practice. Mark on one occasion described himself as being like "a cake with one slice missing," and, when I prompted him to find a power animal who could go off on a search for the missing slice, the animal that appeared was a dog. The dog led him to the lovely spot in Norway where he had had childhood holidays, and where he could sense the presence of his spirit guides even though he was unable to see them. It then set off on its own, returning promptly with a boy whom Mark recognized as his twelve-year-old self. I asked him to give the boy a hug and then ask whether there was anything he was afraid of. The initial reply was "A lot," and then this was gradually whittled down to "I'm afraid of being myself." So we did a bit of work on that.

Sometimes, I am glad to say, Deep Memory Process therapy can, with time and perseverance, enable people to work through their anger and let go of it, but sadly in Mark's case there was insufficient time before I moved away from the area. I urged him to keep in touch – or even to come for further sessions with me in either Ripon or Shropshire – but alas he did not so. It may be that he has now dealt with it satisfactorily, but there remains in my mind a fear that the anger was too deep seated for him to feel ready finally to deal with it this time round. At least I can hope that our sessions will have done something to prepare him for dealing with his anger in the not too distant future.

Mark when we got to know each other was in a relationship with a lovely Portuguese girl, whom he had met when on a training course in Portugal. Lidia was a few years his junior and they sincerely believed themselves to be soul mates of some sort.[1] She, however, was badly missing her family and also feeling frustrated at not being able to get any work in the Hull area apart from cleaning. Another real problem for the couple was Mark's inability to settle in a career that he felt to be intellectually satisfying for him. Despite the very deep love they felt for one another, and their shared interests in spiritual subjects, the relationship was very tempestuous, and I was never confident that it would last. Lidia also came to me for just one session, when she was trying desperately to decide whether to stay with her partner or return home to her family and the promise of more fulfilling work, but, much though I empathized with her situation, no conclusion was reached at that time. We did, however, find a past life in which she and Mark had been together before very happily, so I am quite sure that that will happen again at some point. In the meantime I hope and pray that they will both find ways of putting their very real gifts to good use.

Note

1. See my book *Souls United – The Power of Divine Connection*, Llewellyn Worldwide, USA, 2009.

CHAPTER TWENTY-TWO

THREE SIBLINGS' STORIES

Adopted children are self-invented because we have to be; there is an absence, a void, a question mark at the very beginning of our lives. A crucial part of our story is gone, and violently, like a bomb in the womb.
Jeanette Winterson – *Why Be Happy When You Could be Normal?*

Although the main focus of this book is people who were adopted or fostered and all the parents, siblings are also an important element of the full picture and should not be forgotten. Having a brother or sister who is not closely related by blood can never be the same, however well integrated into the family the additional member has become. I preferred to let my own children give their own point of view, and recount their personal experiences themselves, but this brief chapter is devoted to three, very varied, stories, given to me by three, totally different people of my acquaintance.

Siobahn is a therapist, who was the eldest of a Catholic family of five. Like myself, she has come to believe in reincarnation and the fact that families are planned in advance on the other side, though she has not yet had reason to find out about the nature of her karmic links with any of the other members of her family. Yet her story is a rather curious, and I'm sure very unusual, one, which shows not only how we hold our Life Plan in our subconscious, but also how it – or a bit of it – sometimes leaks through into the conscious mind.

After Siobahn had been born, Moira, her mother, declared that she knew that she would only conceive girls and so, since she very much wanted a boy as well, their next child should be adopted. Her husband – perhaps surprisingly since the couple were quite fertile and there had been no particular problems with the first pregnancy and birth – agreed, and there was at the time in Ireland no shortage of Catholic babies needing new homes. So little Dermot was adopted when Siobahn was still a toddler and, after he had himself stepped into the toddler shoes, Moira did indeed successively give birth to another three girls! Siobahn told me that in adulthood the family was still well united and that, although Dermot had exhibited a few 'normal' problems that are common among adoptees, he had grown up well and was for her fully a real brother.

The same is not alas true for Phyllida, who is in effect an only child. When she was still quite young, Audrey, her mother, was working in a children's home and she became particularly attached to a three-year-old boy named Declan. Phyllida does not share my belief system and so the notion that Audrey and Declan had a strong karmic link would be foreign to her, but to my mind the fact that her mother felt such a strong desire to adopt the child indicates that coming together was part of both their Life Plans. With Phyllida's father's agreement, an application for adoption was made, and Declan joined the family when Phyllida was seven years old. Seven can be a tricky age in any circumstances for a child suddenly to cease being the sole center of her parents' attention, but for Phyllida the difficulties were compounded by her younger brother not being a lovely little baby whose nappies she could learn to help change and so on, but rather a child with numerous behavioral problems caused inevitably by his difficult background.

Phyllida says nevertheless that, although many things that Declan did, such as steal her sweets and take her parents' attention away from her from time to time, she doesn't recall ever being seriously resentful of his presence in the family. At seven she was fully able to understand her parents' explanation of Declan's problems, but that did not of course make growing up with him easy for her. In later life, despite the family doing all they could to help him, Declan got into various bits of trouble – again none of which were abnormal for an adopted child, especially one who had spent his earliest years in a children's home – and the sad end to this little tale is that Phyllida no longer has any contact with Declan and doesn't even know where he is. The fact that both her parents are now dead obviously does nothing to help her to resume contact. She herself now has a full life, with a supportive partner and a job that she enjoys, but the question mark about Declan's fate can never completely leave the back of her mind. Her story is by no means unique – I have a friend whose blood brother has lost touch with all four of his sisters – and one has to face up to such things as facts of life. Where belief in reincarnation and understanding of adopted people's problems help is that they give assurance that no soul is ever really 'lost' and that someone who has been overwhelmed by difficulties in one life will learn from them in preparation for a much happier and rewarding life on Earth another time.

Maisie's story is different again. She too was an only child, but she found out some time after both her parents had died that she had an older half-sister. Hazel had been born out of wedlock in the days when illegitimacy still entailed enormous stigma, and so Emma, Maisie's mother, had had Hazel adopted at birth. She never breathed a word about this to Maisie, who does not even know whether her father knew about it, and so, when Hazel suddenly got in touch with her completely out of the blue, she was initially very reluctant to believe the story. She nevertheless agreed to meet Hazel, and doing so forced her to accept what she had been told. "Quite apart from anything else," Maisie told me, "Hazel looks even more like my mother than I do. Besides, the more I thought about it, the more it seemed to explain so much of my mother's behavior that had often seemed strange to me." Maisie went on to say that her father had been a wonderful man, and a wonderful husband and father, but that, despite her parents' apparent devotion to one another, Emma had always been prone to bouts of depression and impenetrable gloom which had no apparent cause. Maisie had also always found it easier to communicate intimately with her father than with her mother.

We saw in the Birth Mothers section of this book, and in my own family's story, how difficult or impossible it is for a woman ever to get over giving a child up for adoption, so what Maisie told me about her mother did not surprise me at all. Fortunately what happened in the now distant past appears to have had no ill effect on Maisie herself, who had a happy childhood and has since led a full and successful life. She married a man considerably older than herself and is now sadly a widow, but she says that the marriage was a blissfully happy one and, rather than focusing on her loss, she treasures the many good memories of her life with Peter and, now in retirement, devotes a great deal of her time to helping other people in the Christian community in which she is involved. She says that her only real problem at the moment is her sister Hazel, whom she finds difficult to like, yet towards whom she feels obliged to be sisterly.

It seems that Hazel's adoption was never a happy one, and the adoptive parents, like Maisie's, are both long dead. She has never married, never found any motivating force to make her life seem worthwhile, and is consequently extremely envious of Maisie, whom she feels to have had everything of which she herself was deprived. It was only very late in life that Hazel decided to try to trace her birth parents, but her hopes of finding a ready-made family to which to belong were quickly shattered. Emma was already dead when Hazel traced her and, since the surname on her original birth certificate was her mother's, she had no way of finding out who her natural father had been. Besides, since Maisie is, as I said, now a widow and since she had no children, Maisie is quite literally Hazel's only family. Now that she has got over the shock of discovering that she has an older half-sister,

Maisie feels sorry for Hazel and, good Christian that she is, she never denies her a meeting so long as she is available, but the relationship is far from easy. Those who appreciate the fact that everyone from time to time has lifetimes whose purpose is to learn to stand on their own – as well as lifetimes which give them a great opportunity for showing compassion – will not see either Maisie's or Hazel's 'problem' as something which should have been avoided. But for those whom the Churches have brain-washed into disbelief in multiple lives and 'Heaven-made Plans', such difficulties tend to be less easy to accept.

CHAPTER TWENTY-THREE

'ADOPTED' TWICE OVER!

Amanda's Story

The search for the lost father runs through much of modern literature. The father may have disappeared for a myriad of reasons: divorce, illness, desertion, death. The child who grows up without the father who gave him life will feel abandoned and unprotected in the world.

Betty Jean Lifton, *Journey of the Adopted Self – A Quest for Wholeness*

Iptisam was terrified; she was all alone in a dark cave and it felt like hours and hours since her father had hurriedly carried her there on his shoulders. She was only a toddler and so it was hard for her to understand everything that was said, but she was sure that her father had promised he'd be coming back for her very soon. Now it was obviously morning and she was having trouble breathing. She was also thirsty and she thought she could hear running water outside the cave. So she crept out and drank greedily until she could drink no more. The hills all around were bare, it was hot, and oh, how desperately alone she felt! She decided to try to run home, but before she'd got very far someone she didn't know picked her up, carried her to a tent where there were some other children, and gave her something to eat. Everyone seemed to be talking gibberish, but after a little while she came across a boy a bit older than her who spoke her language. That was a bit of a relief, but she still didn't know where she was, or why.

A year later she was living in the same area, no longer in a tent, but in a little square house, and Hassan, the older boy who spoke her language was living there as well, along with a man, a woman and an older woman. The grandmother figure was teaching her to spin wool and she was slowly learning to speak the 'gibberish' that they all spoke around there, at the same time as improving her own language with Hassan's help . She asked the grandmother, "Why am I here? Where are my parents? I'm sure Daddy said he was going to come and fetch me home from that horrid cave!" The gentle, kindly reply was "There was a terrible earthquake in your village and I'm afraid your parents and just about everyone else there got killed. So Allah's looking after them all now. Everyone's fine, and you were lucky that your father took you to safety. Now we're lucky too that both you and Hassan are in our family! You see my son and his wife hadn't got any children of their own and so they were really happy to adopt you both."

Iptisam had a good think to herself. It was sad to lose your parents and she missed them badly, but her new parents were very good to her and Hassan was a nice person to have as an older brother. He seemed to understand her perfectly and he didn't bully or tease like so many boys his age did. She was getting quite used to the new environment, which was hot and sandy like her own, and the people weren't too different either, even though they spoke a different tongue.

After another five years had passed, Hassan was old enough to go off to the hills looking after the sheep. As for Iptisam herself, she had now learnt to speak the new language very well and to bake bread with 'Mummy'. Sometimes she was sent to pick up things in the village for the family and she was learning to dye wool as well. Soon she also learnt to weave. Life was peaceful and she was content.

When she got to fourteen, her adoptive parents told Iptisam that she was now grown up and so could get engaged to be married to a boy in the village. It was exciting! She didn't know Abdul very well yet, but they would meet at family events when everyone was there. He was seventeen, lived with his family, and his mother was a healer. Everyone was very happy about the engagement, which would last a year, and now for the engagement celebration she was wearing red with her hair bound up in a hat. She did indeed feel very grown up!

The wedding day was really wonderful. The whole village was involved because it wasn't only Iptisam and Abdul getting married, but lots of couples. An auspicious day was always chosen for this annual event, and it was Iptisam's mother-in-law to be who was responsible for working out which was the right day for the ceremony. Everyone in the village helped with the cooking and everything else to do with the marriages. Each couple wore the same, unique color, and she and Abdul were both wearing a beautiful shade of deep blue. After the wedding ceremony was over, there was dancing, feasting and lots of music. Iptisam and Abdul felt really happy and were looking forward to spending the rest of their lives together.

Abdul was a cobbler by trade; he made beautiful shoes from animal skins. He had an older brother who was already married with one child, and two younger sisters. The family had built an extra room onto their home for the newly-weds, and Abdul's mother had promised to teach Iptisam her healing skills. Iptisam learnt well and she found it very satisfying being able to help people who were sick. Before two years were up, however, she had had a baby boy and so the new family needed a home of their own. The community helped to build them a house, and Abdul and Iptisam gave them goods in exchange for the work and the materials. By the time another five years had passed the couple had three children – a second son followed by a daughter – and so they needed to build another room onto their house. Again the community helped with this.

Then great sadness fell upon the family: Iptisam's adoptive mother fell seriously ill. Iptisam helped to look after her until she died, even though she was also now working as the village midwife besides looking after her own family. But Abdul, who was a really good, kind man, gave her much support. He was also very skilled and made all sorts of wonderful things with his animal hides. The three children grew up nicely and brought the couple much joy. One son went into his father's trade, while the other became a shepherd like Hassan, Iptisam's adopted brother, who was also never very far away.

When the daughter became engaged, another great sadness fell upon the family. Iptisam, who was not yet even approaching forty but feeling a lot older than her years, fell seriously ill with chest trouble. So now it was her turn to be cared for, and she felt thankful to have a wonderful daughter to do this, sad though she was to be leaving Abdul and the rest of her family. The whole village were very upset at her dying, and they lovingly gave her a very beautiful funeral.

After watching her funeral, Iptisam floated up to a wonderful, peaceful place, where she was overjoyed to meet "all my people." She was told that it had been necessary for her to leave that life early in order to enable her family to take a different direction. She met both her birth parents, and her father explained to her that he had realized that an earthquake was coming when he saw all the animals fleeing the area. So he had carried her to the safety of the cave before going off to look for a safe place for them all to live in, but then the earthquake had come too fast for him and Iptisam's mother to be saved. She was absolutely overjoyed to see them both again, and she also realized that her lesson from the life that had just finished was that "I am capable and spirit goes on forever."

Amanda (previously Iptisam) then opened her eyes. She was lying on the floor in the Ripon Natural Health Centre and I, as her therapist, was congratulating her on such a successful first regression. Amanda had not had an easy life this time round either, and it was a desire to get to the bottom of her constant feeling of "being with and yet not with" that had brought her to come to see me for a Deep Memory Process therapy session. Born early in 1945 and the fruit of a "wartime liaison," her single mother had brought up her up on her own, and Amanda herself had since been widowed twice over. Both her parents had been working in the Army when they had had the affair, and she had never met her father, who was already married with three sons.

Although originally Jewish, Amanda's mother had converted to Christianity in adulthood and she brought her daughter up Presbyterian. Yet Amanda herself, even at a very early age, had had memories of what she describes as "things that are not of this life." In adulthood she moved away from Presbyterianism towards a more spiritually oriented philosophy that incorporated belief in reincarnation, at the same time as going into caring professions. At seventeen she moved from Scotland to Yorkshire, where she started off working as a nanny and then trained as a nurse. Nursing was something that she was able to continue with off and on for fifteen years at the same time as bringing up two children from her first marriage. She married at nineteen, but Neil sadly developed multiple sclerosis when she was first pregnant, and he died some years later. Stephen her second husband, then died in 2009, two years after suffering a major stroke.

Amanda's mother worked as a cook and in catering management until she was in her seventies. They were always close right up until her death and, when she met her mother in the Bardo, Amanda recognized her as having been her birth mother too when she was Iptisam somewhere in the Middle East. She also immediately recognized Iptisam's birth father as Neil, her first husband, and she saw that her second husband, Stephen, had been Iptisam's husband. Hassan she recognized as someone who has been part of her life as a soul friend for the past seven years, and she recognized Iptisam's brother-in-law, her husband Abdul's older brother, as David, now Amanda's close friend of forty years, whom she has always regarded as her 'soul brother'.

Amanda's grandparents had been close to her too and, although they occasionally 'took it out' on her mother for having had an illegitimate child, they were always kindly towards Amanda herself. In the Bardo she recognized Iptisam's adoptive grandmother as the same soul as Amanda's natural grandmother in her present life. Sadly this grandmother died when Amanda was only about seven, but she told me that she had taught her to knit, sew and so on. This was interesting since she was clearly the same soul as had taught Iptisam to dye wool and weave. Perhaps more interestingly still, Amanda saw that Iptisam's adoptive parents were in her present life the doctor and his wife who had as good as 'adopted' her when her mother was working for them for ten years when Amanda was a little girl! She still felt an immense fondness for them.

"Yes," Amanda commented to me at the end of the session, "learning that 'I am capable and that spirit goes on forever' is my big lesson for this life too!" After her first husband's death, Amanda had given up nursing and worked for the elderly with Social Services. Early retirement had enabled her to undergo therapy training, and she had then worked for quite some time as a counsellor with families who had suffered abuse. Now that she had gone past normal retirement age, and that her children and three grandchildren were all living in London, she felt ready to move further north again. While still of course missing both her deceased husbands, she was very self-sufficient and not seeking a further relationship.

She further told me that she had spent a lot of her life waiting and thought that she maybe overdid the patience. Although she had never intended to remain in Leeds for so long, her present house had now been on the market for three years and she wondered whether her feeling of being "close to but not there" was possibly blocking the sale. She has always wished that her mother had told her more about her father, who must now be long dead (especially since she knew that he was rather older than her mother), but she felt confident that communication between them would soon begin. Although it must be perfectly normal for an illegitimate, fatherless child to feel something of an 'outsider', Amanda had always suspected that there was "something deeper" to it as well. The regression that we did showed her to be right there, and hopefully she will now be able completely to let go of her feelings of 'not belonging'. Hopefully too her house sale will shortly go through and she will find a new one to buy in a place where she can feel more at home. However, she says cheerily, "If it doesn't work out, I can always just move back to Leeds, where I have a number of good friends, and my family will always come and visit me wherever I am."

CHAPTER TWENTY-FOUR

ADOPTION WITHIN THE FAMILY

Ushma's Story

> *Family is the most important functional unit in the world. If the family is running on sound lines, the world will also run smoothly. If the unity among the family members suffers even to a small extent, the world will face the repercussions. Every family should strive for achieving unity and harmonious relationship among its members. There is nothing that cannot be achieved with unity.*
> Sathya Sai Baba – Discourse

Adoption within the family was no doubt much more common in the past than it is now, and I am sure that it is also more common in countries such as India than it is in Britain and the rest of Western Europe. Certainly in this country I think it would have always been much more likely to happen in cases of an unintended pregnancy. One hears of children who have been brought up by their grandparents in the belief that they are their parents and that their mother is an older sister. That must make for numerous difficulties, but I have no experience that would enable me to elaborate on this topic.

Ushma's case, however, is not one of an unexpected pregnancy. She was born in England, but into an entirely Indian family and her parents were unable to conceive. When her uncle's wife gave birth to a third girl after they had been hoping for a son, the couple offered Ushma to the childless couple, who were delighted to accept her as their own daughter. So Ushma, who has always known that she was adopted, has also known her natural parents all her life. However, although, when she was in her late teens and wanted to make a trip to India, they generously paid her fare because her adoptive parents could not afford it, her birth parents have never taken any great interest in her. And when they in due course acquired the son for whom they had been yearning, this gave them still less reason for regretting their decision to give Ushma away. She too has never felt any great affection for them and, although her father sadly died when she was quite young, she has always felt very close indeed to her adoptive parents.

Having been brought up as a Hindu, Ushma takes for granted that the reason she feels a stronger bond with her adoptive parents than with her birth parents is that she has much stronger karmic links with them. She came to me for a regression on the advice of her mother, who had read my first book, *Karmic Release*, but her reason for wanting this was not to find out the nature of her previous links with her four parents. Of much greater concern was her marriage, which was very difficult because of her husband's volatility and the aggressive way in which he often treated their three fairly young children. She was seriously torn between leaving him and a fear that, if she did so, she would entail a karmic debt, which she would then have to pay by marrying him again in a future life.

Ushma and her mother are, as I said, extremely close, and her mother felt strongly that she should remain in the marriage for the reason just mentioned. Ushma therefore very much wanted to find out what was the nature of the karma between herself and her husband, as she believed that this would help her to make the decision that would be most satisfactory for the whole family. However, people who come for regression vary greatly in the ease with which they get into a previous life, and it is naturally often more difficult the first time. Also, the subconscious always knows best what one is ready to deal with at any given moment, and so obtaining an answer to the main question one is bringing to a session can never be guaranteed. Sometimes it is necessary to deal with present-life issues before going further back in time.

Sadly Ushma was so disappointed at not immediately getting into a past life, and obtaining the answer she was hoping for in order to resolve her problem, that she has not to date made another appointment with me. I told her that regression often takes more practice, but she also does not live very close by and has the difficulty faced by so many mothers of arranging for childcare when they need to leave home for a matter of hours. So at the time of writing I do not know the end of this story. I find the case a very interesting one, however, since it is such a clear demonstration of the importance of karmic links in parent-child relationships. I personally find it hard to imagine how any parent could so willingly give a child away, but on the other hand I do know that I myself have very strong past-life bonds with all three of my children. Maybe I would have felt differently if I had given birth to a 'stranger'. When one looks at the broader picture, it is clear that Ushma's Life Plan was to be reared by her adoptive parents (with whom, interestingly, there is an element of blood since her birth father is her uncle), and – unlike most cases of adoptees that I have dealt with – she does not *appear* to have any difficulties caused by having been adopted. I cannot help wondering whether, if continued contact with birth parents following the handing over of a child were more common, it would sometimes offer a good solution.

PART SIX – STEP FAMILIES

> *Every step family is the result of a loss. To one person it may be a glorious new beginning. To another it can be an ending – a painful reminder of what has been lost or taken away from them.*
> Suzie Hayman[1]

In the West nowadays the normal practice seems to have become to fall in love, have a child or two, get married, fall out of love and then either get divorced or "live unhappily ever after." In India, on the other hand, it is still more common to get married (normally to someone selected for compatibility by an astrologer), then fall in love, then have children, then remain with your spouse until death. Which is better? Surely the Indian system is better for the children at least. Of course there are exceptions to every rule: I personally know of three Indian marriages that ended because the couples were patently obviously ill-matched, and my own older son seems fortunately to have made an excellent marriage (*and* before having their two lovely children!).

But facts of life have to be accepted, and – especially with my understanding of karma – I would never want to be judgmental. In her excellent and comprehensive guide to step-parenting in the 'Teach Yourself' series, Suzie Hayman observes that stepfamilies come from all socio-economic groups and most cultures, and that you do not either have to be married or have your partner's children living with you to be affected by stepfamily issues. In any case, she says that, according to government figures, by 2010 the traditional family of two adults living with and bringing up their own children would no longer be in the majority. She certainly seems to have been proved right.

So what is it that has brought about this radical change of recent years? Personally – while not denying the symptoms of what Indians call the *Kali Yuga* (the age in which so much of the world's evil is being brought to the surface in order to be purged) – I do not believe it to be an indication of a serious decline in moral values. Nor do I believe that marriages in the past were on average any happier. Women who were oppressed simply had to put up with the existence of their husbands' mistresses, and in any case how many of them were given a choice of spouse in the first place? *Of course* children suffer when their mother or father is sufficiently assertive to leave an abusive relationship (and please note that abuse can come in many forms besides physical), but did they suffer so much less in the past, when everyone stayed together however much disharmony there was in the household?

Some of the biggest changes that I have seen in my lifetime are the differences in attitudes towards marriage and relationships between not only my parents' generation and my own, but also mine and that of my children. Divorce did occasionally occur among my parents' acquaintances, but it was much frowned upon, and on the whole the attitude was "You've made your bed. Now you must lie on it." When my youngest sister got engaged, my husband as soon as he met her fiancé said that he gave the marriage six months. He was spot on, but even in this day and age getting out is often incredibly difficult for a woman who has no independent means of supporting herself and the children. Several years later my sister arrived on our mother's doorstep with her third child in her arms and announced, "I've left J..." My good mother's reply was "Would you like a cup of tea?" A couple of hours later she said, "Well, you'd better be getting back home now." So my poor sister, feeling totally unsupported, did so – remaining with J… for a few more years, until he had finally made her situation totally unbearable.

Lack of the same need for commitment than of yore is sometimes cited as a reason for the increasing rate of marriage break ups, but personally I wonder how much this really has to do with it. Ever since the beginning of humanity we have all wanted love and to find our 'perfect other half'.[2] I believe that most couples who decide to 'tie the knot' do so with the conviction that it is going to be a life commitment and that their current bliss will be 'everlasting'. I also, however, know firstly that people change, and secondly that life is all about learning, and that part of our learning comes through making 'mistakes'. Many people get married for the wrong reasons. As a therapist I have become used to hearing such things as "I was looking for security," or "I needed to escape from my parents and marriage was the easiest way to do this," and "I only married her because she's so manipulative and so good at making me feel guilty," and so on. Often people repeat the mistakes they make rather than learning from them straight away, but the universe ensures that all lessons are learnt eventually. When someone recognizes that they have become trapped in a repeated pattern, a therapy such as DMP can prove invaluable.

Although the statistics for failed marriages unfortunately increase with subsequent marriages, I feel we should be grateful that nowadays so many people *are* given a second, or even a third or fourth, chance to find happiness in a relationship. Step parent/child relationships are an inevitable consequence of this and so, rather than running away from the fact, I believe with Susie Hayman that it should be faced squarely in the face and dealt with creatively. She says that, although it may take some work, putting effort into it can make a stepfamily just as happy as any other family.

This last point supports my personal belief that all our major relationships are planned beforehand, and are made with people we have known before and with whom we have something to work out this time round. "There are no mistakes, only learning" is my philosophy, and so a child who is the so-called 'fruit of a mistake' should not be considered unlucky, but rather to have chosen both her birth parents and any subsequent parents for good reasons. But I am very well aware that not everyone – particularly in the West – shares this belief. Would Jan and his stepdaughter in the forthcoming story be such good friends if they had not already known each other well in at least one previous lifetime? I would say "No," but he would say "Yes." So it has been my aim in this book to cover a wide spectrum of people. If the bias of the book appears to be in my favor, that is simply because, owing to the nature of my work, I tend these days to mix mostly with people who share my views. Jan's story shows just as much as does Alan's (someone who, like me, has been thrown firmly onto a spiritual path) that people can make successful and happy step families whether or not they feel they understand the deeper reasons behind their being together. Obviously there are likely to be more problems when a child has not known a parent from birth, but if 'problems' are seen simply as worthwhile challenges to be overcome, all those involved can learn and grow from them. As I said in the Introduction, step parenting may or may not involve adoption, but whether or not it does, many of the issues are similar. That is why I feel this section of the book to be as important as any other.

CHAPTER TWENTY-FIVE

JAN'S STORY

Art is worship or divine service inasmuch as it places Beauty (which is the same thing as Goodness) in the heart of Man.
Vincent van Gogh

Jan is the most wonderful artist, who nowadays specializes in stained glass and etchings. We met after I had seen samples of his work at an exhibition and decided to fulfil a long held dream by getting my 'Life Seal', given me by Aron Abrahamsen[3], converted into stained glass. Jan's spirituality lies in his art, his love of nature and his sensitivity to personalities plus everything else around him that is wonderful. Although he often uses Biblical themes in his work, he was not brought up in a religious family. He is well travelled and interested in and open to the philosophies of different cultures, yet he feels no need to believe in any force outside himself such as a Creator. Nor does he think that he has been here before, or that any part of him apart from his works of art and people's memories will remain here after he has departed this life.

Jan grew up and trained in the Netherlands and, though he was not particularly drawn to teaching, his mother encouraged him to qualify in teaching Art. This was no doubt a good idea, since one has to be either exceptionally skilled or exceptionally fortunate to make a living as an artist. Jan is probably both since, though he has taught at all levels from elementary school through to adults, he is now able to live his dream and support himself entirely by selling his works. On the other hand, I see immense originality and delightful humor as two of his hallmarks, and I personally suspect that it is these (plus – in my book at least! – a good dose of excellent karma combined with numerous artistic past lives which gave him lots of practice) that have largely contributed to his success.

Jan was thirty-one years of age and had already moved to England when he met his ex-wife, Margaret, and she had a three-year-old daughter, who was consequently part of the equation from the word 'go'. The little Cindy's father was around, but he had never lived with them, so there was no question of 'rivalry' as far as the child was concerned. Consequently for Cindy the loss to which Suzie Hayman refers was not of a person, but rather of the vacant space that had been there when her family had consisted of only her mother and herself. There were inevitable difficulties, but Jan was used to children not only from his teaching experience but also from mixing with friends who had children. So he was not in the least put off by any of the possible problems, commenting, "One simply had to find a way through, and some things were resolved more easily than others." One of his biggest battles was caused by the fact that Cindy had the habit of sleeping in her mother's bed. She did *not* appreciate being ousted from it but, gentle and tactful though he is, Jan would not allow himself to be defeated on that one!

Cindy is exceedingly bright, and also a very strong character. This made her in some ways more difficult to bring up than Jan's natural son, Costyn, who was born when she was ten, and is more artistic and practical than academic, and also a more relaxed character. Jan comments, "Since Cindy was already there, one had to make up the rules as one went along, whereas with Costyn we could plan beforehand and we had already worked out what worked and what didn't." Yet, despite one or two minor problems (such as grinding her teeth in her sleep), Cindy had an extremely happy childhood, and she was overjoyed when Costyn arrived. They still get on "like a house on fire," as do they both with Margaret's second son by her new partner, who was born another ten years later.

As both an adoptive and a birth mother myself, who

sometimes find that people assume it to be impossible to love 'another' child as much as one loves one's 'blood' children, I was delighted to find that Jan shared my feelings on this subject. His comment was that he loved the two of them equally but differently, and that this was simply because they are totally different personalities, and the relationship with each of them is consequently quite different. He says that his feelings for each of them have nothing to do with blood.

Jan's love of the countryside and a peaceful life drew the family at an early stage from London to beautiful rural Shropshire, which is where Costyn was born and where Jan is still living. Since his home is not far from my own, he granted me when I requested it the immense privilege of watching him do some of the work on my stained glass piece. Never having seen anything of the sort being created before, I was totally fascinated! As Jan "badgered" the paint on the back of a glass panel, he explained to me that it had the very same (highly toxic!) ingredients as glass and therefore turned to glass when fired at six hundred and fifty degrees Celsius. At the same time as watching and listening, I was looking with half an eye through the window immediately in front of him. It was easy for me to appreciate how he could draw inspiration from the trees, the high hill, the birds and other creatures that lay within his immediate gaze. A few days later, after he had come and hung my wonderful piece in our sitting room window and I had seen the sun shining through it the next morning, I emailed Jan saying that I would never have believed that glass flowers could look "so extraordinarily flower-like"!

Afterwards, while the newly created panel had replaced its predecessor for its half hour in the kiln, we talked some more over a cup of tea in Jan's pleasant kitchen. "Undoubtedly there were various worries over the years," he said, "but looking back over it all now, I can see that everything has worked out for the best." For someone who clearly does not share my belief in a Life

Plan made before conception, I greatly admire his acceptance of things and his sense of there being a good reason for them.

While the little panel was still 'cooking', we talked in more general terms. He told me how, when he has momentarily had enough of working in his studio, he just jumps onto his bike and wanders off exploring the Shropshire hills. We discussed creativity and related it to getting older (something in which neither of us is alone!). We both expect to be around for a good few years longer but, when I commented that I should be happy to go so long as I had all my books published, he replied, "Oh no! You should never let your creativity dry up." I really like that sentiment!

Although Jan's relationship with Cindy was very good indeed when she was a young child, things became much more difficult when she got into her teens. At that time she was seeing quite a lot of her birth father, who had a well-paid job and was able to treat her to such things as expensive holidays. Teenage rebellion caused her sometimes to say hurtful things such as "You're not my father!", and she even at one point conceived a project of getting rid of Jan. Painful though it must have been for him, I doubt whether this was symptomatic of anything other than natural growing up. After all, how many teenagers rebel against their birth parents?! In any case Jan says that Cindy no longer remembers very much about having been so difficult before, and neither does she realize how much she hurt him.

He weathered the pain well, and then things improved greatly when, at the age of sixteen, Cindy won a scholarship to do an International Baccalauréat in Oxford. That necessitated her living away from home during term time; and moving on straight from school to university meant that she never lived with Jan all the time again, thus easing any tension between them. She was nineteen when he and Margaret decided to separate, and that did not cause any big problem for her either, since she had already sensed that things were no longer going well between the two of them. Jan now has a new partner too, and they are all good friends.

Cindy married not long after completing her first degree, and she now has a six-year-old son. Jan says that, though he was initially somewhat alarmed at the thought of her becoming a mother, she is in fact very good at it and very organized, which he could never have imagined when she was a teenager. He has long since got over the pain of those years and, now that Cindy is thirty-one, he feels that, since he has no role as a father, the two of them can be really good friends.

She has recently embarked on training for a new career, and her new university is in a city very close to Shropshire. Although Jan still sees the family regularly, and has an excellent relationship with his step grandson, he says that the hearing problem that he now has makes it impossible for him to look after the child on his own for a whole day. (Having both poor hearing and grandchildren myself, I can sympathize!) Jan still has equally close contact with Costyn, who is also studying not very far away. So all in all we seem to have here a highly successful stepfamily.

Notes

1. From *Successful Parenting*, Suzie Hayman, Teach Yourself (The McGraw-Hill Companies Inc.), USA, 2008.
2. See my book *Souls United – The Power of Divine Connection*, Ann Merivale, Llewellyn, USA, 2009.
3. I wrote about Aron and explained about the 'Life Seals' that he gave in his readings in the above book. My third book, *Discovering the Life Plan – Eleven Steps to Your Destiny*, 6th Books, 2012, has my Life Seal on the front cover.

CHAPTER TWENTY-SIX

ALAN'S STORY

> *...the desire to know God, to love God and be loved by God is a desire that does not bind. When awareness of God dawns in all its splendor, every worldly, sensual desire is reduced to ashes. The individual Self will then turn towards Universal Self and delight itself in supreme everlasting peace.*
>
> Sathya Sai Baba

Often in one lifetime couples come together in order to complete something that they had been unable to complete in a previous one. I have more than once had evidence of this in regressions I have performed. One of these was Alan's, who had already experienced two previous regressions. What he discovered in all three was very interesting – and relevant to this book – because it revealed past life connections with his stepdaughter, Bryony, as well as with his wife Rosalind. Though he has not to date found out any details of past life connections with his stepson, Robin, he knows them to be strong too, and he has further been told that the bonds between himself and his natural son Nicholas (Rosalind's third born) date back a very long time.

Alan came to visit me after reading my book on twinsoulship and realizing that we lived in the same county. Though widowed, he was not at the time preoccupied in looking for a soul mate, but was more interested in the reference I had made in the book to my shamanic soul rescue work. He felt called to do that himself, and my book[1] on the subject was at the time not yet complete. We had a good chat, found that we had many interests in common, and he subsequently came to my house again to make his first attempt at performing soul rescue jointly with me. In between these two visits, however, Alan decided that a regression could be useful for him because of an issue that had arisen following his dear wife's death nearly four years previously.

Alan's childhood was happy; he and his sister had supportive parents and, at the time that we first met, their ninety-seven-year-old mother was living near to him and he was giving her a great deal of care. He always worked hard at school and was so reliable that he ended up as head boy. His only fears were of getting something wrong or not doing it properly and thus letting his parents down. He started work as soon as he had left school, ultimately becoming a successful businessman, and fell in love with Rosalind when he was only eighteen. Initially, however, he felt that he did not deserve her and was troubled by his lack of sexual experience.

Rosalind, who already had two children, was seven years older than Alan, but his fears of inadequacy, and puzzlement at what she saw in him, were quite unfounded. They could not, however, marry for five years because of the difficulty for such a young man to support a family. Rosalind's story regarding the birth of her two children was a painful one: she had fallen in love with a man, whom I will call Joe, who was already involved with another woman. Oddly enough, this other woman shared her name, so I will refer to her as 'Ros' to avoid confusion. Initially torn between them, he took Alan's Rosalind to meet his parents, and after he had made the decision to marry Ros, his father commented, "You're marrying the wrong Rosalind." The realization that his father had been right dawned on Joe too late and, on two occasions, after he had convinced Rosalind of the sincerity of his promise to leave Ros for her, resulted in the conception of a child. He had even gone so far as to buy Rosalind a gold wedding ring, and it was this very ring that brought Alan to me for the regression. When they were courting she promised to get rid of it, and so finding it in one of her drawers after her death had naturally caused Alan considerable distress. "It had been bad enough losing her," he commented, "but then finding the ring caused me to imagine that she had never really given up her attachment to Joe. When one's in a state of bereavement it's all too easy for one's imagination to work overtime!"

Alan clearly remembers having had, at the age of about seven or eight, an awareness of having lived on Earth many times before, and also a strong sense that this was his last time here. A couple of years or so after that he went through a rather religious phase. At one point some foreign missionaries came and talked at his school and he was so inspired by them that he even informed his parents (to their dismay, though they did their best to conceal it!) that he wanted to become a missionary. Later still, however, he began to feel some disenchantment with the Church – so much so that he felt uncomfortable and even guilty whenever he had cause to go inside a church. Religion simply did not make sense to him anymore, and a great deal of what went on in Christianity seemed to him to be hypocritical. When Rosalind died he was open-minded regarding such things as the afterlife, but would still have described himself as an agnostic. He failed at that point to make a connection between his early knowledge of having lived before and its implications – i.e. that the fact of many lives necessitates an afterlife and a between life state. Until, that is, Rosalind's discarded wedding ring started him on the spiritual search that he has been ardently pursuing ever since.

Bryony was out of the country when Alan happened on the ring hidden in a pouch in his wife's jewelry drawer. His daughter-in-law, Josie, had volunteered to come and help him to sort out Rosalind's clothes, but she was out when he decided to start going through the drawers. He had seen the ring on Rosalind's right hand when they first met and, after they had started courting, she had told him the whole sad story of how Robin, and subsequently Bryony, had been conceived. He says, "We were sitting on a bench in a square in the center of the town, near to where we were both working at the time, and I well remember the compassion that I felt for her, my desire to make amends for someone else's wrongdoing, and at the same time my feeling of being inadequate because of my youth and inexperience. My joy when it gradually became clear that Rosalind had begun to love me more than she had ever loved Joe was unbounded, and I trusted her totally when she promised to get rid of the ring."

Alan then went on to explain, "I empathized with Rosalind's suffering and wanted desperately to protect her from it, which was completely illogical since there was really nothing I could do about what had already happened. However, following that initial disclosure of her heartbreak, I always felt the whole subject to be a 'no go area.' Some time later I asked Rosalind what she had done with the ring, and for some strange reason I never pursued the matter even though she replied in a somewhat non-committal way."

When Josie returned to Alan's house after visiting his mother, she was sympathetic to his dilemma and did her utmost to rationalize the discovery and console him. However, he had to await Bryony's return from abroad for some concrete advice as to what to do next. Rosalind's children by her former lover were aged three years and twenty months at the start of the courtship and they both took to Alan at their very first meeting. He has always found Robin, who is very calm and intelligent, easy to relate to, whereas Bryony when she was very small was difficult with anyone other than Rosalind. So it took longer for Alan to feel close to her, but by the time they got married both children were ready to start calling him "Dad" immediately and the bond between Alan and Bryony has grown ever stronger.

Bryony was already open spiritually when her mother died, and her immediate reaction when her distressed father told her about the ring that her natural father had given to Rosalind was to encourage him to consult a medium. She also told him that she remembered as a child having noticed the ring in her mother's jewelry box but that, since Rosalind had made no comment about it, she had assumed that it had belonged to her grandmother.

Alan initially felt somewhat uneasy with Bryony's idea and so did not respond in any way, but, after she had returned home, he realized at some level that he had to do what she had suggested. He then boldly took the plunge and telephoned a medium whom I will call Jane. All his doubts were soon dispersed when Jane quickly started giving him indisputable evidence that she was communicating with Rosalind and, when he voiced his distress about the ring, she immediately assured him that "it doesn't mean what you think it means." Rosalind then came through again herself and told Alan that, because of her great love for him and her disillusionment with Joe, she had tried many times to get rid of the ring but had been unable to "since it was the only tangible thing I had to justify what I had done." Alan explained to me that this made a lot of sense to him because Rosalind had always been someone with a very strong moral sense and desire to do the right thing. She had for some time been a Sunday school teacher, and she would never have agreed to sleep with Joe if he had not convinced her very firmly that he had made the wrong choice of partner and intended to rectify it.

Jane went on to tell Alan that he and Rosalind had planned all this together before they came in and that, in a previous life, their roles had been reversed (i.e. that Alan had been a deserted woman with children and that Rosalind had been the man who had married him [then her]. Alan subsequently did a regression in which he saw some details of that life: the children's father was the Lord of the Manor and Rosalind was a carpenter. He also recognized the Lord of the Manor as a former colleague in his present life to whom he had always felt a particularly strong connection.) He told me, "It was only after speaking to Jane many years later that I realized the reason why Rosalind's account of what had happened with Joe had affected me so profoundly. Obviously it stirred memories deep in my subconscious of when I myself had been in the same predicament."

Rosalind then instructed Alan to take the ring to a favorite family holiday place in the south of the country and to throw it into a lake that was special to the two of them. And she added, "By the time you've done this you'll know the reason." Jane further advised Alan to go for some Emotional Freedom Technique treatment to help him to deal with his emotions. He did this and found it extremely helpful; he took to waking in the night and writing things down, then he would read what he had written to Rosalind before going to bed the next evening. He trained in Reiki, which he still uses regularly, and also bought and read his first book about the Afterlife[2].

Thanks to all this spiritual development, by the time he had carried out Rosalind's request to dispose of the ring at their favorite spot in the area in which they had so often holidayed together, Alan had a full understanding of what the whole experience was about. He explains, "When Jane told me of the Life Plan that Rosalind and I had made together, it made total sense to me, and I quickly realized that finding the ring was the trigger for the spiritual quest that I needed to make during this lifetime, which I believe to be my last lifetime on Earth." Since then, while still of course mourning Rosalind's comparatively early death, he has read more and more spiritual books and gone from strength to strength.

Cancer (not swine 'flu!) is the pandemic of our present times and the cause of innumerable 'premature' bereavements. But those who are spiritually aware know that there is a reason for everything that happens, and in Alan's case the involvement with his local hospice caused by Rosalind's illness led him to train in Bereavement Counselling. Now his voluntary services are proving invaluable at the hospice, and an early retirement package has given him the freedom not only for that, but also to widen his reading, develop meditation skills and generally develop his innate strongly spiritual nature. He is encouraging his son Nicholas in his present major career change and move to ecological living, and supporting Bryony, who has recently left her husband. Once his mother has died, he intends to move to a part of the country where he can be closer to both of them and their children.

Alan's first glimpse of a past life came not in the regression I have mentioned above, but spontaneously in meditation. (This is far from being a rare occurrence; it has happened to me many times now, but the first time was in Mexico, when I was meditating at the Cenote at Chichén Itzá. It was very significant because I saw a past life in which my present adopted son had been my natural son, whom I had lost at an early age.) Alan saw himself as a cabin boy crossing the Atlantic and found that, after reaching Latin America, he had fallen in love with an Indian princess and they had both been killed. He felt sure that the princess was either Rosalind or Bryony in a previous life, but was unable to decide which of the two of it had been. When I dowsed for an answer to that question, my pendulum said that the princess was now Bryony, which rang true for Alan when I told him. Both are equally likely, and either would be a contributory factor to Alan's love for her in his present life. Someone I once talked to, who did not want her story to be in this book, told me that she had in a previous life been married to her present adoptive father.

Despite Alan's spiritual growth since his wife's death, he did not when we first met feel able to communicate with Rosalind. The communication that had come through Jane did of course feel real to him, but he felt that towards the end of her life there had been difficulties between the two of them that he would now like to see resolved. I suggested that if he did a Deep Memory Process session with me he would probably find himself able to talk to Rosalind in the Bardo.

When we worked together Alan had no difficulty at all in

getting into a previous life in which he had also fallen in love with Rosalind. He found himself as a young Roman asking for the hand of someone called Celia, who was above him in status. Her father's reply was that he was unworthy of being a husband to his daughter and that he must first go away and prove himself. Since he was already in the Army, he went abroad to fight, and after only a year we found that he had been promoted. He was, however, unable to return home for another five years and, by the time he did so, he learned that his beloved was married to someone else.

I then took him further back to find out about Marcus' (as his name then seemed to be) first meeting with Celia. He led a tranquil life outside the city, in a happy farming family without a great deal of money, and they met in the countryside at a very young age. In the next scene that Alan saw he was in the city in his late teens, and he saw Celia walking to an event in the arena. She acknowledged him and he followed her, keeping well behind. During the event Celia watched him from afar, and afterwards they managed to talk outside at some length and to arrange a subsequent secret meeting in a sort of park. Even though Celia did not dare stay for long, Marcus declared his love, which she reciprocated despite being aware of his 'inferior' background. They then continued to have sporadic secret meetings over about a year prior to his departure with the Army.

Marcus was naturally bitterly disappointed when he learnt of Celia's marriage, but on the other hand not surprised because he realized that she had never really been attainable. So he went off to fight another battle, and ten years on we found him very senior in the Army, well respected and still a bachelor. He had no news of Celia, for whom he was still pining and, when I asked him to go the next significant event, he saw himself paying one of Celia's servants for information about her. He found out that she was living in the same city, had a family, but was not happy.

A bit later we found Marcus going to Celia's house – not in the hope of meeting her, but because he had business to do with her husband in his capacity as the controller of the Army's finances. The husband turned out to be considerably older than Celia, dictatorial, and to have no regard for other people's views. He saw Celia in the background; she recognized him immediately, looked surprised and gave him a smile and a nod. Soon it became clear that she knew that he had been obtaining information about her, and she managed to get a letter to him. In the letter she said that she had never been happy in the marriage, but that she had not had any choice, and she told him to whom it was safe to give his reply. She also told him that, despite her unhappiness, she loved her three children very dearly.

Marcus' doing business with the husband caused him to continue to visit the house regularly for some time, and it was always tantalizing for him seeing Celia in the background. But then he got sent off elsewhere, and by the time he was in his mid-forties he had become a Governor. Upon being directed to another significant event, Alan saw himself as Marcus organizing a flotilla of ships for an invasion of Egypt. This invasion was successful, even though the Roman Army lost a lot of people in it, and Marcus then remained there for several years until his death when he was in his mid-fifties. While in Egypt he felt connected to it and at peace with himself.

Why is it that so many people have a strong feeling of connection to Egypt even without having gone there? I found myself identifying with what Alan was saying at this point in the regression because I was at the time just back from my first trip to Egypt and it had affected me profoundly. Since the Ancient Egyptian civilization lasted for such a very long time and was so advanced and enlightened, I am sure that it is only very young souls indeed who have not had previous lives in Ancient Egypt. So is it the fact of having Egypt's knowledge and wisdom buried deep in our psyches that is responsible for causing so many people in all corners of the globe to study its history with a passion probably unrivalled by that for any other country? Certainly my husband and I had wanted to visit Egypt for many years before we were finally able to do so, and Alan says too that he has always felt a fascination for it even though he has never been there. Without having studied this ancient civilization in any depth, he shares my regret that much of it is sadly misunderstood these days – perhaps particularly by Egyptologists, most of whom fail to acknowledge their ancestors' belief in reincarnation! Alan had been interested in what I had written in *Souls United* about Joan Grant, and so I advised him to read some of her books[3]. Since all her so called 'novels' are actually autobiographical, having been written as a result of delving extremely deeply into her own past lives, Grant's understanding of the knowledge and philosophy held in Ancient Egypt greatly exceeds, in my opinion, that of the average Egyptologist.

When I took Marcus into the Bardo after a death for which he felt ready, his first desire was to find out what had become of Celia. He was told that her husband had died, but that she was still unhappy. In beautiful, bright countryside he met his guide, who was a man called Joseph. Asked about Marcus' purpose for that lifetime, Joseph replied, "To learn that you can achieve things even from humble beginnings." Then he added, "But not everything is attainable in one lifetime."

I then moved Marcus on to the end of the life of his beloved, so that they could meet in the Bardo. As soon as he looked into Celia's eyes, Alan had no doubt whatsoever that she was the same soul as Rosalind. It was a moving moment for me, the therapist, when they were able to embrace and say to each other, "I've always loved you and I always shall." Further conversation, combined with Joseph's occasional intervention, revealed that they were companion soul mates, and that any differences or disagreements that they might have had in their most recent life were immaterial. As I explained in *Souls United*, though less close than twin soul ones, companion soul mate relationships tend to be the most comfortable, being based on many lifetimes of close acquaintance and friendship.

Alan/Marcus then asked Rosalind/Celia about her three children, who were two girls and a boy. She took a good look and then replied that the first daughter was now Alan's mother, the second was his sister, and the boy was now Joe, her unfaithful lover and Robin and Bryony's natural father. What a fascinating example of how people come together over and over in varying patterns of relationships! And it was of course no surprise to me to learn that Rosalind had always felt very much at home with her husband's family, who had loved and cherished her, grieving her loss with Alan himself. Many mothers would be far from overjoyed at their son taking on an older woman and someone else's two children, but not so Alan's.

As for the son who in this life became Rosalind's lover, that is a rather sadder story, but it is also part of the learning and of the Life Plans that they all made. In that same Bardo session Alan and Rosalind were told that Joe had agreed to be instrumental in the reversal of roles that the two of them had decided they needed to experience, but that he had unfortunately failed to learn the lesson that he chose to learn before coming in. When Joe first met Rosalind, he was already engaged to Ros but, being attracted to Rosalind's sparkle, which made her so different from Ros, was torn between them. When he realized soon after his marriage that it had been the wrong decision, selfishness caused him to take the line of least resistance and to fail to give Rosalind the full financial support that she needed for the children.

Though Robin has never had any desire to meet his birth father, Bryony in adulthood decided to get in touch with him, and they did actually meet at one point. She found herself, however, quite unable to relate to him. In fact she told Alan that he appeared to "have no personality and to be completely self-oriented," and that it was even very hard for her to believe that he really was her father. He had obviously "closed the lid on that part of his life and it wouldn't open," and he claimed not to remember about the ring. He promised to get back to Bryony but then failed to do so and, when she reminded him about her birthday, he acknowledged it merely by a text message three days late. Books on adoption abound in similar tales of reunions with birth parents, and it must always be incredibly painful for the person who feels rejected a second time. At least Bryony is fortunate in having had a 'real father' from an early age. Now both she and Alan, with their spiritual inclinations, would really like to be able to help Joe since the scar of what he did to Rosalind has always affected him. It appears, however, not to be possible in this lifetime because of his inability to escape from the box into which he has put himself.

The regression that Alan did with me explained his feelings of "unworthiness" when he first got to know Rosalind. Fortunately this time round there was no social status factor to divide them and so it was lovely that in this life they were able to consummate their love in marriage and complete what they had failed to do in Roman Italy. Seeing this reinforced Alan's appreciation that he did in fact deserve Rosalind, and in her conversation with him in the Bardo she encouraged him to develop the spiritual work upon which he had already embarked. It was not yet clear exactly what direction this would mainly take, but he is drawn to the idea of running a hospice with a spiritual orientation (something that is undoubtedly greatly needed in England!). Clairvoyants with whom Alan has spoken have foreseen a new woman coming into his life, and that the two of them will have a "big task" to perform together. Rosalind with her broader view from the other side no doubt has a clearer idea than he has concerning his future but, apart from hinting that his new partner might be a friend of hers, she was not giving the game away! Instead she simply advised him to continue following his intuitions: "If you go with the flow, it will come," she assured him. Though Alan always regarded his marriage as a happy one, Rosalind's painful past inevitably affected their relationship, and he says that a clairvoyant in a very recent reading "really put her finger on it." The comment was "Even though you and Rosalind really loved each other, you never felt cherished." And the clairvoyant added encouragingly, "Your new partner will cherish you." So Alan feels grateful now for the communication that is becoming possible with Rosalind's higher self, who, he feels sure, is helping him in the valuable work that he does in the hospice. "Because," he says, "when we were together on Earth her need to blot out her painful past made her unable to express appreciation of what I did for her, and my lack of feeling cherished gave me a slight unease."

Another thing that Alan talked to me about when he came for the regression was a piece of information that he had been given in a previous clairvoyant reading. This reading revealed a lifetime he had had as a very gifted priest in Atlantis. Though he began with good intent, as he got older his life changed and he slowly began to use his abilities for self-gain and power instead of for help and healing. This was not done in a malicious way, as he believed himself to be doing good and could not see that what he was doing with others, who were using him as a puppet, was somewhat harmful to the people of the island. A consequence of this was that his energy burnt out by going beyond his capacity, and this damaged his third eye. One of the victims of these Atlantean 'misdeeds' was his stepdaughter Bryony, and so it seems that this is another thing that has drawn the two of them together this time round – so that Alan could pay a karmic debt by helping her. This he has obviously already done by being (unlike her natural father), a real father to her, and more recently she has been eagerly following his rapidly developing spiritual interests. At the moment, too, he is giving her still more help during the break up of her marriage. Bryony's developing spiritual interests made her able to see how her relationship had always been flawed – something of which Alan had always been aware – and he comments with some regret that, whereas Bryony is learning the lessons that she needed to learn, her husband has not yet understood them.

So, of all the stepfamilies that I have come across, Alan's is the one that was most clearly planned carefully beforehand. To summarize: Firstly, Alan had one lifetime in which he had borne children to a man who would not marry him (then her), and Rosalind (then a man) married him subsequently and helped care for the children. So they decided this time round to reverse the roles, and Joe, who had once been Rosalind's son, agreed to play the role of the deserter. Secondly, the two of them had another life in which they had fallen in love but not been able to marry, and so they decided this time round to enjoy the marriage they had missed out on then. The two children that Rosalind bore to Joe were both old acquaintances of Alan's and consequently welcomed him as their 'adoptive' father. (He did not actually adopt them legally, but to my mind what he did amounts to exactly the same thing.) He has not found out about his previous connections to Robin, but feels them to be strong, while firstly he has been told that he had a karmic debt to Bryony dating from Atlantis, and secondly he himself saw a lifetime in which he fell in love with a princess who was probably Bryony as well. He paid his debt to her by taking her on as a young child and later guiding her in a spiritual direction, and now that she is a mature woman, they are able to give a great deal of support to one another.

When Alan and Rosalind married, even though he had not fathered the two children, the four of them molded very quickly into a 'normal family'. The youngsters commented that it felt completely natural, and Robin later said to him, "I can't think of a time when you weren't there in my life." Nowadays Robin is absorbed in his career and his own family and, "though he would come at the drop of a hat if he were needed," Alan sees less of him than of his other two children, but his relationship with Bryony, and with all his seven grandchildren plus one great grandchild, is very close indeed. Having a second son together, which Marcus and Celia had been unable to do in the Roman era, was a bonus – especially since Nicholas is a soul with whom Alan already had particularly strong bonds. (He has been told in a clairvoyant reading that, in a previous life in which he had lost Nicholas and mourned him terribly, he had tried too much to help him. Consequently this time round he needs to stand back and let him find his own way, which he is at present doing at the same time as always being there for him with support and encouragement.)

So Alan was overjoyed at having a son born to him, but this in no way diminished his love for the older two. In fact his great regret was always the fact that they were not his blood children, and he will say in all honesty that he has always loved all three of his children equally, though of course differently since they are each such very different characters. All the grandchildren too mean a great deal to him and, while still mourning the loss of his wife, he feels very blessed these days to have their support and company. As for the damage to his third eye, which happened so very long ago, he has been assured that the spiritual and care work that he is doing now will gradually heal it. And once it is fully healed, his ability to help others will doubtless be even greater!

Notes

1. *Delayed Departure – A Beginner's Guide to Soul Rescue,* Ann Merivale, 6th Books, 2013.
2. *What To Do When You Are Dead: Living Better in the Afterlife,* Craig Hamilton-Parker, Sterling Publishing, New York, 2001.
3. The books of Joan Grant that I recommend the most strongly to those interested in Ancient Egypt are *Winged Pharaoh,* Duckworth Press, London, 2007, and *Eyes of Horus,* Ariel Press, USA, 1988. I also recommend my own book, *Souls United,* for a brief account of this amazing woman's life.

CHAPTER TWENTY-SEVEN

ALICE'S STORY

No sound nor silence but one equal music.
John Donne

In November 1938, when Alice was only two and a half years old, her mother, Marie, committed suicide by swallowing some corrosive fluid. Alice, who remembers the death but has virtually no earlier memories, came when she was older to believe that it was not pre-meditated and that her mother was probably suffering from post-natal depression (which was not recognized then as it is nowadays), as well as being worried about the state of the world at the time. She still has a strong memory of her father sobbing, and she recalls being hastily put into her cot while the doctor was called, but after that her memory is a blank until the appearance in May 1941 of the glamorous Daphne, who was soon to become her stepmother.

Daphne was working as a secretary to a London solicitor when she was introduced to Henry, Alice's father, by a cousin of his. The attraction was mutual and instant, even though Daphne had a boyfriend at the time. Alice recalls bursting into tears when Henry gave her the news of the engagement, and replying, "Why can't you marry Auntie?" 'Auntie' was the housekeeper, who represented security to the young Alice, while Daphne seemed both to her and to her own mother's family to be "like an exotic bird flying into their house." Her mother's youngest sister Helen, who had been very close to her, never hit it off at all with Daphne.

Despite a strong personality clash between them, Alice came to accept Daphne as a mother figure quite quickly, and her tremendous sense of humor and her ability to make Alice, who was a serious child, laugh a lot, was an asset to her development.

She was also something of a disciplinarian, which was probably a good thing as Alice had become a bit wayward since her mother's death. Also, her step grandmother, who she says was a lovely, very gentle person, and who later came to live with them for a lot of the time, was a huge influence on Alice. She was very spiritual, and one of Alice's earliest memories is of this grandmother teaching her to play cards. Although Alice felt loved by her father, their relationship was never very easy, since he had been one of three boys, wanted to have sons himself, and felt that he did not know anything about girls.

The fact that Daphne's character was totally different from Alice's caused various difficulties between them right up until Daphne's death at the age of ninety-four, but another asset of Alice having her for a mother was the fact that Daphne was a good singer. For Alice, who has made music her career, started playing the piano at the age of seven and her stepmother quickly recognized and encouraged her talent. Her father, who was a bank manager, was not musical, and so Alice feels that, had her birth mother lived, her musical abilities might not have been recognized so readily.

When Alice was six years old, Daphne sadly gave birth to a stillborn daughter. Alice had not been given any information at all about the facts of life, but she has a vivid memory of getting really excited when she was told that her stepmother was going away and would come back with a baby. In fact Daphne was very ill following the birth and a year later had to have a hysterectomy, which in the difficult wartime circumstances was a very traumatic experience for her. When she came home after losing the baby, nobody explained anything to the young Alice, but she knows that there was a lot of sadness around in the household and that her step grandmother was a great help to them all.

Daphne's response to the loss both of her own child and the chance of another pregnancy was to bend over backwards to be a real mother to Alice. Later on she even went so far as to try to prevent people knowing that she was a stepmother rather than a natural one. Alice feels that by the time she had become a teenager Daphne had somewhat supplanted her father as a parent. This was perhaps not difficult in view of Henry's attitude towards girls (many years later Daphne told Alice that it was a good thing that the child they lost was a girl since losing a boy would have been even worse for him!), but poor Alice found her strictness and her domineering rather difficult to live with. She consequently pleaded to be sent to boarding school and her parents acquiesced to this request when she was ten years old. Her first boarding school was a Quaker one and, although she felt homesick initially, she soon found that Quakerism suited her temperament very well, even though she was being brought up as a Baptist. Her parents, however, gave up Baptism when they moved to a different town four years later, and at the same time they moved Alice to a school nearer their new home – ostensibly because it was known to have a brilliant piano teacher.

The new school was an Anglican one, and Alice felt claustrophobic there because they were never allowed outside the school gate except on Sundays after church in the school gym. She began to enjoy the church services, however, started playing the organ, and at fifteen asked to be confirmed. An attack of chickenpox prevented her from getting confirmed at the same time as her classmates, but the bishop kindly let her receive the sacrament later, when he was performing it somewhere else. She remembers this as a very powerful spiritual experience, and nowadays (about sixty years on), although she only likes going to church in order to play the organ and finds herself unable to say the words of the Creed, she still regards churches as a sort of spiritual haven.

When Alice's step grandmother died, Daphne missed coming to the school concert in order to attend the funeral. Since she was playing, this was of course painful for Alice, and her pain was compounded by the fact that she was only told about it all afterwards and would have loved to be at home at the time. Many years later, her father, who had retired early because of a weak heart, died suddenly of a heart attack at the age of sixty-seven. He was on the way back from collecting gear for a cricket club fête at the time and it grieved Daphne immensely not to have been able to say "goodbye" to her husband. She phoned Alice in distress immediately after the policeman had called, and Alice had hastily to make arrangements for her three-and-a-half-year-old daughter to be looked after while she herself rushed down to the West Country. Interestingly, Alice's husband George had that very day had a vision of Henry and got the feeling that he would never see him again.

Daphne, who was only five months younger than Alice's father, remained independent right to the end, but the fact that she bought a little house round the corner from where she lived made it impossible for Alice ever to break free from her entirely. Even when she had left school for the Royal College of Music, her parents had insisted that Alice live at home since they did not like the thought of her living in London.

Alice feels that she has always known about having lived before, and by the time we made friends in 2009, she had for long been making the same sort of spiritual explorations as I had. She was keen to get to the root of what she saw as her difficult karmic relationship with Daphne, and neither of us was in the least surprised when Daphne appeared in the first regression that we did as Alice's father in a previous life. Some time before we met, however, she had brought up a family and left a very difficult marriage. (Despite his intuition re Henry mentioned above, George was a rather difficult person to live with and over the years Alice found that they had less and less in common.)

Alice met George when she was nineteen and they married eleven months after she had completed her studies at the Royal College of Music. Daphne didn't get on that well with George, but Alice at the time believed herself to be in love with him. When she lost her third child, Daphne was sympathetic, but commented nevertheless that it was not quite so heart-breaking as it had been for her as she already had two children.

Besides doing much spiritual reading, Alice got into holistic healing before making the brave decision to get a divorce from the incompatible George. Thanks to her musical training, she has always been able to support herself by teaching, and she has also over the years gained much enjoyment from singing in various choirs as well as from playing the organ. Now in her mid-seventies and with a tremendous zest for life, she shows no thought of retirement, and her energy is enviable.

The regression in which Alice recognized Daphne as her father in a previous life was a fascinating one, and it relates also to her present interests. It was a male incarnation, possibly among the Essenes but earlier than Jesus' time. Born into a simple family, the young man that Alice saw herself as was always a bit of a dreamer, and his mother regarded him as lazy. In the first scene we found that the lad's father had gone away to work and he and his mother had just had an argument which caused him to clear off. He walked some way away from home before having an accident in which a beam fell on him and damaged his left leg. Fortunately he was near to some sort of religious institution when it happened, and he found himself being cared for by some monk-like figures. Although they tried to persuade him to stay, he was scared to do so and set off home again once the sun had got a bit cooler. Home was a sort of tent, and his mother was more relieved than angry when he reappeared. He then resigned himself for a while to staying at home.

One year or so on we found that the father had returned with a bit of money and they had bought a stone house to live in. But by this time the young man had had more than enough of looking after goats and wanted to do something else. Since his parents completely failed to understand why he wanted to go away, he was indecisive for a while and, when he did finally leave about six months later, his parents were very unhappy about it. This past life therefore seemed to explain Alice's feelings of guilt about not having been present when her stepmother finally died. These feelings were irrational since she led a very busy life, had nevertheless kept a constant eye on Daphne and had no way of knowing the precise moment at which she would die.

The young goatherd set off from home, taking supplies with him, and after three or four days' walking, finding wild fruit and other things to eat en route, he reached the city. He knew that he wanted to do things with his hands and, after going to see a man that he knew, he in due course found himself happily making things such as chairs with raffia seats. It definitely felt to Alice like Biblical times, and she saw that the young man was working in some sort of craft center and that there were other people around doing various artistic things.

Two years on found our gifted young man painting frescoes in a church or temple, together with two or three others. These frescoes had a hidden meaning that no one must know; they were intended for people in the future. After a while, however, he decided it was time to leave because what they were doing was subversive and he was afraid of getting found out. So he went off in a boat with a couple of other people, but the sea was rough and dangerous and they soon drowned.

This early death turned out to be not as traumatic as it might seem. When the artist who was now Alice went to the light, he met some angels who told him that he could not have done any more in that life because he was ahead of his time. He had been channeling a being of light, and the painting was a secret code which it would take a while for people to understand. It concerned something that was better than what everybody was being told at the time. He was told in the Bardo that he had learnt the chief lesson from that life, which was how to escape from a humdrum existence in which he was not appreciated for what he had to give to the world.

Alice was then able, still as the young man, to look back and see that after he had left home his mother had fallen sick and his father had looked after her. It soon became clear that this mother was the same soul as Alice's birth mother in her present life, and also that she was not at peace. Alice asked her, "Why did you leave me when I was only two?", pointing out that it had been cruel to her father as well. The reply was "I was overwhelmed and couldn't cope with things. But I really didn't mean to leave you. I wanted to come back, but it was too late." When Marie made it clear that she wanted forgiveness, Alice assured her that she had already forgiven her anyway, and she told her, "It was part of the Plan for me and it's all worked out, although I found it difficult to understand." She further explained to her mother that her anger had been with the people in her family who had failed to tell her what had happened, and that it was only in later life that she had managed to ask the right questions and eventually figure things out for herself. Now her mother clearly needed help to enable her to cross over, and so Alice called for her Aunt Helen, her mother's younger sister, who had been close to her in this life, to come and lead her to the other side.

After that bit of soul rescue work had been successfully completed, Alice felt that it would now be a good moment to meet Daphne, to whom she felt she owed an apology. She explained to her, "I didn't mean to be ungrateful, since you loved me so deeply and considered me as your own, but it was difficult, especially towards the end of your life. I'm really sorry not to have been there when you died." Daphne replied that she thought Alice had been selfish to go out that particular evening, so Alice then explained to her that she had been hanging on to her too much and that there had been no obvious reason for Daphne's last evening to have been different from any of the others during the previous two to three weeks. Getting Daphne to understand this brought some healing in their relationship. I was then rather amused by Daphne's reaction to the question "Have you previously been my father?" because her Christianity in her last life made her skeptical about reincarnation. We don't always re-remember everything as soon as we die, but the angels to whom Alice had just been talking in the Bardo then assured her that Daphne had indeed previously been the young man's father. She then returned to the end of the young man's life and spoke to his father, who had a full understanding of the situation. How very interesting that Alice's two mothers in this life had been married to each other, and were her (then his) parents in an earlier life!

All that was enough for one session, but Alice felt that there was something else she needed to look at another time. This dated back to 1990, when she had first been beginning to explore spiritual questions seriously and had done a trip to Egypt with the Wrekin Trust. The experience of a channeling performed in the desert had been an amazing, and very new, one for her, but when she had entered Rameses' tomb in the Valley of the Kings, she had found herself unable to continue and had come straight out again. She felt sure that the unpleasant, scary feelings and emotions that overpowered her in that tomb were caused by a traumatic past life experience, and so we agreed to look into this at the next available opportunity.

In Deep Memory Process therapy we often start a session by getting the client to focus on a particular pain or sensation in their body, and in Alice's case she felt pins and needles in her higher right arm, lower left arm, and then – even more strongly – in her right leg below the knee. She had no difficulty in going straight to Egypt, where she quickly found herself falling down some steps and collapsing onto her leg. Looking further into the life, we again found a young goatherd! This time, however, he was not an only child, but had several younger siblings, and by the time he was twelve he had a great deal of responsibility because his father had died. The fall occurred when a goat ran away and he went looking for it. He was in a great deal of pain and lost consciousness, but a wise man found him and took him to a doctor, who felt himself forced to amputate the boy's lower right leg. Eventually he was able to explain where he came from, and the man who had found him then took him home. His mother was relieved when he was brought back, but shocked by his condition, and he felt himself to be a burden – especially since his hands were hurt as well, which made him feel totally useless. However, the wise man kept an eye on the whole family and helped them, as well as making sure that the boy got on all right.

A couple of years or so on, when the mother was feeling better, the wise man took the ex-goatherd to the place where he had had the fall. This turned out to be a Mystery school, where he was one of the teachers, and the boy was enrolled in the classes as well as being given a place to live (sleeping on a rug in a dormitory). He had by this time got used to managing with only one and a half legs, and he now learnt to write. Since it was difficult for him to hold a pen with his injured arm, he was given a lump of stone with which to draw on a slate, and he learnt to read stuff on papyrus.

The next scene saw our former goatherd in his fifties. He had grown a big beard, wore a headdress, and was teaching in the same school where he had been a pupil. The teaching, which was sacred and secret, had to do with the Mysteries in Egypt and was carrying on a long tradition. Alice felt that the area could well have been that of Rameses's tomb, and she saw that the school was a fairly big stone building a bit like a monastery. I asked her as the Egyptian man to ask her former teacher who was the Pharaoh and the reply was that it was Rameses II, but that they did not have very much to do with him. When this rescuer-teacher died, the hero of our story succeeded him as Head Teacher of the school.

When I moved the man on to the 'next significant event', some armed men appeared with horses and chariots to destroy what they were doing. There was a lot of bloodshed and unpleasantness, and he was taken prisoner. He was then taken to a large city, where they tried to make him tell the secrets of the mysteries, but he refused to do so and was thrown into the Nile.

Looking back after he had died, Alice as the Egyptian teacher was able to see that he had been strong enough to resist the mental torture imposed upon him, had gone into a trance, and his persecutors had consequently got frustrated and knocked him on the head. This meant that he was already unconscious when he drowned, but it did not prevent him from going straight to meet a Teacher in the Bardo, whose name was Akbar, and he turned out to be a spirit guide to Alice in her present life. From Akbar this Egyptian learnt that the purpose of that life had been to accept that being crippled did not mean that one could not do anything worthwhile. It was in fact an extremely worthwhile life because, whereas the Essene life we had looked at in the first regression had been cut short before he had been able to finish what he was doing, this time some of his great knowledge had been passed on. He was told that some of his colleagues had managed to hide and lie low through the period of unrest, pretending that they did not do anything secret, and that the survivors – especially the younger ones – had later been able to resume their work somewhere else. It seemed that Rameses II had seen them as a threat, despite the fact that they took no interest in any Pharaonic goings on. So no wonder that Alice had felt repulsed upon entering Rameses's tomb!

Our Egyptian teacher then met his father, who had died when he was so young, and immediately saw that he was the same soul as Henry, Alice's father in this life. It seemed, however, that in Egypt he had hardly known him, and when Alice asked why she had chosen him as her father twice, he replied, "In order to get to know him better." But this purpose had not been achievable this time round because of Daphne getting in the way! It appeared that Alice's karmic links with her stepmother were stronger than those with her birth mother, and that they still had some unfinished business from the Essene life. But I am sure that this is something that Alice, as an evolved soul, will be able to deal with, whether or not she decides that she needs to do another regression.

The next character to deal with was the Egyptian teacher's mother, who had been very sad when he had gone off to the Mystery School. This turned out to be a case of the tables being turned – something that we often find happening! – because it transpired that the Egyptian's mother was Marie in her most recent life. Alice knew that her suicide had been irrational, and her mother replied, "You left me before, so now it's my turn to leave you!" So then Alice as Alice (rather than the Egyptian) explained to her mother that she did not like her interpreting things that way and told her that rather than wanting a pay back, it would have been better to build bridges. It seemed clear to us (and this was confirmed by communication with spirit in the Bardo) that she was a much younger soul than her now daughter is, but I feel sure that she will have learnt a great deal from Alice already and will continue to do so.

CHAPTER TWENTY-EIGHT

JINNY'S STORY

> *Only gradually could Howard forgive his birth mother by reminding himself that she was, after all a [Holocaust] survivor – a shattered person... But there are positive sides. He always wanted a brother, and now he has one who is in some ways like a double: he has the same large body... And he has a sister who always writes loving letters claiming him as a brother.*
>
> Betty Jean Lifton, *Journey of the Adopted Self – A Quest for Wholeness*

Betty, who was born in 1921 as one of three sisters, was in the Land Army during the Second World War and she met a GI named Bryce when they were both stationed in Exeter. He had very recently married his childhood sweetheart back in America, but fell so deeply in love with Betty that he could not bring himself to tell her about Helen for quite some time. So Jinny was what is known as a 'GI baby' but, rather than being the fruit of a casual affair, her parents' relationship lasted between two and three years, until Bryce had to return to the States when Betty was about six months pregnant. Both the news that Bryce was already married and the pregnancy were a big shock to her – especially since they had been scrupulously taking contraceptive precautions – but she told Jinny much later that "knowing earlier would have made no difference," since she and Bryce were so clearly meant for one another. Jinny grew up to become a very successful maker of documentary films, and she says that when she received a BAFTA award for one of her films, she saw it as a reward to her mother for keeping her. This happened not long before Betty died, and she was able to watch her daughter's award ceremony on television, which naturally gave her much joy.

Bryce of course had no choice regarding his return to the US, and he was desperately and painfully torn between his intense love for Betty and his loyalty to Helen. Jinny was born in 1946, not long after they had parted, and it was revealed many years later that he always kept the baby photo that Betty sent him in his wallet. They corresponded for over a year, until Bryce told Betty (whose letters went to a post office box number) that Helen was expecting their first child. Betty then decided that they should cease communicating.

Betty's father kicked her out when he found out that she was pregnant, and she then moved in with her two sisters, one of whom thought of adopting Jinny. Jinny's grandfather, however, eventually relented in his attitude towards Betty and his granddaughter, and Jinny when she was growing up was very close to her grandmother. The male figures in Jinny's childhood were initially just her two uncles-in-law, but when she was six her mother married Bill, whom she met in the mill where they were both working in the North of England.

When Betty and Bill got married, the three of them went to live just three streets away, and so Jinny remained close to the rest of the family, and her cousins were like sisters to her. Since the romantic aspect of her parents' relationship appealed to her, Jinny never felt rejected by her father, but she was always very protective of her mother. Bill, who had been a prisoner of war, was a good man. He ultimately adopted Jinny legally, and she always felt gratitude to him, but she comments that he was something of a 'stick in the mud', while Betty was much more outgoing. In spite of his wartime experience, which may well have been a factor in his never wanting to go away, Bill never said a single bad word about the Germans. Jinny both respected and liked him and, near to the end of his life, she succeeded in persuading him to pay a visit to London "for Mum's sake." (Betty enjoyed going away, but would never leave Bill for more than a week.) She died in 2002, and Bill in 2008.

Jinny found her father's letters, and also his graduation ring, when she was about nine or ten, and she wore the ring for a while until her grandmother told her that Bryce had broken her mother's heart. At that point also she became conscious of how wearing the ring must have been hurting Bill's feelings. This was a very important emotional realization for her at the time and was another factor in her decision to stop wearing the ring.

Jinny says that she was a difficult child and, when she was seven and a half and her half-sister, Mary, was born, she did not take too kindly to the new arrival. The age gap in any case prevented them from being close as children, but that changed radically later on, and nowadays they are the best of friends. Jinny, who bought her parents' council house for them, also helped Mary, who is now widowed, through breast cancer and, after the aunt who had thought of adopting her had made her a bequest, she gave some of the money to Mary to help her to buy a house. It was also Jinny who was responsible for Mary meeting her husband, then a colleague of hers.

After failing the Eleven Plus exam Jinny went to a Secondary Modern school, but she was in actual fact a lot brighter than her school reports suggested. Her 'failure' spurred her into passing the Thirteen Plus, and she then swatted to get to the top of the class, where she remained until it was time to go to Art College. She then went to Film School in London before embarking on her successful career in filmmaking. When she retired in 2006, she moved from London to a small town in Shropshire with her partner Ann, and the two of them now feel very settled there. Jinny says that earlier in her life, before meeting Ann, she had a few relationships with men, and she describes herself as bisexual but, since her stepfather Bill had less influence on her than did the two strong women (her mother and grandmother) who brought her up, she finds it easier in her emotional life to get on with women than with men. In fact she has realized that she tends to see men as "intruders and a challenge." In Shropshire she enjoys working on an allotment jointly with her partner, as well singing in a choir, and she also fills much of her time with activities that are useful for the town.

Jinny further says that she has always been a seeker, and she was only thirteen when reading Arnold Bloxham's book *Who is Ann Ochenden?*[1] became a huge discovery for her. After discovering that book she carried on reading massively in this sort of area, and so by the time she came for therapy with me she had long taken reincarnation for granted. This knowledge is also basically the reason for her feeling sex and sexuality to be relatively unimportant, since we change regularly from one lifetime to another. It should be apparent from what I have said about Jinny so far that she is not an example of someone who has suffered greatly either from having been fatherless, or from having been in a stepfamily and adopted. Whatever (natural) difficulties she did have during her childhood and youth she dealt with very well on her own, always with the loving support of her mother and the rest of her family. She and I first met at a spiritual type meeting, and her reasons for wanting regression were firstly to find out something about her past and secondly to deal with one or two (perfectly normal!) issues such as anger.

In 1992 Jinny decided that she was keen to obtain more information about her birth father, her mother was unable to help very much in this apart from telling her his date of birth and that he had had three brothers and a sister, and so Jinny then tried to track her American family down on her own. She was unsuccessful initially, but in 2005, thanks to a website she found called ancestry.com, she tracked down Bryce's four siblings and discovered that, though he had died, his wife, Helen, was still alive. She, however, had dementia and passed away just two months later. Jinny's certainty that she had found the right family was increased when she saw that Bryce's birthday was recorded as February 14th, but she then got stuck until she joined GI Trace, which ultimately revealed the names of her four half siblings.

One of Jinny's incentives came from a desire to find out whether her hearing loss – not prevalent in her mother's family – was genetic. By the time that we first met, Jinny had already been accepted into her American family, been over there a couple of times to meet them all, been visited in England by Bryce and Helen's first born, Joyce, and her husband Dan, and discovered that the hearing problem had indeed been inherited from her paternal grandmother.

The first regression that we did took Jinny into a very traumatic past life, which was of great interest to me because in it her stepfather Bill appeared as her natural father. In the previous life, however, it became apparent that he had been a soldier and had had to go off when the child (a girl) had been not more than about nine years old, and he had never returned. The poor mother never heard what happened to him and, when her daughter was about twelve, another man entered her life. After the second child from her first husband had died, she had two more children with the new man, and some time later Jinny as that fatherless young girl found herself kicked out of the house and quite alone with nowhere to go. In the final scene while still incarnate we found her aged about twenty and a victim of multiple rape. She died very soon afterwards with a pain in her stomach (no doubt caused by the rapists kicking her).

Jinny quickly realized that her present anger stemmed from that young girl who had had real cause for it, and the first person that she met in the Bardo was her grandmother, who had looked after her and her baby brother when her mother had had to go out and work as a maid after her husband had gone off to fight. That grandmother told her that the purpose of the life had been to learn to look after herself. The early death gave her little opportunity for that, but Jinny has been making up for this very well this time round. In the Bardo at the end of the regression she met a wise being who told her that she had needed to suffer in that way in order to learn what it feels like. So she had evidently then paid a karmic debt from an earlier life in which she herself had been a rapist. She also learnt that the reason she had been forced to leave home while probably still only in her teens was that her mother's new partner had begun by then to want her sexually as well as her mother.

Jinny saw enough of this previous life to appreciate that she had in it loved both her parents, despite being a little bit scared of her soldier father, and when she met him soon after leaving her body, he told her that he had really loved her and that being unable to return to the family because of getting killed in battle had caused him great distress. Recognizing the soldier as Bill made Jinny appreciate that in both lives he had had some difficulty in expressing love to her, but she also felt that in her present life she "should have shown Bill more love." (She appreciates, however, that the fact of his no longer being incarnate is no hindrance to her doing that and so can now make up for it.) Returning to someone in order to look after them because of having been unable, or failing, to do so in a previous life is a normal law of reincarnation and karma, and Jinny was consequently no more surprised than I was when she met Bill in that earlier, painful life.

During another session I regressed Jinny through Betty's pregnancy and back to the time in which she was making her Life Plan for this time round. When Betty was five months pregnant Jinny was already aware that her father would shortly be returning to America, and at three months she was aware of her mother's difficulties in facing up to the pregnancy and her father's worries about it. Immediately before conception she was apprehensive but aware that, because of having hurt others in the past (just as we all have), she was going to have to learn more about thinking of other people. At that point Jinny met her teacher, who gave his name as Elijah and promised to be there for her during the forthcoming life, and he told her that she needed to grow. He added that, although she had already grown a great deal, her ego sometimes got in the way, and he reminded her to "Remember love for its own sake." As well as telling her to let go of anger, he further said that through her choice of career she would be able both to express herself and to use her talents to share with others. Her sister Mary (whom Jinny describes as "wiser than I am"!) also promised at the planning stage always to be there for her.

As for Bryce, who was naturally also involved in the making of Jinny's Life Plan, it appeared that he needed to question his morals and decision making, and that he needed Jinny's help in this. It was not made clear what had been the nature of their relationship(s) before, but Jinny saw that all three of her parents were old friends. Her maternal grandfather, on the other hand, had been more of an 'old enemy' than a friend, but in the making of Jinny's Life Plan he was seen to be going along with everything, if slightly reluctantly.

Jinny's four American siblings did not appear at this stage, but Bryce said that her role would be to make them think differently about what can happen in life and the challenge of that. This made a lot of sense to her since, whereas she is a socialist, these siblings are not only all Republicans but also Creationists! Also Steve, the oldest son (whom Jinny has only met once) did not get on with Bryce, is said to have been "born angry," and now has drink issues. When Jinny and I had our final session, she had just returned from another very successful visit to Chicago. She stayed with Joyce and Dan, with whom she still got on very well despite their political and religious beliefs which differ so strongly from her own, and she had been welcomed to a reunion of the entire family. She was also very happy to have been shown some videos of Bryce and found to her surprise that, though taller and red headed, he looked remarkably like her stepfather.

Jinny told me that, whereas Mary seems like a full sister to her, she still sees her American family very much as half siblings. She was nevertheless keen to find a karmic link with Joyce, the eldest, to whom she feels the closest. (Joyce and Dan had a disabled daughter, who died at the age of twenty-five, and Jinny feels great compassion for them because of that.) She consequently got into a very short female life in which her father was shot by an arrow and the family's log cabin was burnt down by Native Americans during the conflict over there. The little girl's mother, who turned out to be Joyce in this life, tried gallantly to save the two children by throwing water over the fire, but they got shot too when the six-year-old (now Jinny) emerged from the cabin with her baby brother. In the Bardo the young girl was told that the purpose of the life had been to do with the mother paying a karmic debt by trying to save her, and she also saw that her then father was now Dan, Joyce's husband. Jinny then called for Bryce and asked him "Why did you leave me?" He replied that he had been very sad to do so but that, though he loved Betty more and had a stronger karmic link with her, he was committed to Helen. We also found out that Bryce had eventually told Helen about Jinny's existence shortly after Joyce's birth and that she, who had been a good mother to them all, had forgiven him despite having been upset. Very movingly, Helen told Jinny she was glad about the contact that she now has with the family, commenting, "All that matters is love."

Jinny's conclusion is that, though she feels sad at "the mess of it all," she recognizes that her life circumstances have made her stronger and able to achieve more. The work that we did together made it clear to her that she has previously been creative and a "producer" many times, but she feels that this time round she had a real incentive to prove herself, make full use of her talents and leave something behind.

Note

1. Arnold Bloxham was a pioneer of regression in the 1950s and is probably best known for the 'Bloxham Tapes'.

CHAPTER TWENTY-NINE

ROSA'S STORY OF A STEP GRANDFATHER

More than pleasure, it is pain that awakens the wisdom in man. If you study the lives of great men, you will find that it is out of trouble and pain that they derived wisdom. Without sorrow, there can be no wisdom.
Sathya Sai Baba

Rosa met her present partner over twenty-five years ago and, despite the fact that he has never been able to express love, she knew from the moment she first set eyes on him that they were to be life companions. She and I met in Sai Baba's ashram, and she told me that she would like to have a regression partly because she was keen to understand the reason for the extraordinary bond between Jacques, her partner, and her little granddaughter, who is the fruit of her previous relationship.

Rosa is Slovenian, and she was brought up in Communist Yugoslavia without any religion. When she was in hospital giving birth to her son, her partner took the opportunity to be unfaithful to her. It was her mother who told her about it, and she was so devastated that she virtually left her body and was as though paralyzed for quite some time. Once she had recovered, she refused to have her partner back, and she brought Dimitri up completely on her own. Although Dimitri and his father did have a little bit of contact when he was between three and four, they never made a proper relationship, and he subsequently disappeared completely out of both their lives.

The outbreak of the Balkans War brought obvious difficulties for Rosa and her son, and so she moved to Brussels, where she was able to obtain a good job, which enabled her to support the two of them. This is where she still resides, and so she and I were able to communicate in French (which was useful as she knows no English). Dimitri started to be really difficult around the time of puberty, and Rosa has had constant worries from his excessive drinking, his failure to tell her the truth, and from general uncontrolled behavior on his part. He was nevertheless able to train in real estate, and has worked successfully in that field. He had a relationship for ten years with a girl who came from a problem family, and they have a daughter who was five years old when Rosa and I met. After breaking up with his daughter's mother, Dimitri returned to Slovenia, where he met up with a childhood friend, who is the daughter of one of Rosa's closest friends. Now thirty-seven, he is living with this girl and working in Slovenia.

Rosa's partner, Jacques, is considerably older than she is, a widower with two children and several grandchildren, and he has his own house in a different part of Brussels from Rosa's apartment. They consequently only meet at weekends, and sometimes mid-week just for a meal. They met when she was thirty-five, very attractive, independent and career minded, and had a good job in property development. Jacques had a piece of land to sell, and when Rosa went with a partner to look at it, the partner noticed the instant attraction between the two of them. The second time that they met for business purposes, Jacques said to her, "If you don't do a deal with me, I shall court you!" This proved to be the beginning of what they have both always seen as a life commitment, and she says emphatically, "C'est l'homme de ma vie!" ("He's the man of my life!")

At eighty-three Jacques was still in excellent health. Although he had always seen his family regularly, he had never been able to demonstrate affection towards any of them, nor even towards Rosa herself. The main cause of this in his present life is no doubt the fact that his mother died when she was giving birth to him, and he was brought up by a childless aunt. Rosa was therefore pleasantly surprised by the way in which he reacted to the arrival of her granddaughter, Elise, with whom he has an extraordinary bond, and who is the only person who has ever been able to make him express deep feelings. She was sure that this indicated a strong past-life bond between the two of them, which she was keen to explore, and she also wanted to know the causes of firstly the burning pain in the middle of her stomach that has troubled her periodically ever since giving birth to Dimitri, and secondly the fact that she has never been able to bear wearing things around her neck. The answers to all these questions were revealed in the single regression that we had time for before Rosa had to leave India.

In the first previous life that came, Rosa found herself as a young boy who was the illegitimate son of an Indian prince. The boy's mother was the daughter of a sage, and it was the sage who brought him up, keeping him incognito because of the shame that would be brought to the family if he were discovered. Nothing about his origins was ever talked about in the house, but the sage instructed the boy well until he was about twenty years old. At that point the prince's legitimate sons somehow found out about him and, since he was their father's first born, they imprisoned him and then had him beheaded.

In the Bardo the young man was at first consoled by a woman dressed in white, who later turned out to be the Virgin Mary. When I moved Rosa forward to the sage's death and they met in the Bardo, he told her that he was now her granddaughter and that the prince who had been the boy's father was now her partner Jacques. Furthermore, the boy's mother (the sage's daughter) was now Rosa's great friend, who had accompanied her on the trip to Sai Baba's ashram, and who always gives her good advice. We then went back to a life at the time of the Crusades for further explanation.

In the second life that she found, Rosa was a powerful Christian king and an important figure in a war, whose son killed very many members of the enemy army. When it came to the crunch, the king deserted, leaving his son to go forward and be killed. The king, however, was then so filled with remorse that he promptly killed himself, plunging his sword in the very spot where Rosa has had the constant pain. The queen then poisoned herself because of her grief at losing both her husband and her son. At that point the king experienced such terrible grief and remorse that I had to work very hard to get him to forgive himself. This only became possible after he had met all the people for whose deaths he had been responsible and they had forgiven him. It then became clear to Rosa that the king's son was now Dimitri, and that immediately explained to her why she has always tended to be overprotective of him. Jacques, Rosa's partner, was one of the king's colleagues in that life, and it was further explained to her in the Bardo that Jacques had been through many loveless lives and was now desperately seeking love as well as trying to learn how to love. As someone who was previously an Indian sage, Rosa's little granddaughter is a very evolved soul, and her and Rosa's joint task is to help Jacques to learn about love as well as to give love generally.

Rosa commented that she has always been completely phobic about war, which seems very natural after that king's experience, and she also told me that the imprisonment in the first life she had found explained her aversion to small windows and doors, and her need always to have the doors in her house open. She consequently felt that she could now let go of her phobia about doors and windows, as well as work on her over-protectiveness of Dimitri. Hopefully that will help him at least to some extent with his problems – a thing that often happens with regression therapy, even when the other person knows nothing at all about the session. It is also very interesting from my point of view to see how a step grandparent/granddaughter relationship can be of so much significance.

CHAPTER THIRTY

ADONA'S STORY

The best interests of the adopted child can only be served:

When the child is seen as a real person – not a fantasy child, not a special child, not a commodity – but a child with his own genetics, his own talents, and his own identity…
Journey of the Adopted Self, A Quest for Wholeness, Betty Jean Lifton

Adona, who is another American email friend of mine, is also a Baba devotee, which is how we first got in touch. Her story is a sad one with an interestingly happy ending. When she was seventeen she became pregnant with her then long-term boyfriend. They both very much wanted to keep the baby, but Adona's mother refused to allow it and, along with her boyfriend, forced her daughter to have an abortion. Adona told me that she was hysterical throughout the whole procedure and went into a major depression "as soon as that life had been taken from my body." To make matters worse, when she got home she found her mother in deep distress, and apologizing. She had changed her mind and telephoned the hospital to tell them so, but the call had been too late.

"After the abortion," Adona said, "I would feel this tiny spirit hovering around me and I was constantly telling her that I wanted her, I loved her, and that I would make a way for her to come back to me if she wanted to. For a few years I could feel her presence, and then it went away." Six years later Adona was living 200 miles away, in a large apartment block that had a swimming pool. One day while she was sunbathing and reading there, she noticed "the cutest little girl swimming in the pool."

The child was going in and out of the pool, sometimes climbing onto her father's lap to warm up, and Adona found herself watching her, fascinated. After a while Adona's mother came out to the pool and at one point the little girl's father walked past them. Adona's mother then introduced them, saying that Tony had recently moved into the block.

Adona said, "Tony seemed nice, but totally not my type and so my interest was not sparked as far as he was concerned." He then went back to watching his daughter and Adona did the same. She says she thought that "Emmie was one of the cutest little girls I had seen in a long time, and I loved the spirit that exuded from her tiny body." Eighteen months later, however, Tony went into the office, where Adona worked, to pay his rent, bringing the now five-year-old Emmie with him. Adona had a big basket of apples on her desk and, since the little girl was eyeing them, Adona asked her if she would like one. Emmie's eyes lit up and she gave Adona a big hug as a thank you.

It was the fall in America, and Tony then invited Adona to take a drive in the mountains with him to look at the leaves. She happened to be feeling "miffed at her boyfriend" at the time, and the upshot of this autumn excursion was that the two of them subsequently lived together for thirteen years. During these years Adona helped Tony to raise his daughter, and she says, "We developed the most intense bond and to this day – she is now well into her twenties – I am the one she calls when distressed." She continues, "Several years ago in a channeling message I got confirmation of what I had already figured out: that Emmie is the same soul that I was forced to give up when I was in high school. She is my daughter, even though she came physically through other people's bodies. She found a way of coming into existence that would eventually lead her back to me."

Another interesting point is that, although both Adona and Emmie have lived in all sorts of different places in the US during the many years that they have known each other, Emmie went to college in the city where Adona was at high school. She comments, "Sort of full circle. I think that she was meant to experience that city, the one that she would have been born in and grown up in if I had been allowed to keep her." Several years ago Adona told Emmie about the channeled message that she had received, and she says that "before the words even came out of my mouth, she was crying – happy tears – and telling me that she knew that I was her 'real' mother. We had a great talk that day, putting together pieces of a puzzle that only we knew."

PART SEVEN – PETS

CHAPTER THIRTY-ONE

THEY'VE BEEN WITH US BEFORE!

"I live here: 'Wessex' is my name:
I am a dog known rather well:
I guard the house; but how that came
To be my whim I cannot tell…

"No doubt I shall always cross this sill,
And turn the corner, and stand steady,
Gazing back for my mistress till
She reaches where I have run already…"
Thomas Hardy

I hope that my previous chapters have made it clear that people, whether born naturally, adopted, fostered, or in stepfamilies, are always in the family they are in for a reason. And that their life was planned beforehand so that the main characters in their family would be people they had known in a previous life or lives. Well, I believe the same to be true of animals; since their lives are normally shorter than ours, they can sometimes return to their beloved 'owners' in their same life rather than having to wait for another one. In her book *Pets Are Forever*[1], Jenny Smedley has various interesting stories that endorse this view.

While I was in the process of finalizing this manuscript we paid a visit to some old friends whose daughter Anne is a vet. Anne was working abroad but, after becoming a single parent, she obtained a job in the same city as her parents and they are all four now living together. Anne arrived with two noisy parrots as well as her daughter but, following complaints from neighbors, the parrots went to a sanctuary and were replaced by six-week-old twin Border Collies, who had been orphaned on a farm at only two days. Two years on Olivia and Evie are still proving very difficult to deal with, and Anne and her parents have all had to learn how to give them the discipline they missed out on from their mother. Olivia is *so* nervous that she had to be kept right out of our way, and receiving a sharp nip on the behind from Evie forced me to reflect upon the importance for *all* animals of maternal care during the first months or weeks of life. It is not that Evie is a 'nasty' dog – she both demands and revels in Anne's physical demonstrations of affection – but the fact of her post-natal deprivation naturally still makes her wary of any 'stranger', and our visit was too brief for me to become accepted. Evie of course received a severe ticking off for having hurt me, but my physical pain was as nothing compared with the commitment and difficulties that our friends have so nobly taken on. This family are for me a clear case of pets and 'owners' coming together for karmic reasons. Fortunately the other stories I have to recount do not involve nips on the behind!

Mary's Story

During the 1970s-80s Mary (not the same Mary as Jinny's sister, but it's the name they both wanted me to use) had a Lakeland terrier called Skip, who was absolutely devoted to her. Sometimes when she was going to work he managed to get out of the house and would lie down in front of the bus that she caught "to teach me to stop going away"! She was devastated when Skip died, at the age of thirteen, but in 2005 Pyxie, her daughter-in-law's Border terrier, had a litter of six and, since Mary lives nearby, she visits her son's family often. They kept one of the female pups, but Ollie 'adopted' Mary as soon as they first met, and eventually she felt she had no choice but to take him to live with her. Nowadays she looks after all three dogs on weekdays when her daughter-in-law goes to work. Ollie's coloring is very similar to that of her beloved Skip, and he has always reminded her of him in other ways as well.

When Mary told me that she was wondering whether Ollie was a reincarnation of her beloved Skip, I offered to consult my pendulum on the question, since, as I have already mentioned, dowsing tends to be more reliable when the person doing it is indifferent to the answer. She was delighted when the answer that came up was "Skip and Ollie are the same soul and he'll be ready to be human next time round," since this rang so very true for her. (She was also keen to know about Buster, a lovely dog that she had had as a child, and was very happy with the pendulum's answer to that question: "he is also ready to be human, but is waiting for you on the other side before coming back.")

Asked what the two dogs had in common, Mary, who has known many dogs in her life, replied that both of them were the most intelligent and the most devoted dogs that she had ever come across. "Also," she told me, "Ollie has Skip's quite uncanny way of knowing what I'm feeling, and both of them have always been better than most dogs are at expressing their own feelings." Of the many dogs she has known, Mary says that none has the gift of 'rapport' as strongly as Skip had and Ollie now has, and she also regards them both as a bit closer to "being human" than any other dogs she has ever known.

Dogs tend to be free spirits (if less so than cats!), and neither Skip nor Ollie is an exception to this, but Mary adds, "Both of them, although friendly and liking people, would defend me to the utmost if they thought I was in danger." She finds nowadays that Ollie is always watchful and says, "When all other dogs are asleep, I'm sure he sleeps with one eye open!" I hope that he will live at least as long as he did when he was Skip, so that Mary can continue to enjoy his company and protection for quite a while to come yet.

Nicky's Story

Nicky has been a huge animal lover all her life. She says that, whereas some describe themselves as 'dog people' and others 'cat people', she herself would never be able to make a choice between the two. While agreeing with me that dogs tend generally to be more "people oriented," she feels that cats can also be very attached to people, but that they are "more selective."

When she was six years old, Nicky went with her family on a visit to her uncle's farm, where she fell instantly in love with a Welsh collie pup that her uncle had recently bred. Although they already had a dog, she succeeded in persuading her parents to let her have the puppy. She named him Patch and he lived to be seventeen; always devoted to Nicky, he died just before she left home to go to university, in Birmingham.

While Nicky was living in digs in Birmingham, she made a habit of feeding the stray cats in the neighborhood and one of these, a beautiful black cat whom she named Puddy, adopted her. When, after a few years, Nicky got a job in Germany, she felt very bad about having to leave Puddy behind. She gave her to some good friends, who looked after her well until she died, but whenever she returned from Germany on a visit and called on the friends, Puddy always showed just the same affection for her as she always had.

Many years later still, Nicky was visiting her mother with her young daughter when they heard a scrawny little black kitten whimpering underneath a car in a car park. Nicky felt somehow sure that this cat was calling *her*, but she noticed that the car contained a cat basket and so, assuming that it had escaped from its owners, she left a note on the window of the car concerned, gave the kitten something to eat and waited with it for a good half hour. When the owner of the car failed to return, she went around from vet to police to another vet, making enquiries, but all in vain. So that night the tiny kitten slept wrapped around Nicky's young daughter's neck and, since she was never claimed, they named her Cobweb and took her home with them, where she lost no time in gaining weight and becoming integrated into the family. Nicky, who is a great reader of spiritual literature and has been studying reincarnation for a long time, gradually came to realize that Cobweb was Puddy come back to her.

Although Nicky and Jasmine were very happy both with Cobweb and another much loved cat, Nicky was very keen for her daughter to have the experience of a pet dog as well. She thought at first that they needed to wait for that until they could move into a house with a garden, but when Jasmine reached twelve she decided that they could not wait any longer. She then heard of a nearby farm where they were breeding shorthaired collies as working dogs and had two pups, one of each sex, that were needing homes.

Before they went to the farm, Nicky told Jasmine that they should definitely take the female because she was quite sure that a female pup would integrate more readily with their female cats. In fact the female turned out to be by far the prettier of the two pups and so to start with Nicky had no difficulty in ignoring her brother. However, Jasmine looked at them both and declared emphatically that she wanted the male. Nicky argued her case for a while, but then she looked into the little male pup's eyes and found herself overwhelmed with an emotion that she could not explain. Then she knew that her daughter was right: they no longer had a choice – this male puppy was theirs!

Nicky has seen one of her spirit guides in meditation and found that he looks like Merlin – a character who had always fascinated her. She had anyway always wanted to have a pet called Merlin, and Jasmine also felt the name to be appropriate for their black and white puppy (who has the unusual feature of his eyes being different colors from one another). The fact that their new dog Merlin was Patch come back to her did not dawn on Nicky instantly; it was more of a gradual realization. After just a few weeks of his living with them (*and* making good friends with the cats!), Nicky observed in Merlin a wisdom that she had never found in any dog other than her beloved Patch. She says that she came to have an indisputable inner knowing that they were one and the same soul. Even at only two years old Nicky found Merlin to have an extraordinary awareness that sometimes proves useful to her. For instance he is able to detect dark energies and this has on occasion caused her to avoid going somewhere that might be dangerous. Nicky even goes so far as to say that she sees Merlin as an enlightened soul who is ready to bypass becoming human!

The Pearson Family's Story

We also once had a dog called Merlin, though he was not of the same breed as Nicky and Jasmine's dog. Unlike my husband, I was not brought up with dogs, and the fact that we have always travelled rather a lot made getting pets for our children seem very difficult. However, the only magazines that our daughter Alice ever wanted when she was very young were animal ones, and she eventually persuaded me to let her have some gerbils. When her fifteenth birthday was approaching she made a plea for a dog, and we succumbed because we knew that she would look after it well. She had read up widely about dogs and decided that only a Cavalier King Charles spaniel would do and, when I took her to choose a puppy, I fully appreciated the reasons for her choice.

Alice, who has always been a great reader, was at the time absorbed in the Terry Pratchett books, and so she named her beautiful tricolor pup after the wizard in his books, changing the spelling to Rincewynd. Rincewynd was completely Alice's dog from the start; she trained him single-handedly, and his main source of exercise was accompanying her on the daily newspaper round that she did after school. Loving and lovable though he was, however, he never appeared to be the most robust of dogs, often going off his food for a day or two, and on occasions when the weather was not to his liking, he would go on strike and insist on staying at home while she braved the elements alone. Sometimes the people in the houses to which she delivered the Hull Daily Mail would ask her where Rincewynd was.

The Christmas of 1983, when Rincewynd was two and a half, we went on a family holiday to Spain, leaving the dog in our house in the care of a good friend of mine who happened to be in need of a home while she was in between houses. Although it was not the first time that we had been away abroad leaving the dog in someone else's care, I felt on this occasion inexplicably nervous about it. We had a wonderful Spanish Christmas together and I tried to dismiss my 'irrational' fears, but these nevertheless increased during our drive home from Manchester airport in the middle of a snowy January night. Alice was greatly looking forward to being greeted by her beloved Rincewynd, and so you can imagine our horror when we opened the kitchen door at four o'clock in the morning to find nothing but an empty dog basket! This was of course in the days before mobile phones and email, and so my poor friend had the unpleasant task of coming downstairs to explain to us how Rincewynd had fallen ill and died during our absence. She had rushed him to the vet, who had diagnosed a severe case of gastro-enteritis and done all he could to save him, but by the time we returned from Spain the cremation was already over and done with.

The story of how my husband saw the dog in the flat in Spain on the day that he died is in my first book, *Karmic Release,* but I would like now to mention the fact of my having had at this point still a great deal of learning to do in connection with pet animals. This sad loss occurred before I had come round to believing in reincarnation and, not having had any previous experience of dog 'ownership' (do people own dogs or vice versa? Nowadays I incline to the latter view!), I failed to appreciate their unique individuality. Though I did not for a moment doubt the fact that animals also had souls, it never occurred to me that they had a history of many previous lives which had gradually led them to progress to their present, highly intelligent, form, and that they had particular reasons for being with us. I consequently made the big mistake of trying to comfort my daughter by telling her that "dogs, unlike human beings, are replaceable." Although I missed Rincewynd's presence in the house dreadfully, my main concern was for Alice's grief and, since she would be going off to university eighteen months later, I felt it imperative to get her another puppy as soon as possible.

The new dog had of course to be another Cavalier and Alice (who had a better understanding than I had about a dog's irreplaceability!) chose a black and tan this time. The breeder was keen to sell him at only six weeks, and he and his sister had been born on New Year's Day (our son Paul's birthday!) – only three days after Rincewynd had died. Alice felt that she should use another wizard's name, which is why she decided to call her new puppy Merlin.

And now my learning really began, since Merlin was from the start so very different in character from Rincewynd. David quickly described him as 'a heavy-duty dog' because he seemed so much less delicate than his predecessor, and at a very early stage Merlin greatly annoyed our neighbor by succeeding in jumping over the fence into his garden! Also, no sort of weather ever bothered him in the slightest. Come heavy rain or excessive shine, Merlin would be out on that newspaper round, and would complain in no uncertain terms when anyone ever had cause to go out without him.

But above all, whereas Rincewynd had always been indisputably *Alice's* dog, Merlin was from the start much more of a *family* dog. Alice is someone who always likes a lie-in in the morning whenever possible, and at weekends and during the school holidays, when she did not have up to get up early, Rincewynd would scratch on the door of her room and, once admitted, would lie curled up on her bed until she eventually came to terms with the fact that it was time to get up. Merlin, on the other hand, would bounce into her room as soon as he had been let out of the kitchen where he slept and, if she showed no inclination to get out of bed, would go looking for someone who was already up and willing to talk to him. So, when it had got into the early nineties and I had become engrossed in my studies of spiritual subjects including reincarnation, it came as no surprise to me to be told by the now famous clairvoyant, Edwin Courtenay, that Rincewynd had previously been a bird that belonged to Alice during an itinerant masculine life and that they had been very attached to one another. As for Merlin, Edwin saw that he had been our family cat in an eighteenth century life! Since I have already recounted the story of that life in my first book, let it suffice for me to explain here that I was then also married to David, that Paul and Alice were both our children, and that Christopher was a family friend.

Alice loved both Rincewynd and Merlin dearly but differently, and I know that even now that she is a mature woman, Rincewynd still holds a very special place in her heart. Although she herself does not share my spiritual beliefs, I am personally quite sure that he will one day return to her – possibly as the rescue dog she hopes to acquire once her living circumstances are more favorable to her keeping a dog. (She no longer sees Cavaliers as "the only possible type of dog" for her!)

Since Alice did indeed go off to university as soon as she left school and has been working in the London area ever since she completed her studies, it is no doubt a good thing that dear Merlin was so very much a family dog. Though of course always delighted when she returned for vacations and later simply weekends, he accepted her departure and David and/or me taking him for his daily walks rather than going on the newspaper round.

He remained a 'heavy duty dog' until round about the time that we moved to Ludlow in 2004. By this time it had become apparent that he was suffering from a heart murmur – a condition that Cavaliers are alas very prone to. The move from his much loved Cottingham home was no doubt stressful for him (just as it was for us, much though we wanted to make it!), and the nice Ludlow vet to whom we soon had to start making regular visits lost no time in putting Merlin on heart pills and diuretics, and he also told us to reduce his walks to a minimum. This was hard for all three of us since Merlin had always loved accompanying on us lengthy walks and we had been so looking forward to introducing him to the Shropshire hills, but in his old age he set what I shall always regard as a first class example in forbearance and patience in adversity. Never did a complaint pass his lips even when we left him at home on his own for a whole day, or when he was clearly suffering a good deal of pain. When we went on a month's holiday to Peru in the autumn of 2005, Alice nobly took charge of him in her London abode, and it was very hard for her when he suddenly had to have emergency treatment. He spent two or three days at the Raynes Park vet's, who waxed lyrical about his strength of character and his courage, and was clearly amazed when he pulled through.

On our return from Peru, the news of what Alice and Merlin had been going through and the vet's bill were something of a shock, but we quickly forgot about the latter in our gratitude for the extra six months that the treatment gave Merlin. I readily forsook my annual January trip to India in order to be sure of not missing his last days or weeks with us. In early May 2006 the weather happened to be unusually warm, and one lovely Wednesday Merlin came with us on our first visit to Hay on Wye, where he enjoyed a picnic lunch by the river. Walking up the hill afterwards, however, was too much for him, and David had to carry him (still uncomplaining) back to the car. We returned to the vet's the very next day and then, after some sad consultation with Alice over the phone, we acquiesced to his recommendation that he come to the house and put Merlin to sleep on the Saturday morning.

David shed bitter tears at Merlin's departure, while I found it easier to accept since he had had a good twelve and a half years, had brought the five of us much joy and was now, I felt sure, ready to move on to other things. I had always said of Merlin that he thought he was a person until he met another dog, which promptly caused him to remember that he was also a dog. Though I have at present no way of proving it, I firmly believe that he will be human in his next incarnation.

This time, even though the house felt horribly empty, we decided to have a much longer break before getting our next Cavalier puppy – partly because we were set on doing a longer trip to India. But on our return from India in March 2007, it was more than time for me to buy David a late birthday present. He rather fancied a Blenheim (the breed's most common color scheme), but a search of the internet for available pups soon revealed a delightful looking litter of five Rubies in North Wales, easily accessible to us by a direct train route. The breeder wanted to keep the only girl, and another buyer had already laid claim to the little boy that had a white patch on his chest, which left us with three identical pups to choose from. Since my dear daughter forbade me to use my pendulum for the choice (thinking that the breeder would think me as mad as Alice does herself!), I said to David, "Well, the puppy will have to choose us." Which the three-week-old Apu undoubtedly did. (He had to have an Indian name following our seven week tour of that wonderful country. David's choice was triggered by Sathyajit Ray's moving *Apu Trilogy*, but we also gave him the surname of Arun, which means 'reddish brown'.) Five weeks later we excitedly went to his birth-place again to collect him, and he was clearly as sure as ever that we were the people he was going to own. Once we had got him home, one of the very first things that I wanted to do was to find out about our karmic links with our new puppy. For, despite being officially David's birthday present, his bond with me was forged just as quickly as his bond with my husband.

It so happened that the good friend Thia I had left behind in Cottingham had recently had a reading from a North Yorkshire shaman concerning a much-loved cat that she had recently lost. So I spoke to this woman on the phone and her reaction to my question was "Well, if you send me his photograph, I'll certainly look, but are you sure that you have a karmic link with your puppy?" I then explained to her my firm belief that animals always came to people they had known before, just the same as children did. I did not have to wait very long for the return phone call, and what this shaman was told by her spirit guide proved to be a huge surprise to both of us. The reading gave the following information: "You and Apu [which, by the way, is pronounced 'Opoo' in the films] were previously sisters in a Native American life. You were the older and were named Brown Wings, while he, then she, was called Small Broken Tree because she was very delicate and had a genetic weakness. Small Broken Tree died at a very early age when a virus swept through the camp. Since she was very attached to you, a soul fragment of hers stayed with you, and that is why she has returned to you now." The shaman then informed me that, with the help of her guide, who had showered him with a lovely waterfall of drops of gold, she had restored that soul part to Apu, and that he was now consequently whole again.

In Mark's story I already mentioned soul retrieval, but another very interesting question – and one which I myself feel very ill qualified to discuss – is that of souls crossing over between human and animal incarnations. Many people see our evolution as a lengthy process from the mineral and vegetable kingdoms through the animal to the human, but many animal lovers will rightly ask the question, "What reason have you to suppose that being human is any way superior to being a dog, cat or dolphin?" It is well known among devotees of Sathya Sai Baba that two of his classmates, who had been particularly devoted to Him and died very young, reincarnated as the dogs Jack and Jill that He kept very close to Him throughout their lives. And near Bikaner in Rajasthan, North India, is the Karni Mata temple, which is home to several thousand rats, about whom there are various legends. When we visited it, our guide told us that Karni Mata had implored Yama, the god of Death, to revive Laxman after he had drowned. Yama then allowed Laxman to reincarnate as a rat, and ever since all those who die in that particular village become rats in that temple, where they gain merit before becoming human again (I think for their final incarnation).

After being given this interesting information about my previous link with little Apu, I found myself wondering, "Do we sometimes make little forays into being human in between progressive animal incarnations?" Certainly it was quickly clear to both of us that Apu was a much less self-sufficient character than his predecessor Merlin. A nervous little dog, who never got over his habit of barking furiously at the ironing board whenever I got it down, and who would cower for a full hour in the garden any time that a bit of burnt toast caused the smoke alarm to go off, he always seemed to us to need more looking after than Merlin ever had.

So we did our best to instill confidence into Apu at the same time as reveling in his constant affection and devotion – not to mention his boundless energy. I felt sure that he must also have a karmic link with David, and my friend Kate, who is an animal communicator as well as a teacher of Reiki healing, saw when I asked her to communicate with Apu our displeasure with his habit of weeing inside the house, that he had had a previous life as a bird with David, at a time when the two of us were not acquainted.

However, when Apu suddenly died unexpectedly in August

2010, at the age of three and a half, it soon became apparent that the learning in his brief life was two way. I had been sad when Rincewynd died, but that was mainly because of my daughter's pain, and when Merlin died I was sadder for David than for myself, because he took it harder than I did. Now I was the one who really needed to learn about grief! I who had never yet, even at the age of seventy, had to suffer the loss of anyone really close to me.

One of the first things that I did while trying to cope with the shock was to ask my dear friend Jane (who works as a healer and has done a lot of shamanic training) to tune into Apu's spirit. This she kindly did the very next day, and everything that she told me made perfect sense to both of us. Jane said that Apu's apparently untimely death was indeed part of his Life Plan and that his purpose was to open my heart. Jane told us that Apu was now happy and with Merlin, who was guiding him and to whom he was both a "son" and a "sun." She further commented that Merlin was an old soul while Apu was a young one. When David heard what Jane said, he agreed with me that this latter point accorded exactly with the comparison of the two dogs that we had just been making to one another. I remembered what the shaman had told me about repairing Apu's soul fragmentation and so I now believe that he only needed to be with us for a short time in order for his healing to be achieved.

Six weeks later, still grieving the death intensely but at the same time aware that the experience was helping me with my writing on the subject of grief as well as with my ability to feel compassion for others who suffer the loss of loved ones, I felt drawn to attend a clairvoyant supper in Shrewsbury. I was not given any particularly meaningful messages while the meal was taking place, but, after missing the ten o'clock train back to Ludlow and having to wait almost an hour for the next one, I got into conversation on the pavement with one of the clairvoyants. She told me that she could see a little brown dog standing beside my right leg and she commented, "Gosh, isn't he friendly?! He'll lead you to the train." I then told her my sad story, and her reply was that she was a hundred percent sure that Apu would come back to us the following year. (We had again decided to have a travel break before getting our next puppy.)

Remembering what Jane had said about Apu being Merlin's "son and sun," I decided in advance to name the new puppy after Surya, the Indian sun god. We were once more seeking a Blenheim since this was the only Cavalier coloring that we had not yet had, but when I heard about a Ruby puppy being for sale not too far from where we lived, we felt compelled to go and see him. Apu had been unusual in that he tended to hold his tail vertically rather than horizontally (a thing which apparently makes a Cavalier ineligible for Crufts!), and so after his death I had made a pact with him to use that as one of the signals to look for in our next puppy. The tail, however, was not the only thing that drew us to the new puppy: we loved his little white beard and the white mark on his chest, and he seemed to be happy with us right from the start.

But before going to have a look at the puppy, I was attending a regression conference in Turkey, where one of the participants was a young girl who was very gifted at Tarot. So many people were asking her questions that I was also drawn to ask, "Is the puppy we're about to go and look at a reincarnation of our dog Apu?" Her reply was not what I was wanting at the time: "No, he isn't, but he is the right puppy for you." For months and months I was uncertain about it, since I was still so badly wanting Apu back again, but gradually I was able to say to myself, "What does it matter? We love Surya for himself rather than for what or who he was before. Clairvoyants aren't always right about everything, and one of the two has to be wrong anyway."

Surya is now three and, though he still tends to hold his tail vertically, he is a totally different character from Apu and, I would guess, a more evolved soul. He is certainly the easiest of our four dogs and the most obedient. It is a great bonus to be able at bedtime to say, "Into bed, Surya," and then not to have the chase the dog all over the house until he finally does what he's been bidden, and also to be able to have the occasional lie-in in the morning without being barked at from downstairs. The young girl I met in Turkey told me that Apu was still with me, so maybe I should look for him on one of my shamanic journeys.

As for my previous connections with Surya, I found the answer myself in May 2014, when I was at a meeting of the 'Mouliners' group[2] in France. The previous year four of us had visited Mary Magdalen's cave at Ste. Baume and, since I had been having trouble with my right leg, I was apprehensive about my ability to manage the climb up to it. As soon as we started up the mountain, however, I found myself precipitated into a Cathar life in which a small group of us were being pursued by the enemy and consequently made it to the top of the mountain without too much difficulty. On that occasion I failed to see how the story ended, and so at our subsequent meeting this year I asked for a regression in order to find it. We then went off exploring Cathar castles, and it was gradually revealed to me that Surya had been my horse not only in that Cathar life, but also shortly beforehand, in the crusader's lifetime that I wrote about in my first book. I consequently believe that we made a joint pact to return quickly into a much 'better' life. And the tremendous greeting he gave me upon my return home confirmed my conviction about our having been together before!

Lynn's Story

Merlin (perhaps not surprisingly) is evidently a popular name for dogs, and I have also heard of both a horse and a cat with the name. My friend Lynn's reason for choosing this name is because of the associations with Camelot around where she lives in Cornwall (Merlin's cave beneath Tintagel Castle) and also all the mythology and reincarnation myths associated with Merlin which, she says, "seems to fit with this wiz of a dog I am going to welcome into my life soon!" Lynn has long associations with the Weimaraner breed and has kindly written her story herself, so here it is:

"My first encounter with a Weimaraner was in the early 1970s when my mother returned from a trip to the compost heap at the bottom of the garden saying she had seen "a lilac colored dog with yellow eyes!" After rubbing Mother down with a damp edition of the parish magazine and giving her a medicinal sherry, then making further enquiries, we found out that the new neighbors were some of the first people in the country to own a recently imported breed of hunt, point, retrieve dog – the Weimaraner, from Germany. Over the next few years I babysat for the family and came to know and love Kurt, their Weimaraner, and determined that should I ever have a dog of my own it could only be a Weimie.

A little over twenty years later, in 1993, Oscar the Weimaraner became chief guard dog, wreaker of havoc and general mischief in my own family. The hard work of training paid off and we were all blessed with a noble, intelligent companion whose steadfastness and loyalty were the stuff of legend. Oscar was a happy, supremely confident dog, who knew his own strength and ability and also exactly what his job/role was in the family. This important combination meant that he never used his considerable strength unnecessarily and only ever as much as was required by the situation; he was always an exponent of minimal force. There are many examples of his incredible character and temperament and, despite the fact that he got attacked several times, he never once bit another dog. Oscar's answer was to clamp his jaws over the top of the other dog's neck in a doggie version of a headlock and stand over them until they submitted; the other dogs always appeared to understand that he would not harm them unnecessarily.

The two incidents that perhaps best illustrate Oscar's relationships with humankind were, firstly, when he captured a suspicious window cleaner who had come into the kitchen, where one of the children was playing, and escorted him to me in another part of the house with his jaws lightly but insistently clamped around his forearm. And secondly the occasion when a thoughtless 'au pair' left one of the children (aged 18 months) in the bath unattended, whilst she went to watch the TV. Oscar sat by the bath and would not leave the toddler until I returned, and then barked to attract my attention.

Oscar simply loved life and all it had to offer, from going shopping into the local town, where he would sit patiently outside any shop, reveling in the admiration of countless passers-by, to his other love, which was a day out shooting with his master. There he would sit patiently at the peg marking birds and then pick them up diligently. His master was not exactly known for his shooting prowess, so if the day was not going well, Oscar used to mark other guns' birds and pick them up too in order to avoid total boredom. The reward of a slurp of ale, a sausage and a snooze in front of a roaring fire made him the happiest dog in the world. He only had one minor shoplifting conviction, which was for removing a large dog chew from an (inadvisably low) basket in the pet shop, but the incident was soon resolved when I paid up, and ever after that the pet shop owner allowed him to select his own chew whenever he went in. He even appeared to enjoy his puppies and would always sneak in to visit his offspring when Maizie (mum) went outside for a while.

Oscar died in 2004, aged eleven and, despite the fact that the Weimaraner family had grown to four by then, he left a huge hole. A week or so after his death, I was at a friend's house, where I met a professional clairvoyant who was staying with her. This clairvoyant said that she realized that I had recently lost someone who was very dear to me, and so I explained that it was the family dog. She then told me that Oscar was fine on the other side and that he would be coming back to me at some time in the future and that he would be a "present."

In February 2011, I left the job I had had since 2005 as a school nurse. In the meantime the remaining three members of the Weimaraner family had also died and, much as I wanted another dog, I had decided against getting another one immediately, as I felt I needed time to see where life was leading and had several invitations to travel and do voluntary work abroad. Unbeknownst to me, the parents and children made a collection, and a few discreet enquiries with that toddler in the bath, who was now a beautiful, nineteen-year-old woman, led to them presenting me with a puppy voucher as my leaving *present*! So I immediately remembered the clairvoyant's words and realized what a special dog this was going to be.

I am now living happily on my own in Cornwall, where amongst many other things I enjoy walking the South West Coastal Path and am looking forward to being joined in January 2012 by Merlin (or perhaps we should say Oscar), a Weimaraner puppy who will then be approximately eight weeks old – my "*present*"! Coincidentally, Merlin's future mother was bred by my friend who had bred Maizie, Oscar's wife, so it is a real family affair! It remains to be seen how he will behave with errant window cleaners, pet shop owners and my daughters when they are taking baths, but one thing that is certain is that a nobler, loyal and more steadfast companion you could not ask for – the return of a true friend to a true friend – reunited through the timeless bond of love.

Kate's Story

You will remember that my good friend Kate in Chapter Two runs a children's home in India, but in that chapter I did not mention the fact that she gives a good home to even more dogs than she does to children! Her many years in India have filled her with revulsion for the way in which dogs are normally treated there, and she feels that part of her life purpose is not only to give a good life to dogs that are on their last canine incarnation and ready to become human next time round, but also to set an example to people in India as to how dogs should be treated. She also feels that the children in her care benefit greatly from learning how to look after animals.

One of the many frustrations that Kate has to endure is the lack of good veterinary facilities available to her where she lives, and she feels that this has over the years caused many unnecessary deaths among her canine friends. These deaths cause her constant heartbreaks, and also the difficulty in getting the dogs treated by a good vet often results in a surfeit of puppies being born on the premises. Not that either she or the children ever mind yet more puppies being born, but sometimes it proves impossible to help them survive, which causes yet more heartbreak all round!

The dog whose memory will probably always be most firmly engraved in Kate's heart is one who was named Binki – after the first toy dog that she got when she was four or five years old. The 'real' Binki came from a family of nine and was the only one with long hair. Binki was always *everybody's* favorite; Kate tells me that even the Indians who normally took no notice of any of her dogs came to really love him. Being a spiritual person, Kate likes to teach the children bhajans (Indian devotional songs), and Binki never failed to attend these sessions, invariably joining in with the 'Aum' in a most convincing and heartfelt manner. Unfortunately one day Binki had an accident that involved one of his front legs, which – again owing to veterinary incompetence – never healed completely and left him with only a stump. But this did nothing to dampen his devotion and, when I had the privilege of visiting Kate's establishment, I was most impressed with the way in which the three-and-a-half-legged dog would walk into the prayer room as soon as it became apparent that a bhajan session was about to commence. He was a truly beautiful dog – quite unlike any of the street dogs one is accustomed to see roaming around in India – with a gorgeous coat in an identical shade of brown to that of our 'Ruby' dogs Apu and Surya, but of a size nearer to that of a collie or a Labrador.

Kate mourned Binki's death more than that of any other dog she has ever known and, talking to me about it again, we even wondered together whether, since he appeared to be so spiritually inclined, he could bypass being human and become self-realized straight away. Or whether perhaps he had already been human and had chosen to return in canine form as a helper both to children in need of stability and love and to Kate herself. One thing that seemed very clear to me, and dowsing once again confirmed it, was that he had already been close to Kate before he came to her as Binki.

Jane's Story

My friend Jane, who was so helpful to us when Apu died, is herself emphatically a cat person. When she and her now deceased partner owned a house in France in which they used to spend their summer holidays, she befriended a wild cat in the vicinity, but one summer that they were there, he failed to appear and so Jane sadly assumed that he had died. This cat, however, reincarnated some years later in London as a tiny female. She was owned initially by Jane's next door neighbors (who happened to be French!) and they named her Charlie. But they treated her as a farm cat and left her out at night and in all weathers and so, after she had become very ill, Jane adopted her. She says, "It was love at first sight for us both. When I held her I used to get images of where I lived in France and the forest that was her home. And then she came to Ludlow with me."

By the time that I first met Jane, she was well settled in

Ludlow and had besides Charlie three other cats living with her, one of whom, Ruby, had been a stray. After we had become friends Jane went through a very rough period of about two years during which not only all four of her cats died, but also some of the people who had been closest to her. The difficult grieving process disinclined her towards looking for any new cats, but living next door to the woman who ran the local Cats Protection League made it difficult for Jane to avoid getting adopted!

She was adopted firstly by one and then by a second, rather elderly cat, neither of whom was in the best of health. She named one of them Quesie and the other Mama Quilla, cared for them both lovingly, and with the help of the vet whom she had already come to trust, made the end of their lives as comfortable as was possible. Losing these two cats was again hard for Jane, and this time she felt like having a rather longer break.

Not too long after the time that she first felt ready for some new pussies to come into her life, Jane heard of a young black and white cat that had been found under a hedge with seven kittens. So she went to visit them in the foster home, saying that she was willing to consider taking the mum plus two kittens, a girl and a boy. Three new cats seemed plenty to Jane, but when the foster mum pointed out the little tomcat that was a little bit quiet and reticent, she agreed to keep them together.

Anyone who wants to succeed as a healer needs to be very intuitive, and Jane made use of her intuition not only when she recognized Charlie as the wild French cat she had loved, but also when she went to visit the foster home for the first time. As soon as she set eyes on the new little mother cat, she sensed that this was Ruby returning to her, and she felt this initial feeling confirmed once her new family were safely installed in her home. So Ruby is now Bella, and what is more, the 'quiet little tomcat' turned out to be a sweet little girl called Tao, who Sue says, "…is Charlie. And of course Charlie goes back to the original wild cat in France, so bless you foster mum for enabling this very special cat to return to me for a second time."

Of the two elderly cats who had had the good fortune of ending their days in her care, Quesie was one whom Jane felt to be particularly close to her. They had had a very special, loving relationship and Jane now feels that she has come back as the other female kitten, whom she has named Tara Quinn. So of her 'new' family, it looks as though only Chet, the kitten that is genuinely a tomcat, is *really* new to Jane!

Rowan's Story

Another great cat lover is my 'Sai Baba devotee' friend Rowan, who has believed in reincarnation for a long time. A cat whom she named Cymbeline, or Cymbie for short, came into Rowan's life at a very crucial point, when she was badly needing some healing. Cats are well known for being wonderful healers, and Rowan says,

"I collected Cymbeline as a tiny kitten from my neighbor, just a few doors up, on a stormy evening in August 1999. As I held her in my arms, looking out at the lightning and driving rain, I decided to call her Cymbeline, as although she was a tiny, cute kitten, I knew she would grow into the beautiful and majestic cat she eventually came to be. Lisa, my neighbor, had pointed her out to me from the large litter of seven, (three sets of twins and then this tiny, seventh cat) as the kitten who liked to go off on her own, exploring; she had a mind of her own. She also looked the most like her father, Titan, a huge black Persian, who, after making Daisy (a dainty white and black female) pregnant, wandered off, never to be seen again. I did worry that Cymbeline might do the same, and for two or three years, she was almost wild, living most of the time outside, only coming in to feed, sleep on my bed, and occasionally allow me a cuddle or two.

Cymbeline was a very 'knowing' cat and she and I had quite a strong psychic connection. Throughout our life together, whenever I felt like I needed to know where she was, if she'd been out a long time, or sometimes if I woke in the night after a bad dream and needed to feel her comforting presence, all I had to do was think, "Cymbeline, please let me know you're around," and within ten to fifteen minutes she would come padding into the house, meowing and saying 'hello', before either setting off again, or settling down nearby. She knew when I needed her around, and although never a 'cuddly' cat, would stick to my side like glue when things got rough.

One night whilst recovering from her neutering operation, Cymbeline crawled onto my bed and into my arms, immediately I felt healing energy flowing down my arms and hands and into Cymbeline as she nestled on my lap. She stayed there for a quarter of an hour, and when she'd had enough, she went off to sleep on her cushion, the healing energy ceased immediately she left my hands. What a wise cat!

She seemed to have an affinity with magpies – a friend once saw Cymbeline lying down in the field next door to where we lived, with several magpies hopping round about her – she was black and white herself, so perhaps they thought she was a bigger furrier version of themselves! I really don't know, but she was very relaxed, on her back and enjoying their company.

My beloved Cymbeline lived to the age of 11. A brain tumor claimed her independence of spirit and eventually power over her own body. After many visits to the vet, I made the heart-rending decision that everyone dreads, and held her in my arms whilst the injection eased her into death. The morning after her release, she came back to tell me she was around – I was lying in bed, feeling totally grief stricken, when I heard the unmistakable sound of a cat shaking it's fur after being out in the rain. It was a very subtle sound, but I heard it very close to my head. When I looked out of the window, I noticed it was raining."

Rowan is convinced that she and Cymbie have been together in several previous lives, and she is also very sure that Cymbie is an old soul with exceptional wisdom. While she was mourning Cymbie and not yet feeling ready for another cat in her life, Rowan decided to volunteer in a cats' rescue home. However, hardly had she started working there when she was captivated by a pair of female sibling kittens. These adorable little creatures, whom she soon named Ruby and Belle, seemed to be saying to her, "Please take us home with you!" and she found herself totally unable to resist their plea. By the time Rowan told me her story, her new adoptees had made her home completely their own, and my pendulum confirmed Rowan's intuitive feeling that she had also known both of them in a previous life. Here, however, the situation is quite different: whereas Cymbie had come into Rowan's life to help *her* to heal, Ruby and Belle feel to her like much younger souls who have come into her care mainly for their own growth. (I was most interested when she told me that, as it sounded to be the same sort of difference as that between our two dogs Merlin and Apu.)

Asante's Story

Asante, who wrote her own story for the Birth Mother section, is a powerful healer and she believes that her esoteric cat story, unusual though it may seem, is worth including in this book since "such things may well happen more often than we think." In the year 2000 she applied for the post of manager of a shelter for stray cats in Vancouver, but shortly before her interview she suffered a herniated disc in her back and so checked that they were still interested in her application. They replied affirmatively and she was duly appointed, but had to resign after six months because her back problem made it too difficult for her to do such things as lifting cats. She thinks, however, that those six months were simply a way of getting her and Cosmo together.

Cosmo was an enormous cat. Asante told me that, when he was taken out of the bag after being brought into the shelter, he "just seemed to keep on coming forever," and even in the underweight state in which he had been found, he weighed eighteen pounds. Everyone there kept talking about him because he seemed so "other-worldly" and, when the other cats saw him, they "freaked out." Cats that first come in to the shelter are put in a separate compartment, and in Cosmo's case the other cats kept trying to attack him through the wire. While he was in this preliminary room, Asante fell in love with Cosmo and decided that she would take him home with her once his eye infection was cleared. Each day as she made her rounds in the morning he would meet her at the door to this room. Although he would walk her back to the door when she was leaving, he would never try to leave it. She decided to let him make his own choice of when to leave this room, and eventually he walked out of his own accord to join the other cats in the open common area of this 'no kill, no cage' shelter. This means that the cats are not kept in cages unless they are ill or have behavioral problems. They all live together roaming freely about the shelter. 'No kill' means that, unlike some shelters which – normally for reasons of space – have rules about how long an animal can remain there if they are not adopted, the cats in the shelter that Asante managed were never euthanized.

The other cats kept picking on Cosmo, but he always refused to retaliate and somehow always managed to elude a fight. After he had moved out into the common area, Asante didn't see him personally each day in the same way. He no longer either met her at the door or walked her back to it, and so she began to think that she might not adopt him after all. She resisted the temptation to take him home because, as she says, "When you have a hundred cats to look after, you have to be firm with yourself." But then one day when she was lying in bed, Cosmo appeared to Asante and said, "Don't forget about me." So that was it: Cosmo was thereafter hers!

People who met him always commented what a "noble and dignified" cat Cosmo was, and he and Asante quickly became extremely close. On one occasion, when she filled his water bowl, freshening it up from room temperature to cold from the well, she distinctly heard him say, "Thank you! I really like my water cold." He had sinus trouble, which Asante could see was sometimes causing him headaches and, when she gave him healing, he never resisted, which she says is unusual. He learnt quickly that the swinging pendulum she uses in healing, which for most cats would seem to be a toy, removed the pain.

Asante works closely with her main spirit guide, an Egyptian named Khonsu, who is the son of Mut and Amun; another name for him is Horus. She told me that the two of them have an agreement that, when she is incarnate, he remains on the other side as her guide, and vice versa. After he had been with her for about eleven years, Cosmo fell ill. Asante was visited by an angel from Mother Mary (with whom she also works closely), and she asked the angel for healing for Cosmo but was given to understand that it was not in his Life Plan. It then soon became clear that the cat had developed cancer and was dying. At that point Khonsu told Asante that a tiny bit of himself had entered Cosmo with the purpose of transferring some of his power to her. She was further told not to have him put down, even though he was clearly dying, and so she then spent two weeks lying on the bed with him more or less continuously. She said, "We had a fantastic time together during that time, and I was aware that there were higher things going on. I got a major charge of energy through Cosmo, and was told that how long he would live was up to him."

Asante knows a British couple in Vancouver who are homoeopaths, and the husband is also an ornithologist. At one point during Cosmo's illness they prescribed a remedy for both of them which they said was Falcon. This is very interesting since

Horus is of course the Falcon god. She said that the effect on both of them was extraordinary: "Both our eyes were altered by the very high state this homeopathic remedy gave us. It made me feel as though I was flying high above everything and I had an exceptional and wonderful view of it all. The feeling of being high was not woozy – or ungrounded – just very expanded." She emailed me photographs of the two of them before and after taking the remedy, and I could see exactly what she meant about their eyes. This remedy, we are both sure, helped Cosmo to leave his body when his time was up, and it also helped Asante to come to terms with losing him after coming fully to appreciate the purpose of their having been together. She finally took him to the vet when the time felt right, and Cosmo died peacefully in her arms.

Amelia's Story

Amelia came to see me for various reasons, including recurrent back injuries. She had all her life had an immense love of horses and had during her teenage years worked at a horse rescue center. Her parents had died when she was quite young and an inheritance had enabled her to buy her own horse. Now she was married, but her husband worked away a lot of the time, which gave her time to indulge her hobby, and she was the happy owner of three horses, of whom the youngest and her latest acquisition was only six years old. In fact she had never previously owned such a young horse and, when she first went to have a look at him, her immediate thought was "This isn't the sort of horse I'm looking for." Yet she somehow knew that he had to come home with her and, when a friend who is a real expert rode him, he thought that he was a very good choice.

Amelia had named her newest horse Brownie, and she loved riding him herself but, for some mysterious reason, found that she could not trust herself to let other people ride him.

Wondering whether this issue could have its origin in a previous life, we agreed to do a regression to try and find out. She got very quickly into a traumatic masculine life with an abusive, alcoholic father and a mother who took men in for a living. By the time he – let's call him Emilio – was fourteen his mother had gone off, taking his younger brother with her, and he was finding living alone with his father very difficult and painful. One day the two of them got into a fight and the youngster smashed a bottle on his father's head. There was a great deal of blood and, being too scared to wait and find out whether the blow had been fatal, he fled.

In the next scene Emilio had got away from the area by hiding in a stagecoach and, after wandering through some cornfields, had been offered a job looking after animals. Then, at sixteen, we found him living reasonably comfortably in the farmhouse and being given a bit of money as well as food. He was very fond of the horses in his care and would buy them treats with some of his earnings. When he had a day off from work he liked to walk to the market, but one day he decided to go there on his favorite horse rather than walking, thinking that no one would notice its absence. Tragedy struck, however, when, after doing a few errands, he returned to where he'd tethered the horse and found it gone. All his enquiries were in vain and, when the news got out, his master gave him a good thrashing with a belt.

Emilio then left the farm of his own accord and went to the city, where he secured a job with a tailor and remained there for the rest of that lifetime. He died from an accident at about sixty and, when I took him into the Bardo, the first people he met were his parents. His mother apologized to him for having run off with another man, and his father (who *had* died from the blow with the bottle) also told Emilio he was sorry. Amelia recognized Emilio's mother as her mother in her present life. In the Bardo too she/he was able to track down the beloved horse and discovered that he had died because of cruelty inflicted on him by the man who had stolen him. Amelia then looked into the horse's eyes and recognized him as Brownie. So she was overjoyed at his having returned to her and then felt ready to let go of her fear about other people riding him!

Marjorie's Story

Finally, Marjorie is another person who recognizes that animals one has loved in either a previous life or one's present one "always come back to you." I think it must have been our spirit guides who prompted her to contact me via Facebook after nearly fifty years and, since during our student days we had known each other in the Catholic Society, it was lovely for me to discover that during the long interim we had both moved in a similar direction spiritually. (Her moving story about her son's death and what happened afterwards is in my third book, *Discovering the Life Plan*.)

Marjorie used to breed border terriers, and her policy when prospective buyers came to look at her puppies was to sit them on the floor and see which of the pups came to them. Then, if they did not agree that "that was the dog for them," she sent them away empty handed. ("But," she told me, "it only ever happened once!") In one litter that she bred was a pup named Terry, but he was simply never around when any buyer turned up. It had not occurred to Marjorie to keep him, but after a while she realized that he had made up his mind that he was staying with her. So she finally agreed to go along with his decision, and then it dawned on her that he was her beloved Frankie returned. Frankie had died many years previously, and in fact Marjorie even thinks that Terry/Frankie might also be a reincarnation of another dog that she had had as a child. That seems to me perfectly likely and is surely a nice conclusion to this chapter!

Notes

1. *Pets Are Forever: Amazing True Stories of Angelic Animals,* Jenny Smedley, Hay House, London, 2011.
2. See *Life Without Elgar – A Tale of a Journeying Soul,* 6th Books, 2014.

PART EIGHT – CONCLUSION

CHAPTER THIRTY-TWO

THE LEARNING

The feeling that something is missing never, ever leaves you and it can't, and it shouldn't because something ***is*** *missing.*

That isn't of its nature negative. The missing part, the missing past, can be an opening, not a void. It can be an entry as well as an exit.

Jeanette Winterson – *Why Be Happy When You could Be Normal?*[1]

The title of this book has a question mark. If you were hoping to find in it an answer to the question, I'm afraid you will either have to look elsewhere or go inside yourself for one. For, following years of studying different cases, talking to numerous different people and reflection of my own, the only conclusion I have come to is that LOVE is stronger than either blood or the ties created by upbringing and from previous lives. And real love between people is, in my experience, built over a succession of lives rather than being simply a 'flash in the pan'. Our own adopted son has told us that, prior to having a child of his own, he had always believed blood to be relatively unimportant, but that Delilah's birth had changed those feelings. I find that completely understandable, but at the same time I hope to have made clear my personal conviction, based on considerable research, that karmic links have just as big a role in family relationships as either blood and genes, or ties made in other ways. (I have, for instance, discovered through one of my own regressions that Delilah was previously Christopher's daughter when he was an Egyptian Pharaoh.)

The issue of blood versus ties of upbringing was crystallized in a Japanese film that won the Jury Prize at the 2013 Cannes Film Festival. I found *Like Father Like Son* intensely moving and, though fictional, the story of two six-year-old boys who had been swapped at birth, and the reactions of the various characters, seemed quite realistic to me. Looked at from a spiritual point of view, the lesson that the wealthy architect father needed to learn was to get in touch with his feelings, and it was the 'unnatural' son who eventually taught him that. On learning that his son was not of his blood, the architect's immediate response was to aim at achieving a complete and final exchange of the two boys, while his wife (who was already suffering from her husband's always putting work first) behaved in a way that seemed to me much more natural for a mother. The poorer family, too, showed from the very beginning more natural emotions. The ending of the story was not made a hundred percent clear, but it looked as though they were going to follow my advice (at least the advice I would have given had I been asked!): to keep their 'own' sons while maintaining regular contact with the respective birth families. A thorny question indeed and one to which there is no perfect solution.

The whole topic of Adoption and families wherein not everyone is related by blood has numerous strands to it. On the question of blood ties, Betty Jean Lifton does not shy away from the very tricky subject of 'incestuous' sexual attraction sometimes being an issue when members of the same biological family have not been brought up together. She has found that it can even happen between birth parents and their offspring. I did in fact once have such a case with a client who had half-siblings with whom she had never lived. A mutual sexual attraction with a rather older half-brother dated from when she was very young indeed and, in a regression that she did with me, she found its root in a lifetime when they had not been related by blood. So here again I believe karmic links to be another important factor.

When communicating with my friend Barbara, who, as I mentioned in the prologue to the section on Adoptees, has one natural daughter and one who was adopted, she asked me, "Have you put a chapter in about the guilt of the adoptive mother?" Barbara went on to say, "I know I felt very guilty that I had another woman's child, and talking to Fred about your email prompted him to tell me that he felt very guilty too." She continued, "I know I felt very guilty that I had another woman's child. This was especially driven home to me when I was training to be a psychotherapist. The hard-nosed feminists would say that I had stolen another woman's child. Although at the time I stood firm and fought my ground, I nevertheless found it interesting to recognize that I did indeed carry guilt. I would watch myself trying to make up for that by the way in which I treated my younger daughter. I was stricter with our natural child than I was with her."

Everyone is different and, though Barbara and I are in complete agreement about having always loved our adopted and natural children absolutely equally, Josie behaved very differently from Christopher, who *needed* much more discipline and control than his older brother and sister did. Barbara continued, "Josie did tell me in later life that she had decided at a tender age that she had better be a very good child if we were to keep her and not give her away, and on the whole she was." Perhaps that is why Barbara says, "I was much softer on our adopted child; my heart would melt when faced with delivering the consequences of her actions, or saying 'no' to her requests." I expect many adoptive mothers have the same problem, but in my case guilt feelings about rearing another woman's child were somewhat overridden both by the difficulties of coping with him and the intense gratitude I felt towards his birth mother for having entrusted him to us.

Betty Jean Lifton wrote so very competently and extensively

about reunions between adoptees and their birth mothers that I feel I have little to add. I do, however, recognize that there is an enormous difference in the situations of parents who have both natural and adopted children and those who adopt because of being unable to conceive. Lifton talks about adoptive parents who feel "threatened" if their child decides to seek out her birth mother, and I of course have a case (Loraine's) of an adoptee who never told her mother Madge about making contact because she knew that she would react very adversely. As someone who adopted through 'choice' rather than 'necessity', I can appreciate that it would be harder for someone who had been unable to conceive to accept contact with a birth mother, yet did Madge really love Loraine? Personally I don't believe that she was capable of love. No more than was Jeanette Winterson's mother[1], yet she went on to become both a highly successful novelist and – like the poet Jackie Kay, who is also an adoptee – a professor of creative writing. Loraine and Jeanette are two excellent examples of women who, for their growth, were given enormous hurdles to overcome and did so brilliantly!

Barbara, on the other hand, says of her adopted daughter, "She left it very late to seek her birth mother; she told me she felt very disloyal to us. I told her it was her birthright, and there was no reason she couldn't have both. I did all I could to help her overcome the obstacles she encountered in that process. I helped her track her mother down, and she went to visit her." That really *is* love on Barbara's part! She went on to say, "Josie watched her walk down the road and knew instantly that she was her mother. They were parted on the day of her birth and she was never held by her birth mother, yet she recognized her immediately."

We may be unusual in that our adopted son was the *last* person to reach the point of desiring a meeting with his birth mother. Geraldine has expressed gratitude for our "generosity of spirit," but to me it is not generosity at all, but rather a strong desire to fill holes and complete the circle. Even before she had got in touch with us via Barnardo's, she was ever present – as it were an invisible member of our family – and so when she finally 'took flesh and blood', at our first meeting in 1997, it was wonderful for me to be able to dispel the ghost. Now we are looking forward to the circle being completed, when Thomas Christopher and Geraldine finally meet face to face.

When they do, perhaps we shall find out more about the influence of his genes. We were interested to see, when we re-read the information given us by Barnardo's after Christopher had got seriously into basketball, that it had been a hobby of his birth father's. And, while David and I enjoy only classical music whereas Christopher listens mostly to Rap, Geraldine has told me that she does enjoy some Rap music, "though not too much all at once." She commented, "I think that Rap music is often very powerful and very clever," and said that she really enjoyed the film *8 Mile* starring Eminem. (I wouldn't even *think* of going to see a film like that!)

Barbara recounts, "I remember in her early teens when Josie had become withdrawn and was moving into a depression. We had recently moved to the outskirts of the urban area, and I noticed how she brightened up when she saw girls coming down the road on horseback and also when she went to the fence to talk to the foals next door. She had fallen in love with a palomino foal and looked at him with such longing that I knew she needed something of her own to love. So I talked to the owner of the foals, who insisted we took two foals! She was a natural. She simply climbed on his back and rode him down the paddock. He turned things around for her and she and her foal became devoted close friends. We had no such trends in our family, so this was a new interest for us, and later we learnt that horses were a great part of her birth mother's life." For us too basketball was something completely new – I would previously never have dreamt that I would get so excited watching a match!

Athene mentioned the emotion she had felt upon discovering

that her birth mother's favorite type of cake was mocha, just like her own, and I already know that Geraldine likes lemon cake as much as her son does. Genes, however, do not *always* play a massive role: apart from our mutual passion for music, I can think of no way in which I resemble my mother, and Alice in turn is extremely different from me. Christopher, on the other hand, seems to have 'inherited' David's distinctly quirky sense of humor, which Alice certainly has not! And, even though Paul is the only one of our children to have followed in his father's footsteps by studying Mathematics at university, all three of them got As in A Level Maths. Although when Christopher was about eleven we encouraged and admired his own Rap compositions, that type of music is, as I just said, not to our taste, but then neither of his siblings at present enjoys Bach, Beethoven (or of course Elgar![2]) even though they had them in the womb.

In these 'permissive' days when in many countries there is little or no stigma attached either to 'illegitimacy' or to abortion, there is a general shortage of babies for adoption, and so people who have no choice other than adopting older children have much greater difficulties to face than either we or Barbara and Fred had. And there is at present a massive problem caused by the shortage of both adoptive and foster families for these older children – especially if they are black. Policies on interracial adoption change periodically – only a few years after Christopher was born he would not have been placed with us – but are non-white children better off in children's homes or with loving parents who really want a first, second or third child? Nancy Newton Verrier[3] believes it to be preferable for children to remain with their birth mothers whatever her circumstances, which some people will no doubt see as a bit extreme. Barbara says, "Like you, I would now do everything I could to keep the child with its mother rather than adopt it out, but what if the mother simply doesn't want to have the child? There is no way of solving this dilemma. Josie used to say (though she is in therapy these days so may have changed her mind) that if she had been able to stay with her mother she wouldn't have had such a nice time growing up." Our son's birth mother has told me that at twenty-two both she and her partner were "too vulnerable" to have been able to give him a good home. Now, however, that she has matured, had therapy and herself become a therapist, she feels ready to relate to him in a way that we hope will be constructive for both of them. I hope that the present tendency towards 'open' adoptions, rather than the 'closed' ones that the deceased Betty Jean Lifton campaigned against, will grow until the adoptee having contact with both sets of parents has become the norm and it no longer ever happens that an adoptee knows nothing at all about his or her birth parents.

But the main point of this book has been to show every possible scenario as being a good thing since it is what all those concerned need – and indeed chose before incarnating – for their learning. Obviously those who believe in karma will see all this differently from those who do not, but, whatever your beliefs, if you are not fully content with your own life, is it not advisable to make the best of your circumstances and look for the lessons that can be learnt therein, rather than simply bemoaning your fate?

The possibilities in life are endless and it is up to us to look for them. If you yearn for a child, or for more children, have you considered training as a nursery nurse or setting up your own crèche? Of course it isn't the same by any means, but appreciating that circumstances in your next life are likely to be completely different could shed a different light on your situation. If you were adopted yourself and have not got over your feelings of 'rejection', then why not seek counselling or therapy? Though individuals are unique, problems are rarely so, and these days there is real help available for those who make up their minds to help themselves.

The older of my younger sisters, who was born on my second birthday, in 1942, has a 'War baby's' admirable economical instincts. Among the useful or attractive Christmas and birthday presents she has given me over the years is something called a Soap Sam. A simple, but ingenious, device, it consists of a smallish plastic cylinder with a lid at either end. The idea is to put into it all your little soap ends (i.e. the bits that are really too small to use) and then soak the whole thing in warm water until all the little bits have joined together to form a new bar of soap. Once dried, the new 'rainbow bar' can be quite attractive looking. However, I tend to buy my soap all over the place (normally when I travel abroad – ecologically friendly soap is cheaper in France as well as in India and of course I am also a 'War baby'!), and I find that the little soap ends tend to break apart once I have been using the newly-made bar for a few days. A symbol of what goes on between the varied peoples of our world, many of whom were forcibly made to live together as a single country by colonizers or other outsiders? Maybe if I stuck faithfully to just one brand of soap my little bits would meld together more permanently.

Well, in this book I have attempted to meld together differing points of view as well as numerous, very different, stories. I just hope that I have been a trifle more successful than is my Soap Sam! And, even if you disagree with some of my arguments, I hope you can nevertheless relate to one or two of the stories, or at least find them interesting. My own three children share neither my spiritual interests nor my firm belief in reincarnation and Life Plans, yet we nevertheless meld together very well as a family and are the very best of friends. I too had a difficult start in life, but now that I am on the last lap I have an enormous amount for which to be thankful. May you be equally rewarded.

Notes

1. The title of this novelist's autobiographical book, which I cannot recommend more highly, is an extraordinary remark

made to her by her adoptive mother.

2. See my book *Life Without Elgar – A Tale of a Journeying Soul,* 6th Books, 2014.
3. *The Primal Wound* came to me at a crucial time, but Nancy Newton Verrier's second book, *The Adopted Child Grows Up – Coming Home To Self,* Gateway Press, USA, 2003 is equally to be recommended.

By the same author

Discovering the Life Plan – Eleven Steps to your Destiny, 6th Books, 2012. ISBN 978-84694-821-3

Delayed Departure – A Beginner's Guide to Soul Rescue, 6th Books, 2013. ISBN 978-1-78279-011-2

Life Without Elgar – A Tale of a Journeying Soul, 6th Books, 2014. ISBN 978-1-78279-526-1

6th BOOKS

6th Books investigates the paranormal, supernatural, explainable or unexplainable. Titles cover everything included within parapsychology: how to, lifestyles, beliefs, myths, theories and memoir.

www.6th-books.com

If this book has helped you to clarify an idea, solve a problem or extend your knowledge, you may like to read other 6th Books titles on parapsychology. Recent bestsellers are:

The Afterlife Unveiled – *Stafford Betty*
What the dead are telling us about their world
What happens after we die? Spirits speaking through mediums know. They want us to know. This book unveils their world.
Paperback: 2011 978-1-84694-496-3 $16.95 £9.99.
eBook: 978-1-84694-926-5 $9.99 £6.99.

Less Incomplete – *Sandie Gustus*
A Guide to Experiencing the Human Condition beyond the Physical Body
Based on 40 years of scientific research, this book is a dynamic guide to understanding life beyond the physical body.
Paperback: 2011 978-1-84694-351-5 $26.95 £15.99.
eBook: 978-1-84694-892-3 $9.99 £6.99.

I'm Still With You – *Carole J. Obley*
True Stories of Healing Grief Through Spirit Communication
These stories uplift, comfort and heal and show how love helps us grieve.
Paperback: 2008 978-1-84694-107-8 $22.95 £11.99.
eBook: 978-1-84694-639-4 $9.99 £6.99.

Spirit Release – *Sue Allen*
A guide to psychic attack, curses, witchcraft, spirit attachment, possession, soul retrieval, haunting, soul rescue, deliverance, exorcism and others as taught at the College of Psychic Studies in London.
Paperback: 2007 978-1-84694-033-0 $24.95 £11.99.
eBook: 978-1-84694-651-6 $9.99 £6.99.

Advanced Psychic Development – *Becky Walsh*
Learn how to practise as a professional contemporary spiritual medium.
Paperback: 2007 978-1-84694-062-0 $22.95 £9.99.
eBook: , 2012 978-1-78099-941-8 $9.99 £6.99.

The Audible Life Stream – *Alistair Conwel*
Ancient Secret of Dying While Living
The secret to unlocking your purpose in life is solving the mystery of death while still living.
Paperback: 2010 978-1-84694-329-4 $24.95 £11.99.

Divine Guidance – *Stephanie J. King*
The answers you need to make miracles
Ask a question - any question – and the answer will immediately be presented, like a direct line – a telephone link – to the higher realms...
Paperback: 2013 978-1-78099-794-0 $11.95 £7.99.
eBook: 2013 978-1-78099-793-3 $9.99 £6.99.

The End of Death – *Admir Serrano*
How Near-Death Experiences Prove the Afterlife
A compelling examination of Near Death Experience, proving immortality in every page.
Paperback: 2013 978-1-78279-233-8 $19.95 £11.99.
eBook: 2013 978-1-78279-232-1 $9.99 £6.99.

The Miracle Workers Handbook – *Sherrie Dillard*
Seven Levels of Power and Manifestation of the Virgin Mary
Teaches how to invoke the Virgin Marys presence, communicate with her, receive her grace and miracles and become a miracle worker.
Paperback: 2012 978-1-84694-920-3 $22.95 £12.99.
eBook: 2012 978-1-84694-921-0 $9.99 £6.99.